Beyond the Hostage Child

Towards Empowering Protective Parents

Second Edition

Leora N. Rosen, Ph.D.

ISBN-13: 978-1514274170
ISBN-10: 1514274175

CreateSpace
an Amazon company
https://www.createspace.com

In loving memory of my parents,
Abe and Miriam Rosen

TABLE OF CONTENTS

Acknowledgements

Beyond the Hostage Child: Towards Empowering Protective Parents, was planned as an update of *The Hostage Child: Sex Abuse Allegations in Custody Dispute,* originally published in 1996. However, as I began the project in 2013, it soon became apparent that a simple update would not allow me to do justice to the new research and new material that had accumulated in the intervening 20 years. I realized that in order to address these developments, a completely new book would have to be written. That task was made less daunting by the encouragement and support of Connie Valentine, whose upbeat attitude and perseverance as an advocate for protective parents despite grim realities, has been an inspiration. Connie provided me with ongoing advice, and feedback on early drafts of the manuscript and also introduced me to other advocates who provided me with valuable input including Vicki Masotti, Marivic Mabanag, Helen Lynn, Anne Grant, Kathy Lee, and Karen Anderson.

My decision to update the first edition of *Beyond the Hostage Child* was precipitated by Doreen Ludwig, whose book *Motherless America* drew my attention to important areas that I realized required further work. Doreen's research on fatherhood programs and the divorce industry, and her sharp insightful analyses sent me back to the drawing board to look more carefully at these topics, and gather more information. I am grateful to Doreen not only for opening my eyes to these important areas, but in addition for reviewing and editing drafts of the updated manuscript and providing critical feedback. Through Doreen I met other protective mothers who have been fiercely fighting the system in new and creative ways and I gratefully acknowledge the informational input, advice and insights from Susan Skipp and Elizabeth Richter.

In addition, my gratitude goes to the protective parents, advocates, researchers and authors who provided me with information, advice and encouragement during the course of my work on this project. These include Elizabeth Richards, Joan Meier, Joyanna Silberg, Kiersten Stewart, Sue Osthoff, Eileen King, Evan Stark, Joan Zorza, Jeffrey Edelson, Barry Goldstein, Talia Carner, Maralee McLean, Karin Huffer and David Mandel.

Finally, I would like to thank all those professionals, advocates and scholars whose works have guided and informed me in the writing of this book, and to the protective parents whose stories have inspired me and many others to take on this issue. First and foremost among these is Michelle Etlin, my friend since 1982, and my co-author on the *Hostage Child*, whose own case taught me about family court corruption and its use as an instrument of coercive control. Our friendship and collaboration has extended over decades, and led me to devote my energy to this cause.

Leora N. Rosen, Ph.D.
March 2017

Introduction

More than twenty years have passed since the publication of *The Hostage Child: Sex Abuse Allegations in Custody Disputes*, which described a phenomenon that had emerged in the late 1980s and early 1990s – children alleging incest were being taken from their non-offending parents, and placed in the custody of the parents they had identified as their abusers.[1] Family court judges were viewed as chiefly responsible for this outrage, as protest and advocacy movements sprang up in response to specific cases. With the passage of two decades, more books, films and scholarly research have documented growing evidence that battered mothers are losing custody of their children and sexually abused children are being placed in the sole control of their named abusers – sometimes even denied any contact with their protective parents. The most vulnerable citizens petitioning family court for relief – abused women and their children – are being betrayed and further victimized by the government that is supposed to protect them.

Feminist scholar, Phyllis Chesler was the first to identify the problem in 1986, and framed it in terms of a historic gender bias regarding parental rights.[2] In her landmark book, *Mothers on Trial*, Chesler claimed that for more than five thousand years, fathers were legally entitled to sole custody of their children, and it was only in the nineteenth century that the state began to allow mothers with impeccable qualifications to provide very young children with the "maternal tenderness" they required. Since then for the most part, mothers retained custody of children only if fathers did not challenge them. While fathers rarely challenged mothers for custody prior to the 1970s, the turning point came in 1975, when Lee Salk, a famous scientist, challenged his homemaker wife for custody of their children and won because his career was more exciting than hers. Subsequently, Chesler found, fathers who challenged good enough mothers for custody won 70% of the time, even if they were absent, or violent. This was because mothers were held to an impossibly high standard of parenting compared to fathers, who were favored over mothers simply for showing a minimal interest in their children.

One of the proposed sources of the problem is gender bias in the courts, documented in numerous reports by gender bias task forces that were established in the 1980s and 1990s. Karen Winner in her 1996 book, *Divorced from Justice: Abuse of Women and Children by Divorce Lawyers and Judges*,[3] provided divorcing women with a chilling description of the kinds of injustices and indignities they were likely to experience at the hands of family court practitioners, especially lawyers, who she claimed were more interested in pursuing money than justice. Yet despite alleged efforts to improve gender-related discrimination against women in the courts, advocates believe that battered women in custody disputes are worse off today than they were 20 or 30 years ago.

An important contributor to the problem is the fathers' rights movement, which, since the mid-1970s, has greatly influenced the courts and state legislators to favor fathers in custody litigation. Although the stated goal of the movement is the promotion of joint custody and shared parenting, a centerpiece and focus of the fathers' rights strategy is the denial of the validity of claims of domestic violence and child abuse, and the discrediting of those claiming to be its victims. Fathers' rights advocates have successfully promoted a theory that women frequently make false allegations of abuse to gain advantage in custody disputes, despite research showing that such false allegations are quite rare.[4] In doing so they have been successful in influencing courts to deny the validity of abuse claims, often in the face of overwhelming evidence that the claims are true, with resulting custody awards to the alleged abuser, and sometimes loss of visitation rights for the mother.

In the early days of the protective parents' movement, survivors and advocates faced a monumental challenge of disproving a pervasive myth that mothers always win custody unless they are unfit, as well as proving the growing reality that battered women and mothers of sexually abused children were in fact losing custody to abusers. Facing total societal disbelief, advocates, writers, survivors and dedicated researchers set about to prove the existence of unjust court practices, and to provide detailed case histories, documenting the evidence of abuse and how the different players in the system dealt with it. That is what we attempted to accomplish in our book, *The Hostage Child* published in 1996.[5] The book centered around five case histories selected from over 200 cases of protective mothers that were known to us and had sought help and support from grassroots organizations in the late 1980s and early 1990s. Although the facts of these cases were compelling, and were not called into question even by the most skeptical of readers, detractors nevertheless claimed that these were unusual isolated cases, and not representative of a broader problem.

That argument can no longer be made. In the intervening years since the publication of *The Hostage Child*, the documentation of compelling case histories has steadily increased, while broader surveys support the conclusion that the problem is not confined to isolated cases. In 1999, the Wellesley Center on Women began the Battered Mothers' Testimony Project to determine whether the Massachusetts family court system was acting in accordance with internationally accepted human rights standards.[6] Based on testimonies from 39 battered mothers, as well as surveys and interviews with court practitioners, the Project concluded that state court practices violate the human rights of battered mothers and their children including the right to bodily integrity, security of person, equal protection of the law, freedom from torture, and other rights guaranteed under international human rights law. Arizona and California followed with similar projects that replicated these findings.[7] Another project, the Battered Women's Custody Conference, began in 2004, initiated by Professor Mo Therese Hannah of Sienna College, Loudonville, New York.[8] A centerpiece of the conference involves detailed testimony from a selected group of battered mothers who, together with their children, have experienced similar violations of their human rights in state family courts from around the nation. In 2005, Amy Neustein and Michael Lesher published *From Madness to Mutiny: Why Mothers are Running from the Family Courts and What Can Be Done About It.*[9] This book comprises a detailed analysis of over 1,000 cases of protective mothers victimized in a hostile family court system. These mothers were not punished for being abusive, neglectful or violent, but for believing their children's outcries of abuse and for attempting to protect them.

Other compelling case histories have been documented by independent film producer Garland Waller in her 2001 film, *Small Justice: Little Justice in America's Family Courts*, about how abusive men obtain custody of their children in family court.[10] Her second film on this subject, produced in 2011, *No Way Out But One*, tells the story of Holly Collins, an American mother who kidnapped her children in 1994 and fled the country to protect them from being forced into the custody of their violent father.[11] She became the first U.S. citizen to be granted asylum by the government of the Netherlands, which recognized that the U.S. government would be unable to protect her if she returned home. Although the mainstream media have been reluctant to address this issue, exceptions include the 2005 PBS production *Breaking The Silence: Children's Stories*[12] chronicling the impact of domestic violence on children and their continued experience of trauma in the family courts, and the 2012 four-part Los Angeles Fox affiliate TV news series, *Children Lost in the System* about abuses of women and children in the California family courts.[13] In addition, some independent investigative journalists have doggedly pursued stories about the struggles of protective parents in family court, determined to throw light on corrupt practices and the systematic betrayal of children.[14]

The purpose of this book is not to provide further documentation of this phenomenon, which is no longer in question. Rather, our goal here is to present a comprehensive blueprint for action by Congress and the federal government to resolve the problem. This may seem strange, since the problem appears to be firmly located in the state court system, over which Congress and the executive branch of the federal government have no control. But that is not entirely true, and it may be that federal leadership is the only way to bring an end to these systematic human rights violations.

The first half of the book explores the historical roots of the present problem beginning with an important but misunderstood piece of nineteenth century British legislation commonly referred to as the Tender Years Doctrine. Addressed in Chapter 1, this "doctrine" has been interpreted by fathers' rights advocates as representing a historical bias against fathers, and it has also been maligned by feminists as a form of gender stereotyping that discriminates against women seeking careers outside the home, or as representing a brief respite for mothers in an otherwise unbroken patriarchal tradition. The Tender Years Doctrine is in fact none of the above. Rather, it was the first legislative initiative to protect battered mothers from losing custody of their children to abusers.

Chapter 2 examines the origins of the modern protective parents movement, showing that it stands at the intersection of three other victims' rights movements – the child protection movement, the incest survivor movement, and the battered women's movement. Remaining an outsider to all three movements, the protective parents movement has shared few of the considerable government resources allocated to them – especially resources allocated to the child protection movement and the battered women's movement. Only very recently has the protective parents' movement been somewhat incorporated into the battered women's movement, but it still remains at the fringes with regard to funding for research and programs, and official recognition by government leaders.

Chapter 3 develops on the theme of the previous chapter, showing how the interrelationships among key social movements have contributed towards the current battered mothers custody crisis. These include divorce reform, the victims' rights movements of the 1970s and 1980s, the influence of feminism on changes in child custody policy, and the rise of the fathers' rights movement.

Chapter 4 discusses legislative and legal remedies that advocates and survivors have sought in the hopes of redressing the injustices that battered mothers face in family court. We discuss state statutes addressing domestic violence and custody, and especially the Model Code presumption against awarding sole or joint custody to a perpetrator of domestic violence. We review the results of a study that examined the effects of Model Code statutes on custody determinations across six states and develop a method of determining how many custody decisions provided adequate protection for battered mothers in these states. This chapter also discusses three relevant federal lawsuits, two of which went all the way to the Supreme Court, concerning the responsibility of state actors in protecting women and child victims of domestic violence, and whether failure to protect constitutes a violation of civil rights. Two Supreme Court decisions have said that state actors are not responsible for protecting the most vulnerable citizens in our society. One of these cases was brought before an international human rights tribunal, which determined that the victims' human rights had been violated based on standards encoded in its Charter. We try to answer the question of how it has been possible for the United States to ignore and deny the widespread violation of the human rights of so many of its citizens, calling on a concept articulated by mothers' rights advocate Michelle Etlin, which she refers to as the Life Interest. This is a missing quantity that should be – but is not – embedded in the concept of civil rights. Its absence explains how human rights abuses can run rampant in family court, in a country claiming that the protection of fundamental human rights was a foundation stone of its establishment over 200 years ago, and that holds other governments accountable for their failures to abide by their obligations to uphold universal standards of human rights.[15]

Chapter 5 deals with the divorce industry, which has increasingly assumed a prominent role in perpetuating the problem of battered mothers losing custody to their abusers. This industry comprises a variety of auxiliary court-appointed professionals including custody evaluators, mediators and guardians ad litem, who not only influence judicial custody decisions, but also sometimes make those decisions, which are then rubber-stamped by the judge. Many of these professionals subscribe to unscientific syndromes, promoted by the fathers' rights movement, that portray protective mothers as alienators who deliberately lie about abuse in order to damage their children's relationship with their fathers. Such syndromes are often invoked without first establishing whether or not there is a factual basis for the allegations, but once invoked, the syndrome makes fact-finding unnecessary.

The second half of the book deals with past efforts to help protective parents undertaken by Congress, the federal and state governments, and outlines proposals for future directions. Chapter 6 discusses the impact of the Violence Against Women Act (VAWA) of 1994 and its subsequent reauthorizations, as well as legislative efforts on the part of state governments designed to improve safety and justice for protective parents. This chapter also describes key civil rights actions brought by protective parents in federal court, and suggests a reason why these lawsuits have, for the most part, not succeeded.

Chapter 7 deals with specific programs related to the promotion of fatherhood, and it describes how these programs are encouraging practices that may harm battered women and may even be assisting dangerous fathers in obtaining custody of their children. This chapter ends with recommendations that include comprehensive screening for domestic violence and ongoing assessment for threat and lethality throughout these programs, as well as a holistic approach to addressing domestic violence once it is identified, which would include interventions with the perpetrator as well as services for victims.

In Chapter 8, the focus is on battered mothers who have fled a jurisdiction with their children to protect themselves and their children from further violence, and who are accused of parental kidnapping – as portrayed in the film, *No Way Out But One*. In the early 2000s, lawmakers attempted to address this issue by commissioning a study and a report to Congress, but those efforts were stalled. Chapter 8 proposes that the report to Congress and its recommendations be revisited and that further data be collected if necessary to enable Congress to act.

Chapter 9 describes some of the models that have been proposed by professionals and victims' advocates for restructuring the family court system in ways that would be more protective of battered mothers and their children. This includes our own proposal for the establishment of a Child At Risk Classification Office, first mentioned in *The Hostage Child*. All of these models place the safety of the non-offending parent and child at the highest level of priority, and all would require enabling legislation at the state level.

Chapter 10 deals with specific actions that Congress and the federal government could take to bring about a resolution to the problem, beginning with the establishment of an Office on Children of Domestic Violence within the Department of Justice. The chapter lays out a mission and specific duties of such an office. It also discusses other Congressional initiatives including reforming fatherhood programming, and requiring states to enact protective legislation and abide by established standards in order to receive certain types of federal funding. The central theme of this final chapter, as it pulls together the various threads running through the rest of the book, is that the protective parent movement, while allied with other movements, is a political movement all on its own, rooted in ending the human rights violations being perpetrated against some of society's most vulnerable members.

Chapter 1

The Infant Custody Act

History seems to teach us that for the better part of the past twenty-five hundred years of human existence, the inherent rights of the individual were not recognized. Only within the past 250 years, according to one view, have such rights received some recognition; only within the past 100 years has this recognition included women and children; and only within the past 25 years has there been any enforcement of legal protections for battered women. This is the perspective that Marvin Timothy Gray suggests we take in trying to understand the current crisis facing battered mothers in the family court system. There has been progress, but it has not gone far enough. For the better part of our history, the dominant ruling principle in our society has been something called "patriarchy" – a family-based system of male-centered power and privilege that placed the adult male head of household in control of women and children, who had no self-executing rights. An extreme example was the Roman paterfamilias who had the power of life and death over the women and children of his household. Every infant born into his household would be placed at his feet, and he would decide whether the child should live or die. The Roman Law of Persons was based on the property ownership of the head of household over all the family, and as Gray notes, from this culture, much of our modern law developed.[1]

However, there is historical evidence that progress has not centered solely on the issue of patriarchy and gender roles, and perhaps for that reason has not been linear. Concerns for the health, wellbeing and humane treatment of the parties has, at times, also been a factor. It may come as a surprise to some that the earliest documented rule about child custody based on the Tender Years Doctrine came from the Talmud, books of law representing an important component of the Jewish Oral Tradition first published about 1,500 years ago.[2] The doctrine is laid out in Tractate Ketubot 65b2, and 102b4 as follows: children under the age of six require a mother's care, therefore mothers are given custody of all children under the age of six. Fathers take custody of boys over the age of six, while girls over the age of six remain in the custody of their mothers, as the Talmud says a girl's place is always with her mother.[3] This was a child-centered doctrine based on parental obligations to care for and educate boys and girls of different ages. In those days, when other nations primarily regarded children as the property of the father, Jewish society, though patriarchal, was known for its pro child policies. The Roman historian, Tacitus (56 CE-117CE) said disparagingly of them: *"They will not allow even one child to be killed!"*[4]

There are some theories that attribute the modern Tender Years Doctrine to economic changes following the Industrial Revolution, when children, who had previously helped to work the family farm, were now of less economic value to their parents. Fathers were going off to work in factories, leaving children with their mothers, and this made mothers the *de facto* custodians of children. As a practical matter, however, the modern Tender Years Doctrine can only be understood in the context of laws pertaining to divorce and/or separation, and these followed a slightly different course in Britain compared to America. The British Tender Years Doctrine was established in 1839, when Parliament passed specific legislation giving mothers access to their young children upon marital separation or divorce.[5] Prior to 1839, upon marital separation, fathers had sole custodial rights to infants *from the time of their birth*, but older children could choose where they wanted to live. If a child around the age of 14 left his father and refused to return, the courts would not compel him to do so. In other words, just at the time when a child would be of economic value to his father, he could choose to live with his mother, whereas an infant who was only an economic liability, could be taken from his mother at birth.[6] Second, divorce was extremely rare, and was a privilege limited to the very wealthy because it required an act of Parliament. Even legal separation required expenses that only the wealthy could afford. Fathers in this class of society hired nursemaids to take care of their infant children, or in some cases would hand them over to their live-in mistresses. Women rarely left their husbands except under extreme circumstances. This is the society in which the British Tender Years Doctrine made its appearance. It was one of the human rights reforms that occurred around the third decade of the nineteenth century. These reforms included the Great Reform Act of 1832 that expanded the number of adult males eligible to vote, and the British Slavery Abolition Act of 1833, which abolished slavery throughout most of the British Empire including the West Indies, Mauritius and South Africa.

The Legacy of Caroline Norton

Caroline Norton was a beautiful, vivacious, talented and accomplished woman married to George Norton, a jealous, controlling, manipulative man who blamed everyone but himself for his perceived failures in life. Although Caroline was instrumental in finding him a good job and helped to support the family with her earnings, George took it out on her every time he felt disrespected by society, and he abused her – including scalding her with a hot kettle, attempting to throw her down the stairs, and strangling her, leaving marks on her neck. Caroline left him twice, but returned each time after he apologized contritely, begging for forgiveness, and promising to reform. The second reconciliation occurred late in her fourth pregnancy, but shortly after her return, the abuse continued and Caroline miscarried.[7]

Caroline's family were understandably outraged and made it clear to George, that they disapproved of the reconciliation and that he was not welcome in their social circle. George reacted to this latest slight by locking Caroline out of the house, refusing to allow her access to her clothing and personal effects, and hiding the children from her. To bolster his position, George accused her of carrying on an adulterous affair in their home while he was away at work, and sued her alleged lover – the British Prime Minister – for "criminal conversation", a term used for adultery. After a sensational trial, the court cleared the Prime Minister (and Caroline) of these charges, in the light of evidence that George Norton's witnesses were disgruntled ex-servants who had been paid to perjure themselves.[8] Following this public humiliation, George commenced a round of attempts at mediation in which he promised to allow Caroline access to her children if she agreed to make certain financial sacrifices, but he kept going back on his word. Eventually even the mediator, who was of George's own choosing, doubted his credibility and gave up on him. For four years Caroline had no contact with her children other than a few snatched moments when she was able to see them very briefly. Caroline was finally allowed visitation with her two surviving sons after the death of her youngest son, aged nine, following a minor accident. The child's death was not directly caused by the accident, but by inadequate medical care, which resulted in sepsis.[9]

This nightmare scenario sounds very much like one of the horror stories that could have been presented at the Truth Commission of the Battered Mothers' Custody Conference. These events, however, occurred more than 175 years ago. The battered mother in this story was a successful poet and author from a prominent English literary family, who turned her personal tragedy into activism for social reform in nineteenth century England. While it is possible that in today's world, George Norton would have been prosecuted for his crimes, or at the very least, Caroline could have obtained a protective order, it is also likely that in the present-day United States of America, Caroline's custody situation could have ended up exactly as it did in England in 1837. Back then, the batterer got custody simply because it was the law. Today, the batterer requires the assistance of judges, court auxiliaries and various "experts" to make his case, but frequently the result is the same as it would have been 175 years ago.

The Infant Custody Act

Changes in the British custody law began in 1835, when Sir Thomas Noon Talfourd, Serjeant-at-law of the British bar and Member of Parliament, represented a father in a custody case. A certain Mr. Greenhill left his young wife, took up residence with his mistress, and sought custody of the couple's three infant daughters, intending for them to be raised by the said mistress. Mrs. Greenhill's appeal to the Court of Chancery was rejected, as there was no provision in the law for a married mother to have any access to her children against her husband's wishes. Furthermore, Mr. Greenhill obtained a writ of attachment for Mrs. Greenhill, as she refused to turn over the children, whereupon Mrs. Greenhill fled England with the children and went to the Continent.[10]

Recognizing the law to be grossly unjust and oppressive to women, Serjeant Talfourd set about to change it. Two years after the Greenhill case, Caroline Norton found herself in similar circumstances, and she teamed up with Talfourd to change the law. Caroline was a devoted political reformer, having been active in earlier reform movements. Thus it was natural for her to turn her attentions to the issue of maternal custody. In 1837 she published a pamphlet entitled: *Observations on the Natural Claims of a Mother to Custody of her Children As Affected by the Common Law Rights of the Father.*[11] This became the basis of the Infant Custody Bill that Talfourd introduced into Parliament in April 1837. The Infant Custody Act finally became law in 1839, making provisions for mothers of unblemished reputation to petition the court for custody of children under the age of seven, and to have access thereafter to older children.

Caroline was a major force in bringing about reforms in custody law for the benefit of women in mid-nineteenth century England. She herself did not benefit from her efforts because her husband had moved to be with his family in

Scotland, which was outside the jurisdiction of the law. In addition, in order to access their newly won rights, women would have had to incur significant legal costs, as they do today, and thus the law would not have benefited poor women. But what did happen was a gradual shift in court practice that presumed women to be the appropriate custodial parent of young children, upon marital dissolution.

It is important to bear in mind that these reforms in England occurred 79 years before women got the vote, 43 years before married women were allowed to own property in their own right, and 20 years before there was even such a thing as civil divorce. Although legal separations did occur, divorce was extremely rare, and could only be granted by the legislature and only on the grounds of adultery. Wives could initiate divorce only if the adultery was compounded by life-threatening cruelty.[12] Caroline was not interested in women's suffrage or in other aspects of women's political rights. She ostensibly accepted women's relative position of inferiority in the family, and did not regard herself as a feminist.

In December 1838 Caroline sent a letter to the Lord Chancellor of England in support of the Infant Custody Bill, writing as Pearce Stevenson Esq., and addressing the major issues raised by detractors of the Bill.[13] She denied that she opposed a husband's authority. But she argued that even members of the military, apprentices and servants, who were subject to strict authority, nevertheless had recourse to justice when those set over them acted with cruelty and oppression. In the case of a father's authority over a mother in the matter of custody, no amount of cruelty could secure her redress.

One of the issues raised by opponents of the Bill was that the custody hardship was just one of many hardships that women had to suffer, such as the right of the husband to dispose of her property as he pleased, including spending it on his kept mistress. Even regarding property, Caroline pointed out that husbands were required to provide for their wives to the amount of one third of their incomes, and assumed responsibility for their wives' debts, thus providing the wife with some protection – a protection which was absent in the case of infant custody. Caroline went so far as to say that even the hardship of not being able to obtain a divorce that would allow a woman to remarry was not as barbaric as the law affecting a mother's claim to custody. She wrote:

> "[I] t was never publically known or understood, that in this free country, a man could take his innocent legitimate child from his wife, and give it to the woman with whom he was living, and that the English Law, the law which boasts a 'remedy for every wrong' – the law of the country which piques itself on the protection of the oppressed – gave that wife no redress, but left her child in the custody of the father's mistress."[14]

She described the operation of the law as aiding the oppressor to tyrannize and punish the innocent while letting the guilty go free.

Some opponents complained that such instances of oppression were rare. Serjeant Talfourd only presented five cases. In other words, the majority of men had already agreed to act as if women had some claim to access *"guided by the principles of natural justice."* Caroline pointed out that the minority of men who made this Bill necessary were base, ferocious and unjust – *"adulterers – men whom the great laws of society could not touch, whom the opinions of the majority could not influence, but who were nevertheless a pest to that society, and object of detestation and horror to that majority, and proper objects for such control as the Bill of Custody would give."*

Another argument against the Bill, which contradicted the previous argument, was that it would result in the prisons being crammed with fathers lying in contempt. Caroline disputed this prediction, but stated, *"whether the instances of injustice which this Bill is intended to remedy be few or many, one thing is very certain, namely that after the passing of this measure the number of those instances will be diminished."*[15]

Domestic violence as a consideration

Caroline doubted that the Bill would be of much benefit to women who left their husbands for no good reason, or who were themselves guilty of misconduct, since she maintained only aggrieved women, who could no longer bear the yoke of violence, tyranny, or infidelity would risk the stigma of making such a rash decision. She argued that the Bill was especially intended to protect "innocent" women – namely those who were able to obtain verdicts against their husbands of adultery or cruelty in the Ecclesiastical Court. She said such women should obtain custody as a "matter of course". But she said that the Bill should also benefit all separated wives since the burden of proof to obtain a divorce, especially on the grounds of cruelty were exceptionally high. She wrote:

> "In cases of cruelty, the chances are still less in favour of the woman obtaining the divorce sought by her; for the law, to guard against the reception of frivolous and vexatious complaints, requires very strong evidence of the husband's cruelty, and it should be cruelty such as may be supposed 'to endanger life or limb;' which (as few men offer personal violence to their wives in the presence of by-standers, and her own single evidence is of no avail,) generally fails of absolute proof. Add to this the absurd law of condonation, which takes away from the woman who has forgiven acts of cruelty and returned home, the power of complaining of them afterwards; and there is scarcely a chance of such divorce left; for I suppose nine women in ten struggle against their resentment of terror of a violent husband for the sake of their children and reputation, do, at the entreaty of the husband, or by the advice of friends, return to their homes after complaints of cruelty, and so condone the past."[16]

Gender bias recognized

Among the Bill's detractors were those who expressed horror at the possibility that an adulterous woman might be able to gain access to her children. In response Caroline wrote:

> "The idea that a sinful *mother* should be allowed to look upon, speak to, or caress the children of an injured husband, was monstrous, was incredible, and called forth eloquent and proud rebukes on the occasion of the discussion of the Bill: but the idea that a sinful *father* should in any way be interfered with, or prevented from disposing of his children as best suited his vengeance or his caprice, was quite incomprehensible to the defenders of his "*right.*" Truly this is straining at a gnat and swallowing a camel."[17]

Coercive control recognized as a motive

Caroline also recognized that the existing child custody law, and the law of "condonation" were significant weapons in the arsenal of coercive controlling men. She asked:

> "[T]he question is, on what principle the legislature should give a man this power to torment; this power to say to his wife 'You shall bear blows, you shall bear inconstancy, you shall give up property, you shall endure insult, and *yet* you shall continue to live under my roof, *or else* I will take your children, and you shall never see them more?' Or, on what principle, if his victim leaves him, he is to say with hard and insolent triumph, 'She shall return to her home, or weep her heart out; I make no promise—I admit no man's right to interfere—I care not what truth there may be in her complaints of my conduct; all I say is, that either she shall *return*, or she shall never again see or hear of her children.' Can the return under such circumstances be deemed a 'reconciliation,' or even a voluntary and spontaneous act?"[18]

The Tender Years Doctrine in the United States

The Tender Years Doctrine in the United States followed a different course from that in England, which was in some ways to the benefit of American women. While in England, until the mid-nineteenth century, only Parliament could grant a full divorce, in America, throughout the nineteenth century, there was an increased movement away from legislative towards judicial divorce.[19] In addition, there does not seem to have been a uniform preference for paternal custody; many early cases demonstrated that both the mother and the father could claim custody, and the predominant rule appears to have been based on fault. Up until the late 1960s, divorce always required a showing of fault by one spouse against the other. Adultery had always been grounds for divorce, but over time more grounds were added and by 1886 there were at least 42, possible reasons for granting divorce, including bigamy, drunkenness, desertion, and public defamation.[20]

Professor Naomi Cahn reviewed documentation of divorces granted in the nineteenth century and found that the definition of "fault" was consistent with stereotypical gender roles, in which men were expected to be providers, and women were expected to conform to the ideal of the good wife and mother. Furthermore, she notes that awards of child custody and spousal support almost always went to the innocent party. So for example, if adultery were proven against the wife, she would lose custody and receive no alimony.[21] If adultery were proven against the husband, he would lose custody and be required to pay alimony. A study of divorce statistics in the United States from 1867 to 1967 found that wives were overwhelmingly the ones to file for divorce, and this tendency increased over time from 65% of divorces granted in 1870 to 73% in 1965.[22] The legal basis for obtaining divorces also changed over time. During the period 1867 to 1886, about two thirds of divorces were granted for adultery (24.6%) and desertion (44.1%). In the 1950s and 1960s, about two thirds of divorces were granted for "cruelty" or "indignities" with very few for adultery.[23]

In addition, the definition of "cruelty" changed over time. In the nineteenth century, it referred rather narrowly to extreme physical violence that caused serious injury, while from the 1930s onwards "mental cruelty" seemed to cover virtually anything that caused marital discord.[24] The concept of mental cruelty was supposed to liberalize divorce by recognizing that psychological acts could endanger life as much as physical acts, but this still maintained the traditional concept of divorce in which an innocent party sought relief from a guilty party. However, many early to mid-twentieth century divorces were de facto "no fault" divorces. When both parties wished to exit the marriage, collusion, in which one spouse, usually the husband, agreed to take the blame, was quite commonly practiced, even though it was strictly speaking illegal.[25] In such cases, it seems likely that couples also worked out other terms of their divorce such as custody. In fact throughout the period under review, only 11% to 14% of divorces were contested.[26]

Explanations of custody awards to mothers during the first half of the twentieth century (the so-called "tender years" period), must take into account the traditional concept of divorce and the fact that wives were overwhelmingly portrayed as the innocent parties entitled to relief. Professor Naomi Cahn notes ironically that while innocent nineteenth century women were entitled to receive alimony, property and custody upon divorce, innocent modern-day women, who comply with traditional gender norms, are disadvantaged.

> "Judges continue to view marital property as belonging primarily to the person who earned it, and to believe that women deserve little compensation for their household and care work during the marriage."[27]

Not only are traditional women disadvantaged with regard to finances, but also with regard to child custody. Caretaking, which was previously considered to be an important female function, is now considered of no importance to the roles of either gender. On the other hand, a consideration of a child's best interests often includes superior financial capability.[28] Thus, primary caretaker mothers may be losers on both counts.

A comparison of the English and American approaches to maternal custody of young children reveals another irony. At one point in history it appears that American women were treated more fairly than Englishwomen with regard to child custody awards following divorce or separation. In England, the historical right of fathers to custody of their children regardless of fault was only challenged and modified legislatively when abusive, controlling men asserted this right. Most separating and divorcing couples assumed that mothers would and should be the caretakers of young children, and the unfairness of the law only became apparent when some men refused to give their wives access. Indeed, despite the absolute legal right of British fathers to custody prior to 1839, most members of the British public believed that mothers had custody of children under the age of seven.[29] This was because most separated and divorced fathers did what they believed was right, and ignoring the law that was in their favor, voluntarily practiced the Tender Years Doctrine. Caroline Norton was the one who educated the public about their misperception that mothers had a right to custody of young children, and thus she was successful in getting the British Parliament to change the law.

Even though the Infant Custody Act specified that only "innocent" mothers should have custody, "innocence" generally meant "non-adulterous", since this was the only ground for divorce at that time. Around the same time in America mothers were already considered entitled to custody if they were the innocent party. The relaxing of gender roles and the acceptance of no fault divorce – considered by most to be major social advancements – have altered the rules in ways that place American caretaker mothers at a huge disadvantage. Women today may choose virtually any career, and can make a life for themselves that does not involve marriage or children. But if they should choose to be stay-at-home moms, they could find themselves in a worse situation than Englishwomen prior to 1839. This means that their husbands could commit adultery, abuse them, divorce them, and take their children away – and require them to pay child support. As in pre-1839 England, most divorcing husbands today would not do this. Yet despite massive changes in gender roles over the past 150 years, and despite resources and laws to protect victims of domestic violence, it has become easier than ever for abusive fathers to take children away from protective mothers. In the next chapter we will explore some of the social conditions that have made this possible.

Chapter 2

Intersecting Pathways

The protective parents movement emerged at the crossroads of three separate but related victim advocacy movements, each with its own unique goals and constituencies. These three movements are: (1) the child advocacy movement, (2) the battered women's movement, and (3) the incest survivor movement. Currently, the protective parents movement is most closely associated with the battered women's movement, which began in the 1970s, influenced by the civil rights movement and the feminist movement of the 1960s. Empowered by these earlier movements, and using consciousness raising groups as a forum for discussion, women began speaking out forcefully about rape and wife battering as male crimes of violence against women, based not on personal relationships, but rather on gender politics derived from the principles of patriarchy and historical male privilege. Grassroots efforts around these issues led to the establishment of rape crisis centers and, later, battered women's shelters, which in time became the beneficiaries of substantial government funding. While the protective parents movement is presently viewed as part of the battered women's movement, it was not always so. In fact it is only in the last decade that the protective parent issue has found legitimacy within the battered women's movement. Even though battered women's shelters and battered women's advocates provided services to protective parents, as a group these women were invisible, not really belonging in any of the categories of activism that provided context and meaning to survivors' efforts to overcome violence and abuse.

The term "protective parents" was first used by H. Joan Pennington to describe mothers trying to protect their children from sexual abuse through custody litigation in family court.[1] Pennington, who founded the National Center for Protective Parents in Trenton, New Jersey in 1990, was among the first to document such cases, noting that family courts not only fail to stop the abuse, but frequently punish mothers for making these allegations. For the many protective parents who were also battered women, their experience with intimate partner violence paled by comparison with their struggles to protect their children. They saw their problems as being mostly about child abuse, but the major organizations and services that promised to protect children from abuse seemed to be more enemy than friend. This was because the child protection movement had a very different course of evolution based on a very different philosophy from the violence against women movement. The result was that advocates and practitioners from these different camps found themselves on a collision course – even becoming adversaries in legal proceedings. In order to understand how this came about, we need to track the different courses of development of three major victim advocacy movements in the United States, beginning with the child protection movement that historically preceded the violence against women movement and the incest survivor movement.

The child protection movement

Prosecution and criminal justice sanctions (although rarely used) were available remedies for egregious cases of physical abuse and rape of children prior to 1875. After this date, the era of child protection came into existence with the establishment of private, charitable organizations devoted entirely to child protection – the first one being the New York Society for the Prevention of Cruelty to Children (NYSPCC). Still in existence today, the society's original goals were –

"To rescue little children from the cruelty and demoralization which neglect, abandonment and improper treatment engender; to aid by all lawful means in the enforcement of the laws intended for their protection and benefit; to secure by like means the prompt conviction and punishment of all persons violating such laws and especially such persons as cruelly ill treat and shamefully neglect such little children of whom they claim the care, custody or control."[2]

By 1922 there were 300 nongovernmental child protection societies scattered across America, but this number was to decline dramatically during the Great Depression of the 1930s, when charitable contributions dried up due to economic circumstances. State involvement in child abuse and neglect cases began with the establishment of juvenile courts. The first juvenile court was established in Chicago in 1899, and by 1919 most states had juvenile courts. While juvenile courts were concerned primarily with delinquency, they had the authority to intervene in cases of abuse and neglect.[3] Federal involvement in child abuse and neglect was still decades away, but the vehicle for this involvement would be the Children's Bureau, created in 1912 within the U.S. Department of Health Education and Welfare.[4] Its role was primarily to deal with tracking infant mortality, and later providing federal funding to improve infant health and nutrition. Federal involvement took a leap forward in 1935 when Congress passed the Social Security Act. One of the provisions of this Act, Aid to Families With Dependent Children (AFDC), allocated funds to help poor families. In addition, the Act authorized the Children's Bureau to cooperate with state public welfare agencies in establishing, strengthening or extending services for the protection of homeless, dependent or neglected children, and children in danger of becoming delinquent.[5]

The battered child syndrome

The discovery of the "battered child" syndrome ushered in the era of state government dominance in the matter of child abuse and neglect. The syndrome was a clinical condition first described by virologist and pediatrician, Henry Kempe, who had immigrated to the United States after escaping from Nazi Germany. Awareness of child battering developed out of improved technology in diagnostic radiology in the 1940s and 1950s, revealing patterns of what the medical profession believed to be intentional injuries.[6] Kempe began to further investigate this issue in 1961, eventually identifying and coining the term "battered child syndrome." He and his colleagues proposed that the syndrome be considered in evaluating any child exhibiting evidence of bone fractures and other injuries, where the degree and type of injury was inconsistent with the given history of the trauma. They argued that physicians have a duty and responsibility to the child to require a full evaluation of the problem and to guarantee that no repetition of trauma will be permitted to occur. Following Kempe's call to action, states began enacting laws requiring physicians to report suspected child abuse, or at least providing immunity from civil or criminal liability for reporting suspected child abuse, and by 1967 all states had such laws.[7] Over time those laws were expanded both to require more people to make reports and to broaden the kinds of conditions or maltreatment that required reporting. By 1974, there were 60,000 reported cases of child abuse and neglect nationwide. By 1980, that number rose to over one million. By 1990 reports exceeded 2 million, and by 2000 they were around 3 million.

The Child Abuse Prevention and Treatment Act (CAPTA)

Federal leadership and oversight of child abuse and neglect became a reality in 1974 with the passage of a landmark piece of federal legislation, the Child Abuse Prevention and Treatment Act (Public Law 93-247).[8] Reporting requirements had always been matters of state law, with statutes and definitions differing from state to state, but CAPTA required state law to include specific elements in their definitions and to establish procedures for investigating reported cases of child abuse and neglect as a condition of receiving federal funds for prevention, assessment, investigation, prosecution, and treatment activities. CAPTA also provided grants to public agencies and nonprofit organizations for demonstration programs and projects, and supported research, evaluation, technical assistance, and data collection activities. CAPTA established the Office on Child Abuse and Neglect, mandating the dissemination of information through the National Clearinghouse on Child Abuse and Neglect Information. CAPTA also set forth a minimum definition of child abuse and neglect, and required certain individuals to be mandated reporters including registered or practical nurses, hospital administrators, medical examiners, social workers, law enforcement officers, school teachers, principals, school attendance counselors or other professional personnel in public or private schools. Child protective agencies were established in all states to respond to reports of abuse and neglect. These agencies, which are partly funded by CAPTA, go by several different names such as "Department of Children and Family Services" or "Department of Social Services" or simply "Social Services." Another major source of state funding for child protection services became available in 1981, with an amendment to Title XX of the Social Security Act to include Social Service Block Grants to States.[9] Annual appropriation levels have varied from $2.8 billion during the 1990s to $1.7 billion more recently. Around 10% of these funds are used by states to fund child protective service. In 2012 CAPTA state grants were funded at $26 million. CAPTA Community-Based Child Abuse Prevention (CBCAP) Grants were funded at $41.5 million and CAPTA Discretionary Grants were funded at $27 million.

Family preservation

Since 1935, the primary source of government funding for child welfare has been Title IV of the Social Security Act, which includes funding for foster care, and cash assistance to needy families added in 1946. The dramatic rise in child abuse reporting resulted in an increase in the number of children in foster care, which raised budgetary concerns. Congress attempted to address this with amendments to Title IV beginning with the Adoption Assistance and Child Welfare Act of 1980, which emphasized reasonable efforts to avoid removing children from abusive parents and, when removal was necessary, to make reasonable efforts to reunite families.[10] This approach was roundly criticized as potentially dangerous to children, notably by Richard Gelles in his 1996 book, *The Book of David: How Preserving Families Can Cost Children's Lives.*[11] Subsequent amendments to Title IV during the 1980s and 1990s continued to emphasize family reunification, although language addressing child safety was also included. Thus the Adoption and Safe Families Act (ASFA) of 1997, which guides much of current practice, showed an interest in both protecting children's safety and developing permanency.[12] This law requires counties to provide "reasonable efforts" (treatment) to preserve or reunify families, but also shortened time lines required for permanence, leading to termination of parental rights should these efforts fail. ASFA introduced the idea of "concurrent planning" which demonstrated attempts to reunify families as the first plan, but to have a back-up plan so as not to delay permanency for children.

In conclusion to this section, the underlying philosophy of the child protection movement is rooted in the fact that children are dependent on adults for support. Without the financial support of their parents they become a burden to the taxpayer – the prime motivation for family reunification even when it is not appropriate or in the child's best interest. Child protection is a paternalistic system that views violence against family members as a symptom of dysfunction rather than as a crime, often placing equal blame on the victim and non-offending parent. As we shall see, it is completely at odds with the philosophy that fuelled the violence against women movement.

The violence against women movement

Susan Schechter, one of the leaders of the battered women's movement wrote that the issue seemed to "come out of nowhere" in the early 1970s.[13]   In fact the civil rights movement of the 1960s had a profound effect on feminism, as women working against racial oppression began to question their own position.   As young women gathered in the thousands to protest racial inequality, they developed the courage and experience to organize against gender inequality. Consciousness-raising groups encouraged women to see that what happened between men and women in the privacy of their homes was in fact deeply political.   This created an atmosphere in which women could speak out and organize against violence, beginning with the anti-rape movement of the early 1970s, followed a few years later by the battered women's movement.

Rape crisis centers began to open in the early 1970s. Myths that victims seduce or provoke their attackers were exposed. Rape was viewed as an expression of the unequal distribution of power between men and women. In her 1975 book, *Against our Will: Men Women and Rape*, Susan Brownmiller argued that rape is a conscious process of intimidation by which men keep women in a state of fear.[14] The following year, feminist and gay rights activist, Del Martin, published *Battered Wives*, which is widely regarded as the first general introduction to the problem of wife abuse.[15]   Martin addressed the legal and political status of battered women and the extent to which their immediate predicament must be understood in broad political terms. She argued that the basis of the problem is not in husband-wife interaction or immediate triggering events, but the institution of marriage itself, historical attitudes toward women, the economy, and inadequacies in legal and social service systems. She proposed reforms to the criminal justice system's approach to wife battering suggesting that judges protect the wife by closing the door to probation and de-emphasizing reconciliation.

These views were a far cry from the perspectives on wife abuse among the experts of previous decades. Susan Schechter noted that medical and social science literature prior to 1970 blamed wife beating on the wife's frigidity or masochistic need to fulfill her husband's aggression. A 1964 study on the wives of 37 men charged with wife-beating, published in the *Archives of General Psychiatry*, concluded that it was the intervention of adolescent children that led to the reporting, which the study's authors described as a disruption of the marital equilibrium that had previously been working more or less satisfactorily.[16]

Battered women soon joined the ranks of those seeking crisis assistance in greater numbers. Shelters proliferated in the mid 1970s, followed by the emergence of state coalitions that addressed legal reforms through state legislation, publicity, training of law enforcement, and legal advocacy and counseling for battered women. The Pennsylvania Coalition Against Domestic Violence opened in Pittsburgh in 1974, followed by the Chicago Abused Women's Coalition in 1976. Battered women's shelters, safe home projects, counseling and hotline services appeared in hundreds of locations after 1976. A 1977 survey of 163 programs found that 46,838 battered women and 14,473 children received shelter. A 1979 survey in Minnesota found that 70% of women had to be turned away because of lack of space. By 1982, there were an estimated 300 to 700 shelters and safe homes nationwide, with enormous variation from state to state. Soon public funding sources became available and facilitated the expansion of services. By 1982, the Pennsylvania Coalition was administering $2 million in Title XX funds from the Pennsylvania Department of Public Welfare. In Massachusetts, Battered Women's Service Groups, formed in 1978, also received Title XX funds, allocated by state bureaus to individual programs. In Minnesota, the state legislature began funding shelters for battered women in 1977, appropriating over $3.5 millions of state funds for 21 shelters over a period of five years.[17]

The rapid expansion of services, and increased availability of funding was accompanied by intense dialogue among battered women's activists regarding the philosophy of the movement, and its place in the human services sector of government. In 1977, a group of activists met at the White House to discuss woman abuse, and argued that it should not be lumped together with drug abuse, alcohol abuse and child abuse. In January 1978 the U.S. Commission on Civil Rights sponsored a consultation on battered women's issues, fulfilling its mandate to investigate denial of equal protection based on sex. Federal legislation, known as the Domestic Violence Prevention and Treatment Act, had been introduced several months earlier in both the House and Senate. Since this Act would authorize funds for services to battered women, activists from around the country converged on Washington, hoping to influence how the money was spent. It was at this consultation that the National Coalition Against Domestic Violence (NCADV) was formed.[18]

The Act failed to pass Congress, but the following year, President Carter established the Office on Domestic Violence (ODV) in the Department of Health Education and Welfare. This Office had no mandate to fund services directly, but was presumed to be the agency that would monitor future funding if federal legislation eventually passed. Meanwhile, ODV's main focus was on policy planning, information dissemination, and technical assistance. A year after it opened, the ODV was dismantled by President Reagan, and its remaining grants were moved to the National Center on Child Abuse and Neglect.[19]

Prior to 1984, federal funding for battered women's shelters and programs came from Social Security Title XX funds, the Law Enforcement Assistance Administration (LEAA) – now Office of Justice Programs (OJP), and occasionally Community Development Block Grants from the U.S. Department of Housing and Urban Development (HUD). It was not until 1984 that Congress finally passed legislation authorizing federal funding specifically for direct services to battered women. This legislation, known as the Family Violence Prevention and Services Act (FVPSA), provides the primary source of federal funding to domestic violence shelters and programs, and is administered by the U.S. Department of Health and Human Services. Congress has reauthorized FVPSA every five years as part of the Child Abuse Prevention and Treatment Act (CAPTA) reauthorization. Currently, over 2,000 local domestic violence agencies rely on FVPSA funding for essential services such as emergency shelters, hotlines, counseling and advocacy.[20] It would be another ten years before Congress would pass, in 1994, the landmark Violence Against Women Act (VAWA), which focused on improving the criminal justice system's response to domestic violence, sexual assault and stalking. VAWA will be discussed further in the next chapter.

How the battered women's movement viewed children

After the closing of ODV, a proposal was made to merge child abuse and domestic violence funding programs under one agency. Supporters of the merger believed it would be both cost effective and treatment effective in the light of new data showing a correlation between child abuse and spouse abuse. The data in question was coming from a national survey conducted in 1975 by Murray Straus and his colleagues at the University of New Hampshire.[21] The measure of abuse used in this survey (and subsequently hundreds of other studies) was the Conflict Tactics Scale, which asks respondents to report on different methods they use for managing conflict between themselves and their spouse or partner including the frequency of their experience of physical acts of violence. Studies using this scale have consistently shown near equal self-reports of the use of violent tactics by both men and women. Critics of this scale have offered numerous arguments as to why it is not an appropriate measure of wife battering, and the reader is referred to research and discussions on this topic for further information.[22] Important aspects of the controversy will be revisited in Chapter 5.

From the perspective of the battered women's movement, the University of New Hampshire research was also suspect because it approached domestic violence as a form of conflict resolution – a product of learned behavior, cultural influences and family dynamics. This research also gave credence to the "couples' counseling" or "family therapy" approach to dealing with domestic violence, since it treated both parties as equally culpable.[23] By contrast, the battered women's movement viewed intimate partner violence as a highly gendered form of power and control, related to sexist attitudes and historical male privilege, and sought more effective criminal justice sanctions, as well as safety and support for victims. Not surprisingly, the leadership of the battered women's movement vehemently opposed a merger with an institution that most likely would depoliticize wife battering and re-cast it as non-gendered "family violence." Susan Schechter prepared a statement to be read at the Fifth National Conference on Child Abuse and Neglect in April, 1981 in which she disputed the data correlating child abuse with spouse abuse, claiming that the correlation was grossly exaggerated. She wrote:

> "Child abuse and violence against women are different phenomena with different historical roots. A major goal of child protection services is to keep the family united, hopefully free from violence. Our goal is to support a woman in creating a violence-free life for herself and her children in whatever way she chooses. You must provide a form of protection and caretaking that is necessary for children but demeaning and debilitating for adults. Child protection services were organized because children are dependent. Battered women's service provision fundamentally challenges women's dependency, asserting the necessity of independence in order to be free from violence. Two clearly different forms of intervention are required. To use only one means women will be treated as incompetent and denied the very autonomy needed to escape victimization."[24]

About seven years after this statement was written, published studies would begin to show that there was indeed an overlap between wife battering and child maltreatment. By 1999, reviews of 36 studies put the overlap as between 30% and 60%.[25] Other studies documented the negative outcomes to children as a result of exposure to domestic violence.[26] Yet it would be another sixteen years before the leadership of the battered women's movement did a 180-degree turnaround and officially recognized that child abuse and battering often coincided and that it did not make sense to treat these as separate issues to be dealt with by separate sets of services. Thus in 1998, the National Council of Juvenile and Family Court Judges obtained a grant to develop guidelines for interventions in cases where domestic violence and child maltreatment coincide. This was known as the Greenbook project and we shall hear more about this later.[27]

To this day, however, there is no widely accepted theoretical connection between child abuse and wife battering. Wife battering is increasingly recognized as just one of many tactics by which men exert coercive control over women. Child abuse is still primarily defined as a form of family dysfunction, amenable to therapeutic interventions, which ideally should lead to family reunification. In order to understand why the theory of male privilege and coercive control never became part of the explanation for child abuse, it is necessary to review the historical development of the most recent form of child abuse to achieve recognition – child sexual abuse and incest. This review will help explain some of the bizarre contradictions in the child protection movement, where protective mothers can lose custody and even visitation if they leave the abuser, but can be charged with neglect and have their children permanently removed from them if they fail to leave.

Child sexual abuse and incest

The recognition of child sexual abuse lagged behind that of physical abuse until the late 1970s, when new child abuse reporting laws began to take effect. Until the middle of the twentieth century, incest was believed to be rare, and cases that were identified, tended to occur among children who came to the attention of the courts, for example prostitutes or "sex delinquents" whose brazen behavior and lack of fear were interpreted as moral defectiveness.[28] This led to the assumption that incest was exclusively a problem of the lower classes, caused in part by overcrowded conditions. Children were also seen as complicit in their own victimization, characterized as being "seductive" perhaps due to their "need for affection."

Another prevailing theory prior to 1970 was that of Freud, who viewed claims of sexual abuse as symptoms of children's repressed incestuous desire. Therefore, Freud claimed that children who reported sexual abuse by adults had either imagined or fantasized the experience, or had been the seducers of adults rather than the victims of sexual exploitation.[29] One of the first professionals to question this theory was Florence Rush, who recognized the problem of childhood sexual abuse while working as a psychiatric social worker at the New York Society for the Prevention of Cruelty to Children, and at a facility for delinquent female adolescents during the 1950s and 1960s. At that time therapists were instructed to avoid discussing incest with their young patients because of the Freudian theory. Rush was the first to challenge Freud's theory, calling it a cover-up of real claims of sexual abuse. Her paper: "*The Sexual Abuse of Children: A Feminist Point of View*" was presented at the April 1971 New York Radical Feminists (NYRF) Rape Conference.[30] Rush's view that Freud intentionally ignored evidence that his patients were victims of sexual abuse was corroborated in 1984 with the publication of Jeffrey Masson's book, *Assault on the Truth: Freud's Suppression of the Seduction Theory.*[31] Masson had been appointed Projects Director of the Freud Archives, with full access to Freud's correspondence and other unpublished papers. While perusing this material, Masson concluded that Freud might have rejected the seduction theory in order to advance the cause of psychoanalysis and to maintain his own place within the psychoanalytic inner circle. He argued that Freud deliberately suppressed his early hypothesis that hysteria is caused by sexual abuse during infancy because his Viennese colleagues viewed it unfavorably.

Reporting laws change the landscape

The awareness of child sexual abuse began to change when CAPTA required all states to include sexual abuse in their definition of child abuse, and by 1976 all states had reporting laws that included sexual abuse. Child sexual abuse awareness was born into a socio-cultural context that viewed child abuse as something treatable, caused by family dysfunction, substance abuse, poverty, ignorance, and other social ills which, when corrected, should ideally lead to family reunification. Since the socially and economically disadvantaged tended to be the primary recipients of child protective services, it was not difficult to add incest to the list of other problems that had come to be expected of this segment of society. Now, blaming the child victim for being complicit was replaced with a more elaborate theory of family dysfunction, centered on a construct called the "incest mother." Medical professionals from the mid to late 1970s described the incest mother as sexually repressed, frigid, rejecting her husband sexually, and giving her tacit consent to a sexual relationship between her husband and daughter. She was also described as powerful and controlling, but unable to function due to illness, and even facilitating and encouraging the sexual relationship between her husband and daughter. The incest father was described as unemployed, drunk, often controlling, and living in a sexually repressed household.[32] At the National Symposium on Child Victimization held in 1990, experts were still touting the incest mother theory, and claiming that incest was not a real crime and required a non-punitive approach because of the close relationship between the victim and the perpetrator. Incest survivor and victims' rights advocate Louise Armstrong, who attended the conference, summarized the theory of one of the presenters:

> "The non-punitive approach, as he went on to describe it, focuses mainly on the mother. By pointing out to her the unusual pattern – of a passive, dependent wife (who may often be absent because she works or is sick), who in any

case is not sexually attractive or cooperative, who invites the child to take over her household responsibilities, and a dominant, controlling husband, who favors the child in any case, which makes him jealous of the child's outside friends – social workers can get the mother to own up to the fact that she has failed in her father-taming role and to challenge the father's denial and to 'get a confession from him.'"[33]

Another speaker at the same conference claimed it was not uncommon for the child to initiate or actively participate in incest and that in most cases both parent and child found erotic gratification in the liaison.[34] This mother-blaming and victim-blaming philosophy thus had secure roots in the very institution that was supposed to protect children. This philosophy, together with the strong financial incentive to keep families together, shaped our nation's approach to dealing with child sexual abuse since it was first "discovered." It was also this philosophy that shaped the "mother-blaming" approach to incest in the child protection system, allowing mothers of incest victims to be charged with "neglect" for failing to protect their children. The only problem was that this perspective was about to be challenged when adult survivors began to speak out about their personal histories, initially, at last placing incest in the arena of gender politics.

Adult survivors take center stage

The stereotypes of the incest mother, and incest father were challenged when adult survivors of incest decided to break their silence, speaking out about their first-hand experiences. The first of these survivors was Louise Armstrong, author of "*Kiss Daddy Goodnight*" published in 1978, based on her own experience and narratives collected from other incest survivors.[35] In the mid-1970s when Armstrong began her research, health professionals regarded incest as something extremely rare – so rare in fact that her publishers even wondered whether there would be anyone to read the book.

At that time, other literature was emerging by clinicians and researchers with a more feminist focus. Judith Herman's study of incest was first published in Signs in 1977.[36] The following year, Sandra Butler published *Conspiracy of Silence; The Trauma of Incest.*[37] David Finkelhor's groundbreaking study, *Sexually Victimized Children*[38] was published in 1979, and Diana Russell's study on incest was published in 1983.[39]

Following these revelations and media coverage on the issue, child sexual abuse awareness was catapulted into public consciousness. Curricula to teach children about "good" and "bad" touch were developed and children were exhorted to tell a trusted adult if anyone touched them in a bad way. These educational programs were often run by law enforcement, and located in schools. Meanwhile, CHILDHELP USA established the first hotline in 1982 to provide referral services for the abused children and "trusted adults" who came forward in response to these educational programs.[40] The immediate consequence of these preventive efforts, said Armstrong, was not prevention of sexual abuse, but rather increased case finding, and many of these newfound cases involved fathers who did not necessarily fit the stereotype of the unemployed, rigid alcoholic with a sick or frigid wife. In fact the belief that incest was the prerogative of the poor and disadvantaged had been replaced with the maxim that incest cuts across all classes and ethnic groups. Middle class men were now getting caught in the improved detection and reporting system previously designed for poor single mothers. Now mothers of alleged victims, empowered by the battered women's movement, and the incest survivor movement, increasingly supported their children's allegations and made efforts to leave the abuser. These developments, however, threatened the stereotype of the middle class abuse-free family, and forces immediately arose to preserve the status quo, more commonly referred to as a backlash.

Beginning of the backlash

The backlash developed from two themes, which eventually converged to give rise to the fathers' rights movement. The first theme began to show itself in the mid to late 1970s and was related to the increased efforts among divorcing fathers to avoid payment of child support through obtaining joint or sole custody of their children. This theme will be developed further in the next chapter. The second theme arose from the banding together of individuals claiming to be victims of false accusations of child abuse. According to Armstrong, it was no coincidence that the backlash first showed its flag just at the time that state intervention began to include middle class white males.[41] Initially, the backlash organized as VOCAL – Victims of Child Abuse Laws, which posited that overzealous child protection workers were breaking up families and bringing false accusations against innocent citizens. Armstrong conceded that a certain number of innocent people had been pulled into the battle with the child protection system, and these people were drawn to VOCAL. However, the major impetus for the backlash had nothing to do with intra-familial violence. It came from accusations of child molestation in daycare beginning in 1984 with the McMartin Preschool Case in Manhattan Beach, California.

McMartin and its aftermath

In the McMartin Preschool case, six daycare workers were accused of abusing over 350 children in bizarre satanic rituals. The case dragged on for seven years, cost the taxpayer over $15 million, and resulted in no convictions. Charges against all but one defendant were dropped, and that defendant was eventually acquitted of most charges in a much-publicized trial. The remaining charges resulted in a mistrial.[42]

Meanwhile, similar types of allegations were occurring in other day care cases that popped up around the country. These cases generated hysteria about a large national and even international network of satanic ritual abusers that were preying on little children, although no evidence was ever found to support these claims. Meanwhile, the damage to children's credibility in general was catastrophic. The maxim that children never lie or make false allegations was in question, particularly as information emerged from the McMartin trial transcripts about how these children were subjected to coercive and manipulative questioning techniques that included shaming, misleading, and punitive, repetitive grilling.[43]

Social workers and mental health practitioners investigating child abuse now came under suspicion of eliciting false allegations through suggestive questioning methods such as the use of anatomically correct dolls. Eventually there would be rigorous scientific research into fair and objective methods of eliciting truthful information from children about sexual abuse, but often those seeking the truth were caught between the backlash and the "true believers." As a result of this polarization, routine incest, according to Armstrong, was being rendered diminutive by contrast to the large-scale satanic abuse cases with multiple defendants. Fifteen years after the publication of *Kiss Daddy Goodnight*, Armstrong expressed profound disappointment at the direction taken by the incest survivor movement. Her vision of incest as a central issue in gender politics, and of survivors as a force for political change and protection for future generations of children had not been realized. Instead, she said, the movement had been taken over by mental health professionals, who turned incest into an illness, infantilizing survivors, and making them dependent.[44] This criticism by no means applied to all therapists. Some such as Judith Herman and Florence Rush maintained their feminist focus. But far too many others jumped on the "treatment" and "recovery" bandwagons, while stories of celebrity incest became endless fodder for talk show entertainment, and the movement further lost its political focus.[45]

As the therapeutic community became increasingly fascinated by the theory of recovered memories especially of ritual abuse, ordinary incest was no longer good enough to warrant attention. Diana Russell reviewed the history and research on recovered memories in the introduction to the second edition of her book *Secret Trauma: Incest in the Lives of Women and Girls.* She concluded that some recovered memories are real, while others, especially those recovered with the use of questionable techniques such as hypnosis and suggestion, are likely false. (She also points out that some memories of individuals claiming not to have been abused in childhood may also be false.[46]) In 1992 the False Memory Foundation was established to advocate for parents who had been accused of satanic ritual abuse based on recovered memories. Russell writes:

> "This movement was led by parents many of whom had been charged with incestuous abuse by their children, who believed that most or all recovered memories of child sexual abuse are false — the product of suggestions by therapists, other incest survivors, and/or suggestive reading material. While the rigorous documentation of very high prevalence rates of incestuous abuse in *The Secret Trauma* indicates that incest continues to be a widespread and urgent problem, I now believe that both sides of "the Great Incest War" have some validity as well as many shortcomings. I also believe that both sides have undermined the feminist effort that first brought incest to public attention."[47]

Battle lines are drawn

The problems that protective parents face today began in the early 1980s through a convergence of powerful social forces. Women and children were given permission to speak about incest, thus challenging for the first time in history an area of male privilege that was previously unassailable, in part because it was invisible. This is what Armstrong referred to as the cradle of sexual politics. It was the moment in history when adult survivors of incest began speaking out, empowered by the feminist-inspired violence against women movement. It was also the point in time when the child protection movement had established a formal infrastructure replete with social workers and hotlines, ready to take reports from children who were being educated in schools about good touch and bad touch. A Pandora's box – the reporting system – had been opened and could not be shut, threatening to derail a historic bastion of male privilege – the power of men to exert coercive control over women and children if they should so choose. The Defender of this privilege became the fathers' rights movement, and its instrument became family court. Scrambling to find a solution, the Defenders came up with a new theory that was a variation on an old theory. The incest mother who had previously served up her daughter on a silver platter to her perpetrator husband now became the vengeful ex-wife making false allegations to gain advantage in a custody dispute. Armstrong wrote:

> "By the mid-to-late-1980s, if there was one thing everyone would verbally have agreed to about incest, it was that it was up to a mother to protect her child from her husband's sexual assault. But – having achieved this universal accord, this coast-to-coast affirmation – along came the increasingly powerful Male Protective Brigade to slam shut all doors that would have made such protection possible (all while we were beckoning kids forward, all the while trumpeting 'help is available!')"[48]

Soon, protective parents would routinely be losing custody of their children to alleged abusers. While some of these cases garnered positive media attention, frequently the mainstream media and the public failed to recognize the context in which these cases occurred. Each case was characterized as a "custody dispute" or an aberration rather than a deliberately staged all out assault on women. By the early 1990s, hundreds of cases had come to Armstrong's attention, many of them involving professional women, who believed with absolute conviction that courts would listen to their children's allegations and would provide them protection. Women who were married at the time of the disclosure were often advised by protective service workers to leave their husbands and file for divorce, which then placed the issue in the context of a custody dispute. If protective services validated the cases, they would tell the mother not to let the child go on court ordered visitation, lest she have the child removed from her for failure to protect. Some mothers defied court orders and were jailed for contempt, while others went into hiding with their children through a developing network of "underground railroads." Armstrong claimed that of the hundreds of cases that came to her attention, all but a few of the mothers ended up losing custody, and often visitation as well.[49]

Grassroots and professional organizations get involved

While media attention may not have had any long-lasting effect on the public's perception of the problem, it did bring together mothers who recognized their common plight and early grass-roots organizations coalesced to protest these grievous injustices. The first of these was Help Us Regain The Children (HURT), which was formed in Brooklyn, New York in 1986 by Dr. Amy Neustein whose daughter had been removed from her custody following allegations of sexual abuse.[50] In 1987 Mothers Against Raping Children (MARC) was formed in Mississippi in support of two mothers who had lost custody of their children for refusing to allow them to go on court ordered visitation with fathers who had allegedly abused them.[51] In 1988, Friends of Elizabeth Morgan, later renamed Alliance for the Rights of Children (ARCH), was formed in Washington, D.C. to protest the lengthy incarceration for civil contempt of Dr. Elizabeth Morgan who refused to reveal the whereabouts of her daughter, whom she claimed had been sexually abused by her ex-husband. That same year the National Coalition for Family Justice was founded in New York, offering support groups and referrals to services for divorcing women and mothers going through custody battles. This is the only organization formed in the 1980s that continues to be active at the present time.

New organizations that emerged in the 1990s and early 2000s, engage in a variety of activities including advocacy, lobbying, education, information dissemination, support, and referrals of battered mothers to legal and other services. In 1994, Mothers of Lost Children was founded by three mothers in Davis California, to protest the human rights violations of children who are removed each year from their safe mothers and ordered to live with or visit their identified abusers. Initially established as a weekly prayer group, the organization gathered strength and by 2010 it was holding biannual demonstrations at the White House to bring attention to the plight of children who are being placed in the custody of identified molesters or batterers. The California Protective Parents Association was founded in Sacramento, in 1998, and has since been in the forefront for effecting changes in state legislation, seeking to strengthen laws that protect victims and hold abusers accountable. Its accomplishments will be discussed more fully in Chapter 4.

In response to the growing backlash during the 1990s against child and adult victims of abuse seeking protection, a group of mental health and legal professionals met in 1998 to search for ways in which they could educate the public about trauma, and counter the increasing stream of misinformation attacking the credibility of abuse victims. This meeting led to the establishment of the Leadership Council on Child Abuse and Interpersonal Violence, a nonprofit scientific organization with an advisory board of over 40 internationally respected researchers, clinicians, legal scholars and public policy analysts. The Leadership Council maintains a web site that serves as a clearinghouse for information on the subject of child abuse, custody and trauma, including original research by its Director, Dr. Joyanna Silberg. The Council writes amicus briefs and refers battered women to knowledgeable professionals and expert witnesses who might be able to help. Council members also work pro bono to educate victims and the general public about the problems related to child abuse, especially sexual abuse, and custody battles.[52]

An important organization, the Battered Mothers Custody Conference (BMCC), founded by Maureen Therese Hannah, held its first meeting in Albany, New York in 2003. Its mission was to draw public and media attention to the injustices faced by battered women and their children in the family court system in the United States, to educate court personnel, legislators, government agencies, policy makers and professionals about this problem, to discuss and disseminate strategies for improvement, and to facilitate communication and collaboration among experts, scholars, advocates, professionals and lay persons who work on behalf of battered women and their children. The centerpiece of the BMCC's strategy was the establishment of a Truth Commission comprising a panel of experts who took testimony from a select group of battered mothers in front of an audience of conference attendees.[53]

Another significant development on the legal side was the founding in 2003 of the Domestic Violence Legal Empowerment and Appeals Project (DVLEAP) in response to the urgent need for expert appellate litigation to reverse unjust trial court decisions with regard to domestic violence and custody. DVLEAP also provides technical assistance to local domestic violence advocates and attorneys, and conducts training and presentations around the country on domestic violence and custody issues.[54] Other important organizations include, but are by no means limited to the following:

- Child Justice, based in Washington, D.C., which refers battered mothers to knowledgeable and experienced pro bono attorneys;[55]

- The Parenting Project, based in Rhode Island, which documents legal abuse in child custody cases, including those with a history of domestic violence and sexual abuse;

- The Protective Parents' Coalition, which advocates for transparency and accountability in the Texas family courts affecting child custody cases with allegations of domestic violence and child abuse;[56]

- Mothers Against Court Custody Abuse based in Pennsylvania, which conducts research and disseminates information on the role of federal funding in family courts' mishandling of custody and abuse cases;[57]

- Safe Kids International, which seeks to raise public awareness of "licensed court abuse" of children, and is actively engaged in lobbying for a law that would mandate that all child sexual assault cases be thoroughly investigated by a special victims unit and heard before a jury with a preponderance of evidence burden of proof.[58]

Professional literature identifies the problem

The earliest professional to identify the problem was Dr. Phyllis Chesler in her 1986 book, *Mothers on Trial: The Battle for Children and Custody*, which exposed the myth that mothers always win custody after divorce.[59] Through a series of case studies, Chesler demonstrated that when challenged for custody, "good enough" mothers were routinely losing their children to fathers, including those who had battered them or abused their children. The next book to come along was Louise Armstrong's 1994 book, *Rocking the Cradle of Sexual Politics*, which has been discussed throughout this chapter.[60] In 1996 investigative journalist Karen Winner published *Divorced from Justice: The Abuse of Women and Children by Divorce Lawyers and Judges*, an exposé of the lawless and unethical practices in the New York family court system that result in abusive fathers winning custody.[61] The same years, Michelle Etlin and I published *The Hostage Child: Sex Abuse Allegations in Custody Disputes*, presenting an in-depth description of five case studies followed by an analysis of the system failure.[62]

In some of the cases described in the earlier literature on this subject, judges acting alone would simply discount evidence of abuse, or say it didn't matter. Armstrong cited one case in which the court found that the father had indeed sexually abused the child, but found insufficient evidence to deny the child the right to a loving father.[63] In another case from the early 1990s a woman judge in Massachusetts awarded sole custody to an alleged abuser, implying that the child had learned to say "no" to her father's sexual advances, but had not yet learned to say "no" to her mother's emotional pressure to see her father through her mother's eyes.[64]

As it became clear that mothers would not back down easily and would continue to seek help, gather evidence, file appeals and pressure the legal system for redress, the system's counter-response became more organized, and efficiently punitive, facilitated by the rising importance of the role of court auxiliaries such as custody evaluators and guardians ad litem. The process whereby these actors develop and enact scripts that cast the victim in the role of abuser, is described in detail by Neustein and Lesher in their 2005 book *From Madness to Mutiny: Why Mothers are Running from the Family Courts and What can be Done About it.*[65]

Domestic Violence, Abuse, and Custody, Legal Strategies and Policy Issues [66] – a textbook published in 2011, co-edited by Hannah and Goldstein – is the most comprehensive resource currently available for legal professionals, advocates, and lay people who represent or assist battered mothers facing custody litigation, or policy makers, academics, or other professionals who wish to educate themselves in the search for solutions. Another textbook for attorneys co-edited by Goldstein and Liu, was published in 2014,[67] and the following year Goldstein published *The Quincy Solution,*[68] which outlines a model for change based on the coordinated community response to domestic violence implemented by prosecutors and law enforcement in Quincy Massachusetts in the 1990s. Protective mothers themselves have begun to publish personal memoirs of their experiences with abuse and custody, providing haunting accounts of systematic cruelties inflicted on them by courts and affiliated personnel, and the devastating losses they have endured.[69]

Parameters of the problem

Most protective parents and their advocates describe the system as having failed, or worse – as being a massive disaster. Neustein and Lesher offer a unique approach to understanding the problem by examining *"the inner dynamics of the ways the family courts have evolved into oppressive, biased dispensers of justice, whose decisions so often run counter to the best interests of children."*[70] Their approach examines the practical reasoning used by actors in the system that produces and gives meaning to a particular social order.[71] Neustein and Lesher's description of how the system's players act purposefully to achieve a certain result is consistent with our own view in *The Hostage Child*, that the system is in fact working as it has chosen to work. We suggested that there are in fact two systems – the overt and the covert – both sustained simultaneously by a process of "double-bookkeeping."[72] The overt system promises child protection though a network of agencies, and family courts, governed by written rules, regulations and procedural guidelines. The covert system is the way things actually work. Attorney Marvin Timothy Gray has another term for this phenomenon, which he refers to as Modern Vulgar or Local Customary Law.[73] These unwritten laws may override statutory or case law binding in that jurisdiction, and judges may even go against their own clearly stated policies. Another attorney suggested that in family court, the Constitution does not apply, and described family court as a "country club" rather than a court.[74] In an environment where the law doesn't matter, it should come as no surprise that facts don't matter either. Another way to understand this is through the concept of "motivated skepticism" developed by political scientists, in which new information is interpreted to support a pre-existing conclusion. This would explain the entrenched belief among matrimonial lawyers and judges – despite evidence to the contrary – that women fabricate allegations of abuse to gain advantage in custody disputes. This would also explain the most puzzling medico-legal phenomenon of our day – the widespread reliance on fictitious syndromes to discredit mothers' reports of abuse. An entire industry of experts has become established around the diagnosis of Parental Alienation Syndrome, parental alienation, Malicious Mother Syndrome, and Munchausen by Proxy Syndrome, despite rejection of the scientific validity of these concepts by mainstream medical science, and the absence of scientific evidence of their existence. This has not prevented family court judges, lawyers, and court auxiliaries from accepting these syndromes as valid. In fact, family court is the only place these syndromes exist. The system is sustained through the almost limitless powers of "judicial discretion", the extraordinary difficulty of appealing decisions, and the backing and support of court auxiliaries described above, who all enjoy immunity from lawsuits. This problem will be discussed in greater depth in Chapter 5.

Coercive control

The purpose of this chapter was to develop some insight into the historical roots of the protective parents movement and thus some of the problems it faces today. The movement stands at a three-way intersection of the battered women's movement, the child protection movement and the incest survivor movement. The oldest of these movements – the child protection movement – has benefited from formal federal leadership and federal funding for 40 years. The battered women's movement has benefited from formal federal leadership and federal funding for 20 years. Protective parents, who are sometimes also battered women, have for the most part been unable to benefit from either of these formal federal programs. Furthermore, while battered women and adult rape survivors have benefited from two decades of research, extensive data collection, legal advocacy, and the development and evaluation of programs designed to benefit them, protective parents are yet to be recognized as a category of victim deserving of special attention.

We have argued that protective parents' battle for recognition was hampered because the early protective parents movement centered on incest, which was never politicized in the same way as wife battering and which is viewed as a children's problem to be handled by the child protection authorities. The early battered women's movement wanted nothing to do with the child protection system, which they associated with dependency and family reunification – the opposite of their philosophy, which defined physical battering as one of several power and control tactics rooted in the enforcement of traditional gender roles. Other tactics recognized and articulated by battered women's advocates included threats, intimidation, isolation, economic abuse, and the manipulation of children. The goal of the movement was to liberate victims from this control and support them in developing independent lives. However, since the criminal justice system became the major vehicle of redress for battered women, programmatic activity focused on those aspects of battering defined as crimes – namely physical and sexual violence, and stalking.

Evan Stark has proposed that the battered women's movement has stalled because of its primary focus on physical violence rather than coercive control – a course of conduct that entraps women in personal life.[75] He points out that unlike physical acts of violence, which may be perpetrated by both men and women, coercive control is almost exclusively perpetrated by men in the context of intimate relationships. Stark compares coercive control to other capture crimes such as hostage taking or kidnapping, linking it to a larger discourse about rights and liberties including human rights, and noting the similarities in techniques used by batterers and by hostage takers to humiliate, degrade, and terrorize their victims. Stark writes:

"The hostage analogy also illuminates the structural dimensions of battering that allow controllers to regulate a woman's behavior, including isolating them from sources of support; taking their money; depriving them of such necessities as food and medicine; suppressing conflict and resistance; closing off opportunities for escape, communication or transportation; and laying down and enforcing rules for everyday conduct." [76]

The result, says Stark, is an entrapment that is gendered in its construction, delivery and consequences. While Stark focuses mainly on coercive control in the context of intimate partner relationships, he notes that children can be both the object and the instrument of coercive control. For a brief period, outspoken leaders of the incest survivor movement articulated a theory of incest rooted in male power over and control of children, before the movement lost its political focus. It is imperative for the sake of our children today that this focus be reinstated. Recently, in a discussion with Dr. Stark about incest and coercive control, he told me that in his experience batterers abuse children to get at their mothers. I wondered however, how this pertained to cases of incest where the mothers never knew it was happening. Armstrong provided some insight into the motivations of incest fathers as related to her by the victims. In many of these cases, the fathers gloated inwardly about the fact that the mother did not know what was going on, deriving satisfaction from imagining how hurt she would be if she found out.[77] These fathers also enjoyed the fact that they had come between mother and daughter, isolating them from each other and damaging their relationship.

But there is also ample evidence from other sources that coercive control of the victim's mother – whether secret or not – is not the only motivating force behind incest perpetration. Many incest perpetrators, unlike predatory child molesters, focus on a small number of children, or even only a single child over whom they believe they have proprietary rights. They reveal a similar sense of ownership over their daughters as they do over their wives, and harbor a similar sense of entitlement to the services of these owned objects.[78] Other similar attitudes and behaviors displayed towards victims of wife battering and incest include sexual jealousy, isolation tactics, victim-blaming narratives, and psychological cruelty and manipulation, all consistent with the dynamics of coercive control. Future research and theoretical development of the concept of coercive control in the violence against women field must address the commonalities between incest and wife battering, and must consider incest as a distinct form of coercive control of women.

A note about terminology

In this chapter we have used a variety of terms related to the gender-based abuse of women and girls – battering, domestic violence, intimate partner violence, coercive control, rape and incest. The term "battering" is usually taken to reflect the gender-oppressive paradigm associated with coercive control and in some views, may involve minimal or no actual physical violence. Throughout the remainder of this book "domestic violence" (hereinafter referred to by its initials DV) is the general term we will use for physical intimate partner violence. "Battering" refers to violence grounded in gender-based coercive control, and may include non-physical forms of abuse such as emotional abuse, financial abuse, threats, intimidation, isolation, and undermining of the parent-child relationship. "Protective parent" refers to a non-offending parent seeking to protect a child who has been abused (or is credibly alleged to have been abused) by the other parent. Protective parents may be of either gender, and may even be grandparents, but in the experience of the advocacy movement, those who bear the brunt of family court injustice are predominantly mothers. We refer to these women as "battered mothers" whether or not they themselves have been the targets of physical violence. Battered mothers are typically victims of ongoing court-sanctioned coercive control, even if they have survived DV.

In recent years, feminists have rejected the term "victim" to refer to women who have been the targets of DV or sexual violence, and prefer the term "survivor," which denotes agency rather than passivity, dependency and weakness. However, feminist journalist Rahila Gupta, has argued that the term "survivor" does a disservice to women who are still entrapped in oppressive circumstances, and fails to recognize the enormity of the oppressive system and its brutalizing potential.[79] While she made these observations in relation to women in third world countries, the same principle is true of women in western countries, especially those battling court-sanctioned abuse of their children, whose ongoing victimization is entrenched in our system of government. In this book, we prefer the term "victim" in reference to those who are still substantially entrapped in abusive relationships, particularly with regard to services, policies and legislation intended to provide them with relief. We use the term "survivor" in reference to those who have left abusive relationships but still battle to secure safety for themselves and their children. These terms underscore the fact that the battle is far from won, and that the help of our government and its leaders is still very much needed.

Chapter 3

A Perfect Storm

The previous chapter tracked the historical development and intersection of three victim advocacy movements that are relevant to issues facing protective parents. The child protection movement, with its paternalistic perspective and its goal of family reunification was at odds with the battered women's movement, grounded in gender politics, with its goal of achieving independence and self-determination for survivors. The incest survivor movement was initially successful in raising consciousness about an age-old and pernicious manifestation of patriarchal abuse. However, it failed to live up to its potential as a vehicle for social change, and morphed into the "recovery" movement, controlled by mental health professionals and becoming bogged down in the "false memory" backlash. In this chapter we drill down into the social conditions that led to the emergence of protective parents as a special group, and explore the forces that kept them entrapped in the private realm of "the family" preventing them from moving into the political realm like the battered women's movement. These forces included the divorce reforms of the 1970s, which, together with the relaxing of norms that determined gender roles, and increased child support enforcement, gave rise to the shared parenting movement. This movement, aided by endemic gender bias in the courts, joined forces with the false allegations backlash, and successfully resisted the feminist characterization of DV as rooted in gender politics. Instead, it promoted the idea of DV as a private matter arising out of relationship conflict. Taken together, these elements found expression in the "fathers' rights" movement, and established the perfect conditions for divorcing abusers to regain and maintain control over their victims.

Divorce reform

"No fault" legislation destigmatized divorce, making it an acceptable way to end unsatisfying relationships without necessarily attributing blame to either party. California was the first state to pass no fault legislation in 1970. By 1983 all but two states had adopted some form of no fault divorce, and in 2010, New York became the last state to adopt no fault divorce. These social changes probably contributed to a spike in the divorce rate, which doubled in the space of a decade going from 2.6 per 1,000 in 1967 to 5.3 in 1979. In the century prior to this, the divorce rate had doubled only about every 30 years. However, the divorce rate has gradually decreased through the 1980s and 1990s, reaching 3.5 per 1,000 in 2008.[1]

With the no-fault divorce revolution came the need for a new set of standards for deciding custody of children. Since there were no longer guilty or innocent parties, how would the custody of children be determined? Under the old system, mothers had typically been the innocent parties, but did this mean that under the new system custody would always automatically go to the mother? Some states began amending their statutes to reflect the "best interest" principle in the 1960s. By the early 1970s, 31 states appeared to have statutes providing for custody to be predicated on the best interests of the child in some form. Some of these statutes specified the kinds of factors that had to be considered, while others combined best interests with the vestiges of the parental fault standard. California, Nebraska, Oregon and Florida amended their statutes to reflect no presumption in favor of either party while Utah, Oklahoma and South Dakota had presumptions in favor of the mother, at least for young children. Some states that did not specify best interests had broad standards calling for determinations based on "what is right and proper," "just and reasonable" or "expedient."[2]

Feminism and the maternal presumption

The feminist movement gave women greater freedom to define their roles outside of marriage and family and increased their economic independence. In addition, the feminists of the 1970s played a significant role in undermining the maternal presumption, and promoting gender-neutral principles for custody determination. They viewed motherhood negatively, as merely involving the physical, menial aspects of childcare, and preventing women from achieving equality in the work-place, and they regarded the Tender Years Doctrine as a symbol of gender stereotyping – a remnant of the old order that prevented women from getting out of the home and seeking employment. In fact it was a feminist and activist for battered women's rights, New York Family Court Judge Sybil Kooper, who is credited with putting the final nail in the coffin of the Tender Years Doctrine, when ruling in the 1973 case Watts v. Watts. Judge Kooper ruled that any presumptive preference in favor of maternal custody violated the father's right to equal protection under the Fourteenth Amendment. In support of her decision she cited a passage from an article by anthropologist Margaret Mead which stated that (1) mother-child separation of even a few days would not damage the child, and that (2) there is no non-cultural reason why fathers should not participate more in childrearing. Judge Kooper concluded that the simple fact of being a mother does not by itself indicate a willingness or capacity to render a quality of care different from that which a father can provide, and that child development studies indicate that the essential experience for the child is that of mothering, not the gender of the person performing the mothering function.[3] However, this line of reasoning is flawed, according to Ramsey Laing Klaff who pointed out that being capable of doing a job is different from actually doing it.

> "Even accepting for the moment that mothering may be a gender-neutral function, this line of argument against the tender years doctrine is flawed. It assumes that the

maternal preference is based solely on gender and/or biological motherhood, while in actuality the preference is based principally on the fact that the mother has performed the mothering function – that is that she has been the primary caregiving parent. In short, the presumption in favor of maternal custody encompasses both a policy presumption against separating a child from his primary caregiving parent (that is, the parent who has mothered him) and a factual presumption that the primary caregiving parent is the mother."[4]

Maccoby and Mnookin present a similar argument in response to a literature review showing that fathers can learn to be primary parents.

" A woman who has served as the primary parent, after all, has already largely developed and demonstrated the skills to care for the child on an everyday basis. While her post-divorce role as custodial parent would require change, she has much less to learn in most cases than the father. Her experience as well as his inexperience strike us as relevant to the custodial issue."[5]

While these early discussions on fathers' fitness for custody centered on the question of his ability to provide – or learn to provide – primary care to his child or children, the debate on best interests drifted away from caregiving towards shared parenting, which in many jurisdictions became the new best interests standard. The reasons for this were primarily financial, and had little to do with the welfare of the child.

Child support and the push for shared parenting

Over the course of a century of rising divorce rates, states and the federal government gradually increased their efforts to enforce child support payments and prevent women and children from becoming dependent on public assistance. The first attempt to enforce child support payment occurred in 1910 when the National Conference of Commissioners on

Uniform State Laws approved the Uniform Desertion and Nonsupport Act that made it a crime for husbands to willfully abandon or refuse to provide support for children under the age of 16.[6] Only 24 jurisdictions adopted this law, and it was easy for fathers to evade the law by moving to a jurisdiction that did not have the law. It was not until 1950 that the Conference approved further model legislation that would allow states to pursue parents across states lines.

Improved welfare payments to poor women in the 1960s are credited with facilitating divorce among low-income families by making it possible for poor women to live by themselves.[7] However, this was accompanied by increased federal involvement in enforcing child support payments. In 1967, the federal government began requiring states to establish paternity and a means for collecting child support from parents of children receiving welfare. Then a major leap forward occurred in 1975 with the creation of Title IV-D of the Social Security Act, which established the federal Office of Child Support Enforcement (OCSE) in the Administration for Children and Families of the U.S. Department of Health and Human Services.[8] We shall discuss Title IV-D and subsequent child support legislation in greater depth in Chapter 7. In this chapter, our focus will be on how the legislation served as a catalyst for fathers' rights activism. Thus, among provisions of Title IV-D was the withholding of child support from the paychecks of federal employees and members of the Armed Services, who became the first groups of workers to experience involuntary wage garnishing for child support.

It should come as no surprise that the most active and influential early fathers' rights groups sprang up in the areas around Washington D.C., which are heavily populated with federal employees and members of the Armed Services. Fathers United for Equal Rights, which originated in Baltimore, Maryland in 1970, opened chapters in Montgomery and Prince George's Counties in 1975 and in Virginia and the District of Columbia in 1976.[9] David Levy, founder of the Children's Rights Council, and staunch advocate for shared parenting, was himself a divorcing federal employee involved in a custody battle, who sought assistance from the Virginia chapter of Fathers United around 1980.[10] Free Men was founded in Columbia, Maryland in 1977, with chapters rapidly expanding to other locations, eventually being renamed the National Coalition for Free Men in 1980 with its headquarters in Missouri. By 2005 there were close to 300 active fathers' rights websites representing distinct organizations with some presence in all 50 states and the District of Columbia.[11] The goal of these groups was primarily to advocate for shared parenting after divorce with a corresponding reduction in child support from fathers.

A landmark piece of legislation in this escalating struggle was the Family Support Act of 1988 (P.L. 100-485), which had two major purposes: (1) to improve the system for administering private child support transfers between parents to help support their children, and (2) to establish work programs and work provisions for parents who participate in the public support or welfare system for children.[12] The goal of child support reforms was to make child support orders more universal, more equitable, and more strictly enforced. The Act mandated uniform guidelines within states for child support orders, and required cases that go through OCSE to be reviewed every three years. Child support orders could be increased if the nonresident parent's income increased and decreased if income decreased.

Another major component of the Family Support Act addressed child support collection. Child support payments could be withheld from the nonresident parent's earnings in the same way that income tax is withheld, as a way of routinely collecting the child support obligation. The child support guideline formulae that were adopted by most states included a calculation that factored parental income and custodial time. It was not long after the adoption of the Family Support Act that noncustodial parents began to realize that if they fought for increased visitation time then child, support payments would be lowered. Thus the movement towards shared parenting gathered steam, as did the adoption of joint custody presumptions in state statutes.[13]

While the rise in popularity of joint custody statutes can be directly correlated to the increased child support enforcement initiatives, the theory behind the statutes is the best interests standard. Best interests in this context are usually defined as frequent and continuing contact with both parents. The first joint custody statutes were enacted in California in 1980, and presently, 35 states and the District of Columbia have some sort of joint custody statute. In August 1989, the American Bar Association approved and urged state legislatures to adopt the Model Joint Custody Statute, which makes joint custody an explicit option for families that have experienced separation or divorce. The Model Statute does state, however, that joint custody is inappropriate in cases in which spouse abuse, child abuse, or parental kidnapping are likely to occur.[14]

Scholars have argued that research contradicts the presumptions that joint custody is always in the best interests of children. A review of early studies examining the impact of joint custody on children's well being concluded that while joint custody could work in certain circumstances, it was totally inappropriate and not in a child's best interests where DV had occurred, where there was continued overt conflict between the parents, and where it was imposed by the courts rather than agreed-to by the parties.[15] A review of more recent studies reached similar conclusions – namely that while joint custody may work in certain circumstances, it is not for everyone – even parents who are highly committed and motivated. It is certainly inappropriate for parents who have abused their child or the other parent, since this abuse is likely to continue in the joint custody situation.[16]

A major study conducted by Maccoby and Mnookin in the late 1980s found evidence that joint custody is used at increasingly higher levels of conflict as a way to resolve that conflict and is thus being imposed in exactly those situations where it is contraindicated. The authors advocate against joint custody where there are high levels of parental conflict:

"We are deeply concerned about the use of joint physical custody in cases where there is substantial parental conflict as such conflict can create grave risks for children. We do not think it good for children to feel caught in the middle of parental conflict, and in those cases where the parents are involved in a bitter dispute we believe a presumption for joint custody would do harm . . . We wish to note, however, that joint custody can work very well when parents are able to cooperate. Thus we are by no means recommending that joint custody be denied to parents who want to try it."[17]

Demographics of single parents

Statistics provided by the U.S. Census seem to show that most custodial single parents (82%) are mothers. This pattern has varied little over the past 17 years. However, of the 14.4 million single parent households in 2011, 3.5 million or 24% had some kind of joint custody arrangement. Breaking this down by gender, we found that 38% of the fathers and 21% of the mothers had some kind of joint custody arrangement with the other parent regarding the children who were residing with them at the time of the survey. Of single parents who had sole custody of their children, 85% were mothers and 15% were fathers. Yet mothers had sole custody in only 64% of the totality of single parent households, fathers in 11%, and 24% involved joint custody.[18] These data are surprisingly consistent with the findings from the longitudinal study conducted by Maccoby and Mnookin in the late 1980s involving over 1,000 divorcing California couples. In that study, 67% of physical custody awards were made to mothers, 9% to fathers, 20% were joint custody awards, and 4% were "other" awards.[19] Maccoby and Mnookin found that their sample was demo-graphically comparable to the rest of the nation, except that the mothers in their sample were slightly better educated, and were earning more at the time of the study's third wave of data collection compared to divorced mothers in the United States as a whole. Also, the census data included single parents who were never married, and a higher proportion of these were mothers (37%) compared to fathers (23%). When we excluded custodial parents living in poverty, 90% of whom were mothers, a very different picture emerged. Only 59% of non-poor custodial parents were mothers, 13% were fathers, and 28% had joint custody. Thus although the census shows that most children are residing with mothers, the combination of joint custody and father custody brings us closer than ever to the 50-50 split envisioned by the shared parenting movement. The canard that mothers always get custody is now only true for the poorest families in our nation.

Dividing the child: what parents want and what they get

Maccoby and Mnookin interviewed divorcing parents before they filed formal requests for custody with the court, and asked them, among other things, about their custody preferences. While over 80% of mothers stated that their preference was for maternal custody, only 29% of fathers stated that maternal custody was their preference. The remainder was fairly evenly split between joint custody (35%) and paternal custody (32%). When filing formal requests, however, 80% of mothers but only 56% of fathers requested their original preference, and overall, 80% of couples did not file conflicting requests.[20]

Maccoby and Mnookin found a variety of reasons why the fathers in their study may have changed their minds. First, men held their views about custody somewhat less strongly than women, and men who pursued non-traditional custody arrangements, held their views more strongly than men who opted for the traditional arrangement. Another reason why men changed their minds was logistical. Most couples agreed that the mother's home would be the children's place of residence after separation for practical reasons such as proximity to the children's school. Most fathers did not want to disrupt their children's lives, and the children's place of residence was a major factor in the final custody outcome. Moreover, the authors noted that over time, children's residential patterns tended to change from that which was initially decreed, and their impression was that these changes were more likely to occur for positive reasons – informal agreements between both parents about the best interests of the child, rather than negative reasons such as allegations of abuse and neglect or attempts to block visitation.[21]

Most divorcing fathers want to continue having a relationship with their children, and also want what is best for their children. These are the factors that contribute to their initial custody preference and the ultimate resolution of any disagreement between themselves and their ex-wives. The problems that we are concerned about here arise in a sub-category of divorcing couples referred to as "high conflict". Maccoby and Mnookin describe conflicted custody requests in terms of a pyramid. The base of the pyramid comprises 50.4% of couples that did not contest custody. At the next level are 29.3% of couples that initially disagreed, but ultimately filed unconflicting requests. Of the couples that filed conflicting requests, 11% settled with mediation, 5.2% settled after a custody evaluation, 2.2% settled during trial, and a judge decided 1.5% of cases. The authors noted that maternal custody awards diminished at successively higher levels of this pyramid. Whereas maternal custody was awarded in 70% of low conflict or no conflict cases, it was awarded in 63% of cases that settled after mediation, and only 44% of cases that were resolved after evaluation.[22]

Most interestingly, when the authors re-interviewed the couples three years after the first court filing, they found a shift towards maternal residence in cases where joint physical custody had originally been decreed. Even more surprising is the fact that the shift towards maternal residence was slightly greater in high conflict families (48%) compared to low conflict families (35%) even though this difference was not statistically significant. These results were unrelated to residential stability, and the authors suggest that some highly conflicted cases are being resolved by adopting the joint physical custody label, although in fact the children's residence is with the mother.[23] Looked at another way, some fathers may be fighting for custody to punish their ex-wives by dragging them through a protracted court battle and not because they want a greater parental role. The authors did not address whether DV was present among these highly conflicted couples, but other studies have found high levels of violence in similarly defined conflicted relationships.

Conflict versus violence

Stanford University sociologist Janet Johnston conducted two small studies of high conflict divorcing families referred for counseling because mandatory mediation had failed. She found that 35% of parents in the one study and 48% in the other study experienced severe aggression such as battering and threatening to use or using a weapon, even though the couples had been separated on average 30 to 42 months.[24] These levels of aggression were 36 times higher than those experienced by divorcing couples drawn from a general sample. In a larger study of randomly selected failed mediation case files in San Diego, Dennis Saccuzzo and colleagues found that 39% (200 out of 512) involved male-perpetrated DV.[25] Thus on average across the three studies, 40% of failed mediation cases involve DV. However, in the world of conflict resolution, DV seems to be irrelevant. In the San Diego study, mediators failed to address DV in 57% of cases where there were clear indications of DV in the mediation file. In some of these cases, the mediators tended to focus on problems other than DV, such as substance abuse, which was seen as the cause of the violence. In other cases, they referred to the violence as "conflict" or "quarrelling" or they ignored the violence altogether. The following is an extreme example of this distorted reasoning process:

> "In a series of mediations, the mother repeatedly attempted to make clear her fear of the father and to utilize safeguards such as separate mediations. Even after the two preschool age children witnessed the father threaten to slit the mother's throat and the father was convicted of making a terrorist threat, the mediator stated that "there was no way of determining the veracity of the mother's report. " It continued to be the mediator's opinion that the mother was simply attempting to minimize the father's time with the children. "[26]

Maccoby and Mnookin acknowledge that some families in their study experienced severe DV including beatings, and threats with knives and gun, but this was mentioned in passing to illustrate the diversity of the population they had studied.[27] One could hypothesize that most of these violent families were at the top of the conflict pyramid, where custody awards to fathers or joint custody awards were more frequent than at the lower levels. Indeed, Maccoby and Mnookin noticed a pattern of intense hostility among a subgroup of fathers whose wives had left them, and who retaliated by asserting control over the children's place of residence at the beginning of the separation. Furthermore, intense hostility of the father towards the mother, but not the mother towards the father, was one of the characteristics of families at the top of the conflict pyramid.[28] While the authors speculate as to why this may be the case, DV is not even considered as a possibility. Interestingly, they point out that a relative absence of conflict at the lower levels of the pyramid did not necessarily mean the absence of hostility, which they illustrate with the following narrative from a mother who had agreed to let her husband have custody of their young son:

> "He threatened to kill me if I took Kevin. You know what? He would have. He's beaten me up twice before. I see Kevin every other weekend now. The only thing I could do to make this divorce easy on Kevin was to give Kevin to his father. It's not worth losing my life over. The next time he would kill me. That's how angry he is at me for leaving."[29]

This case also demonstrates why the equation of DV with conflict tactics fails to capture coercive control – the essence of battering, which involves instilling such fear in the victim that she complies with the abuser's demands.

Divorce professionals also tend to interpret child abuse allegations as evidence of conflict, and for this reason such allegations are often dismissed without any attempt at investigation. Citing a statewide California study of 1,669 mediation sessions by Depner and colleagues, Johnston notes that child neglect allegations arose in 38% of cases, child physical abuse in 18% of cases, and child sexual abuse in 8% of cases. The study did not attempt to address the validity of these allegations, and in fact Johnston views them as signs of hostility, distrust, and negative perceptions.

> "It is commonly believed by family court counselors, however, that these allegations of neglect or abuse often do not meet the criteria for mandatory reporting. In fact, court counselors generally contend that, when such investigations are undertaken by child protective services, the allegations are frequently dismissed by overworked staff as being either indicators of interpersonal spite, impossible to prove, or insufficiently serious to require state intervention."[30]

Even when divorce professionals acknowledge that the allegations of sexual abuse are true they do not necessarily propose parenting arrangements that protect the children, as illustrated in the following case history from the San Diego study:

> "The mediator listened to this family's history, noted his/her belief that the incidents of domestic violence and child sexual abuse perpetrated by the father of the children were factual, and yet came to the conclusion that the father should get a 36% share of unsupervised custody of his two biological children. The mediator gave no explanation of the decision and appeared to regard the division of custody as fair and reasonable."[31]

A criminal justice practitioner would most likely recommend prosecution and jail time for this father based on the facts of the case. So then why would another court-based professional recommend rewarding the same behavior? How could such contradictory views co-exist in the same justice system? The biases of divorce professionals will be addressed more fully in Chapter 5. Our goal here is to establish that these are not isolated cases, and to ask what we know about the extent of the problem.

Gender bias

Before turning to statistics on battered mothers and custody, it is important to address the problem of gender bias in the courts, which has documented disadvantages for women, especially in their role as parent. The unequal treatment of women in the courts became a major concern in the 1980s and spurred the establishment of task forces on gender bias, which we reviewed in our original book, *The Hostage Child*, published in 1996.[32] In summary, some of the key findings of the task forces were that gender stereotypes, influenced by common law and cultural beliefs, resulted in the minimization of the significance of DV, unequal standards of good parenting for mothers versus fathers, and the blaming of victim mothers for the consequences of their victimization, such as frequently having to move or keeping their home addresses or phone numbers unknown.[33]

Preference for fathers over mothers in contested custody cases was clearly documented by the Massachusetts Gender Bias Task Force, which published its findings in 1990.[34] For the custody section of the study, the Task Force sampled 2,100 cases obtained from family law attorneys representing fathers seeking custody in the previous 5 years, and 700 cases from Middlesex County between 1978 and 1984. The Task Force also conducted a survey of family law judges. Results from the attorney survey indicated that in contested cases, fathers obtained primary physical custody in 29% of the cases, and joint *physical* custody in an additional 65% of the cases. Thus, when fathers actively sought physical custody, mothers obtained primary physical custody in only 7% of cases. In the Middlesex sample, when fathers had sought custody mothers received primary physical custody in less than one-quarter of the cases. Although the Task Force did not specifically address violence in the context of custody, three-quarters of the family law attorneys surveyed reported that in cases in which a woman alleges that she has been physically abused, court-affiliated mediators sometimes or often make remarks indicating they are applying a presumption of joint legal custody.[35] Over half the probate judges surveyed agreed that "mothers allege child sexual abuse to gain a bargaining advantage in the divorce process."[36]

The results of this study, as well as many other gender bias studies frequently cited in the literature, are based on data collected before 1990. What if any change has occurred in the past quarter of a century? Feminist author, Phyllis Chesler, who first described the problem of custodially challenged mothers, recently listed some of the changes that have occurred since the 1986 publication of her landmark book, *Mothers on Trial*.[37] Parents, she says, are no longer automatically disqualified because they are gay or because they have high-powered careers; where assets exist, judges have more power to award more of them to mothers and children, and DV does get factored in somewhat more than before. However, she notes certain problems have gotten much worse. Battered mothers are losing custody in record numbers, and children who are reported by mandated reporters for suspected sexual abuse are given to the parent accused of abusing them, while the mothers of these children are viewed as having "coached" or "alienated" the children. In short, in a country that prides itself in being anti-discrimination, where billions of dollars have been spent providing services to battered mothers and promoting programs and policies to hold abusers accountable, and where gay marriage recently became the law of the land – *battered and protective mothers are being marched backwards into the 19th century.*

Battered mothers and custody

Exact statistics on the extent of the problem do not currently exist. However, the Leadership Council on Child Abuse and Interpersonal Violence has estimated that every year, 58,000 children in the United States are court-ordered into the unprotected care of an abuser after their parents' divorce. This is derived as followed: 13% of divorcing families experience allegations of severe DV or child sexual abuse, and conservatively, 60% of these cases are found to be valid; on average, 75% of these valid cases are court ordered into the custody of the abuser. Since divorce affects one million children annually, the number of children ordered into unsafe custody arrangements would be 58,000.[38]

Data for the Leadership Council estimate were obtained in part from a Maryland study, which found that 13% of divorces involved allegations of DV or child abuse.[39] More recently, a study of 2,374 Seattle couples undergoing marriage dissolution found that 11.4% of cases involved substantiated male-perpetrated DV (Seattle Study 1).[40] Another study by the same authors examined Seattle divorces over an 11-year period (29,000) and found that 10% of these cases involved a substantiated history of DV based on police and court records (Seattle Study 2).[41] Thus conservatively, at least 10% of divorces involve valid claims of DV, which would affect 100,000 children. Regarding sexual abuse allegations, the most comprehensive study to date was that conducted by Thoennes and Tjaden in 1986, involving 9,000 contested custody cases in 12 states. Two percent of these cases involved sex abuse allegations, and 50% of these were substantiated.[42] This is consistent with findings from Seattle Study 2, which found about 1% of DV custody cases involved substantiated allegations of child sexual abuse. Seattle Study 2 also found that 13.5% of DV custody cases involved substantiated allegations of any child abuse (physical, sexual and emotional). To date there are no data on how often child abuse is alleged in custody cases with no allegations of DV, but it is safe to say that conservatively, 100,000 children per year in the U.S. are the subject of custody battles involving substantiated DV, with or without child abuse.

Until recently, most studies of custody decisions involving allegations of DV or child abuse were based on non-represen-tative, self-selected, clinical or legal samples. The major findings of these earlier studies are summarized in Table 1. As regards custody, we are fortunate to have one study of judges' rulings in substantiated DV cases obtained systematically from court records in six states.[43] States' selection was based on whether or not they had enacted provisions of the "Model Code" presumptions against awarding custody to a perpetrator of DV. We will discuss the impact of the Model Code presumptions on judges' custody decisions in the next chapter. In the present chapter, we combine custody decisions from all six states to come up with an estimate of a national average. The Model Code study found that on average, 64% of battered mothers were awarded sole physical custody, and for the most part, when mothers received sole physical custody, they also received sole legal custody. An additional 24% received primary or shared physical custody. However, 12% of perpetrators received primary, or sole physical custody. Also, about 34% of fathers who did not receive sole or primary physical custody were awarded visitation without conditions. These percentages varied by state, which we will discuss more fully in the next chapter, but on average, this left a large percentage of children unprotected or inadequately protected. If we combine cases in which fathers received primary, sole or joint physical custody (17.6%) and those in which fathers were awarded visitation with no conditions (34%), we estimate that 51.6% of children in this study lacked adequate protection. Extrapolation of this percentage to the entire country would result in an estimate of 51,600 children in the United States ordered into unsafe custody conditions. In reality, this number could be a lot higher, since not all conditions imposed on fathers' visitation necessarily provided adequate safety.

In Seattle Study 1 mentioned above, most mothers were awarded primary residential custody regardless of whether or not they had experienced DV, (ranging from 86.5% to 92.9%), and in this regard, there were no statistically significant differences between mothers who had experienced DV and those who had not. In cases where the DV was substantiated and known to the court, fathers had a higher likelihood of being denied visitation or of having restrictions placed on their visitation. Thus 16.8% of perpetrator fathers were denied visitation, and 71.2% of perpetrator fathers who received visitation, had restrictions placed on their visitation. If we combine father custody and joint custody with unrestricted visitation in substantiated DV cases, we find that 34% of the children in Seattle Study 1 were unprotected or inadequately protected. This only applies to cases of substantiated DV known to the court. In cases of substantiated DV unknown to the court, 61.5% of children lacked adequate protection. Overall estimates from these two studies are roughly in the same ballpark as the Leadership Council estimates. In addition, as we shall see in the next chapter, there are great variations across states, and even though our estimates are based on systematic sampling methods and documentation of DV from police files and court records, they only cover seven states. We need a lot more information to develop an estimate of a national average.

Table 1: Custody outcomes for battered mothers based on self-selected, clinical or legal samples

Author (date) Institution Sample	Results
Phyllis Chesler (1986)[44] The sample comprised 60 mothers undergoing divorce, who had been married between 1951 and 1974. All mothers were primary caregivers.	In 70% of cases that went to court, judges ordered children into paternal custody. In 70% of cases where custody was privately arranged, fathers also got custody. After two years, 82% of fathers had custody. Only 8% of mothers retained custody, but they had to agree to give up their rights to alimony, child support, or marital assets, and had to agree to whatever paternal visitation was demanded. Over half of the fathers who obtained custody were physically violent.
Kathleen Coulborn Faller and Ellen DeVoe(1995)[45] University of Michigan The sample comprised 214 divorce cases with allegations of sexual abuse that were evaluated by a multidisciplinary team at a university-based clinic.	The researchers categorized the cases as "likely" (72.6%), "unlikely" (20%) and "uncertain" (7.4%). They observed that 40 parents who brought these allegations received negative sanctions from the court including being jailed and losing custody, yet independent investigation found that none of these parents were judged to have made deliberately false allegations, and in fact their cases were judged more likely to be genuine.
Amy Neustein and Ann Goetting (1999)[46] The sample comprised 300 cases of protective mothers collected over a 10-year period.	Seventy percent of cases resulted in unsupervised visitation or shared custody with the alleged abuser. In 20% of cases, the mothers lost custody and in many cases they also lost visitation rights. Only 10% of children reporting sexual abuse were protected by family court.

Table 1 continued:

Author (date) Institution Sample	Results
Jay Silverman et al., (1999) [47] The Wellesley Center for Women The study recruited 39 mothers with documented DV, using snowballing sampling, and interviewed them about their experiences with the Massachusetts family court system.	Mothers reported that the most common problem was judges' refusal to accept or consider documentation of DV when it was presented, an error that was also committed by state-appointed custody evaluators, child protective service workers or both. In over half of the cases where state actors refused to consider documentation, the perpetrators of violence were granted physical custody of their children, and in most of the remaining cases, un-supervised visitation was awarded. In four of the nine cases with documented child abuse, the perpetrator received physical custody, and in the remaining cases unsupervised visitation.
Sheila Heim (2001)[48] California National Organization for Women* The sample comprised over 200 California women who claimed to have been victimized in the family court system, and who responded to a 21-page questionnaire.	Mothers alleged father-perpetrated DV in 86% of cases and child abuse in 76% of cases, but in 73% of such cases they were not permitted to present evidence to the court. In 50% of abuse cases police reports had been filed, and in 36% restraining orders had been issued and violated by the father. The authors were startled to discover that in 69% of the cases where child abuse occurred, the offender was given unsupervised contact or custody of the child despite evidence of the abuse.

Table 1 continued:

Author (date) Institution Sample	Results
Dianne Post (2003)[49] Arizona Coalition Against Domestic Violence* The sample comprised 57 battered mothers who had gone through a custody battle in Arizona family courts during the previous two years.	Seventy-two percent of the mothers said they were not given an adequate chance to tell the court their side of the story and 41% were ordered into mediation although the court knew there was violence. The survey found that courts awarded joint or sole custody to the alleged batterers 56% to 74% of the time (depending on the county). Many of these cases involved documented child abuse.
Joan Meier (2003)[50] George Washington University The sample comprised 38 appellate state court decisions concerning custody and DV.	In 36 of the 38 cases the trial court had awarded joint or sole custody to alleged and adjudicated batterers. Two thirds of these decisions were reversed on appeal.

* These two studies are revisited in Chapter 5, Table 4, dealing with the role of the parental alienation label in mothers' loss of custody to abusive fathers

Chapter 4

Legislative and Legal Remedies

In 1990, Congress passed a resolution encouraging the states to examine their policies regarding DV and child custody.[1] According to the National Council of Juvenile and Family Court Judges (NCJFCJ), as of 2013, 35 states, one territory and the District of Columbia had specifically addressed DV in their state custody statutes.[2] These statutes include: (1) those that give extra weight to consideration of DV in the "best interests of the child" analysis; (2) those that provide DV exceptions to other best interest factors such as relocation; and (3) those based on the Model Code developed by the National Council, which sets forth a rebuttable presumptions that it is not in a child's best interests to be placed in the joint or sole custody of a perpetrator of DV. Many states have multiple statutes addressing DV and custody (see Table 2.) In addition, some states such as California have enacted other laws that specifically address the safety and rights of children of divorcing parents especially where sexual abuse has been alleged. In this chapter we ask what if any benefit victims have derived from these laws and whether they have succeeded in keeping mothers and children safer. Second, we ask to what extent protective parents have been able to seek and obtain redress from higher courts, when lower court verdicts have endangered them and their children.

Table 2: Domestic violence and custody statutes by state

State	Model Code Presumption	Extra Weight To DV	DV Exceptions
Alabama	X	X	X
Alaska	X		X
Arizona	X	X	X
Arkansas	X	X	X
California	X		X
Colorado		X	X
Delaware	X	X	
District of Columbia	X		
Florida	X	X	
Georgia		X	X
Guam		X	X
Hawaii	X	X	X
Idaho	X		
Indiana			X
Iowa	X	X	X
Kentucky			X
Louisiana	X		
Maine			X
Massachusetts	X	X	
Minnesota	X	X	
Mississippi	X		
Missouri		X	
Montana		X	
Nevada	X		
New Hampshire		X	
North Carolina		X	X
North Dakota	X		X
Oklahoma	X	X	X
Oregon	X		
Pennsylvania			X
Rhode Island		X	X
South Carolina		X	X

Table 2 continued:

State	Model Code Presumption	Extra Weight To DV	DV Exceptions
South Dakota	X		
Tennessee	X		X
Texas	X		
Virginia			X
West Virginia			X
Wisconsin	X		
Wyoming		X	

Legislation

The Model Code

In 1991 the National Council for Juvenile and Family Court Judges undertook the drafting of the Model State Code on Domestic and Family Violence in order to assist lawmakers in the development of legislation that would protect battered women.[3] The Model Code was developed with the assistance of an advisory committee composed of leaders in the DV field including judges, prosecutors, defense attorneys, matrimonial lawyers, battered women's advocates, medical and health care professionals, law enforcement personnel, legislators, educators and others. The Code, which was first published in 1994, sets forth procedures for civil protection orders, and principles for child custody determination that assure that the child's safety and wellbeing are of paramount concern.

Specifically, Section 401 states: "*In every proceeding where there is at issue a dispute as to the custody of a child, a determination by the court that domestic or family violence has occurred raises a rebuttable presumption that it is detrimental to the child and not in the best interests of the child to be placed in sole custody, joint legal custody, or joint physical custody with the perpetrator of family violence.*"[4] States that have adopted this provision have "presumption laws." Other sections provide for safety factors such as how to determine when visitation is appropriate and how it can be done safely, and protecting the DV victim and child by keeping their addresses confidential. There are also provisions that require mandatory DV training for judges and for mediators. Ideally the Code prefers that cases involving DV not go to mediation unless the victim desires it and it can be done safely, including by having a supportive person (who could be an attorney or advocate) present. According to a 2013 report, 23 states have adopted a rebuttable presumption against awarding custody to a perpetrator of DV.[5] How do we know if these statutes are working to protect DV victims and achieve justice for them? This question was addressed in a 2001 study funded by the National Institute of Justice.

The Model Code evaluation study

The study, which was conducted Allison Morrill and her colleagues at the University of New England, examined the effectiveness of statutes that address judicial decision-making in custody and visitation cases involving DV, and mandatory judicial education.[6] The researchers categorized all 50 states on the basis of whether or not the state's law included (1) a presumption against giving custody to a batterer (Model Code Section 401) and (2) mandatory judicial education on DV (Model Code Section 510). Initially, four states – two in each quadrant – were selected based on their agreement to participate in the study. When it became apparent that more data would be needed, an additional state was added to each of those two quadrants, making a total of six states. The final sample comprised 393 custody and/or visitation orders where the father perpetrated violence against the mother. Violence was defined in terms of the issuance of a protective or restraining order against the man in favor of the woman within three years of the contested custody case. Judges who entered orders completed a survey about DV education, personal characteristics, knowledge and attitudes about DV.

Four states (Delaware, Florida, Massachusetts and Minnesota) had enacted Model Code provisions involving a presumption against awarding sole or joint legal or physical custody to a perpetrator of family violence. Two states (Kentucky and Rhode Island) had no such presumption. Florida, however, had a competing "friendly parent" statute with no exception for DV except in cases of felony conviction, and was therefore placed in a separate category. The study found that in states with the presumption, significantly more orders gave legal custody to the mother (52%) compared to states without the presumption (31%) and the state with competing provisions (19%). However, there was no difference in the rate of awards of sole physical custody to the mother in states with the presumption (64%) and without the presumption (67%). Furthermore, in the state with competing provisions, more orders gave sole physical custody to the father – the perpetrator of DV (14%) as compared to the mother who was the victim (4%). There were no differences across types of states with regard to the granting of visitation to the father. However, in states without the presumption, fewer visitation orders were structured (54%) compared to states with the presumptions (70%). Additionally, more orders included conditions in states with the presumption (66%) compared to those without the presumption (49%).

Re-analysis of the Model Code study

In February of 2007, two years after the publication of the Model Code study, we requested and received from Dr. Morrill a printout of the frequencies of custody awards broken down by state for further analysis. Our analyses were conducted on a slightly larger sample than that reported in the original publication, which excluded cases decided by judges that did not return a questionnaire. In the present analysis we examine each state individually, and as in the previous chapter, we define adequate protection for children as primary or sole physical custody to the mother with restrictions on visitation for the father in cases where he did not receive primary or joint custody. The results of this analysis are presented in Table 2.

The results show that the state with the worst safety record, Rhode Island, is a no presumption state, providing protection to only 24.3% of children of battered mothers. However, lack of protection comes in varying degrees. Arguably, the worst outcome is sole physical custody to the father followed by joint custody. Rhode Island had the lowest rate of sole or joint custody awards to fathers but rarely imposed restrictions on fathers' visitation. Kentucky is also a no presumption state with the best safety record, but this is accomplished primarily through high rates of conditions imposed on fathers' visitation when custody is awarded to the mother. Interestingly, Washington State, which is a no presumption state, (although not part of the Model Code study), failed to protect only 34% of children of battered mothers when the court knew about the abuse (see previous chapter). In conclusion, it is not clear that the Model Code has any protective benefit to the children of battered mothers. Variations across states appear to be idiosyncratic. A statutory presumption against giving custody of a child or unrestricted visitation to a perpetrator of DV is not necessary in order for judges to conclude that it is not in a child's best interests. For the most part, Washington State judges apparently reach this conclusion without a statutory presumption.

Table 3: Custody and visitation decisions in domestic violence cases across six states

State	FL(+-)	KY(-)	MA(+)	RI (-)	DE(+)	MN(+)
Father sole or joint custody	15%	24.2%	22.7%	8.8%	27%	18%
Father's visitation when he did not get custody						
No conditions imposed	41.3%	15.2%	30.9%	66.9%	17.4%	25%
Some conditions imposed	13.8%	40.1%	17.2%	12.6%	12.7%	34.7%
Visitation supervised	18.4%	16.9%	22.3%	3.9%	38.1%	14%
No visitation	11.5%	3.6%	6.9%	7.7%	4.8%	8.3%
TOTAL	100%	100%	100%	100%	100%	100%
Children considered unsafe*	56.3%	39.4%	53.6%	75.7%	44.8%	43%

+ Model Code Presumption
- No Presumption
+- Presumption with conflicting provisions
*   Derived from adding father sole or joint custody with no conditions imposed on visitation

Legislative accomplishments in California

Since its inception in 1998, the California Protective Parents Association (CPPA) working with the Legislative Coalition to Prevent Child Abuse, PROTECT, and Center for Judicial Excellence, has been helpful in bringing the plight of battered mothers and protective parents engaged in custody litigation to the attention of the California State Legislature, and they have been effective in bringing about some changes to state law. In October 1999 California adopted an amendment to its Family Code specifying that a parent should not be denied custody of or visitation with his or her child solely for lawfully reporting suspected sexual abuse, or otherwise acting lawfully to determine if his or her child was a victim of sexual abuse, or for seeking treatment for the child from a licensed professional. An attempt was made to make the law retroactive to encompass past cases in which mothers lost custody for believing and reporting suspected sexual abuse of their children, but this bill failed because of intense opposition from the California Judges' Association and the Family Law Executive Committee for the State Bar, which maintained that the new bill amounted to undue interference with the courts' discretion. Other court reform accomplishments initiated by CPPA and the victim advocacy organizations mentioned above include:

- Legislation passed in 2000 establishing minimum standards for training in child sexual abuse for custody evaluators, and requiring court-connected and private custody evaluators to refrain from evaluating, investigating or mediating child custody issues unless they have completed child sexual abuse training. [7]

- Legislation passed in 2005 repealing the incest exemption, which had allowed the prosecuting attorney to make a motion to defer entry of judgment in the case of molestation of a minor child, if the perpetrator was a family member.[8]

- Legislation passed in 2006 making it more difficult for convicted sex offenders to obtain custody of a child.[9]

- Legislation introduced in 2007 and 2009 specifying that nonscientific labels and diagnoses that are not consistent with diagnostic or medical standards generally accepted by the medical, psychiatric, and psychological communities are specifically excluded as allowable diagnoses for court use as part of a child custody evaluation. Although the legislation did not pass, the courts began to reduce their use of non-scientific labels due to publicity generated from the bills.[10]

- An audit of the family court resulting in a report by the California Bureau of State Audits in 2011 showing that courts in Sacramento and Marin Counties could not demonstrate that their staff met the minimum qualifications and training requirements to perform mediations and evaluations, and did not log complaints about private mediators and evaluators. The courts also did not ensure that their local rules included all the rules that were required.[11]

- Legislation passed in 2010 requiring multiple reforms in the family court system including: requiring a child's counsel to present the child's wishes to the court if the child so desires; providing that a court order for custody, visitation or support made as part of a protective order, shall survive the termination of the protective order; requiring social workers to draw no inference regarding the credibility of allegations of child abuse from the mere existence of a child custody or visitation dispute; and making an exception to the confidentiality of child welfare agency records for certain participants in family law and probate guardianship cases.[12]

- Legislation passed in 2011 giving children a voice in decisions determining their custody by requiring family court to consider and give due weight to the wishes of a child in making an order granting or modifying custody or visitation if the child is of sufficient age and capacity to form an intelligent preference as to custody and visitation. It further requires the court to permit a child who is 14 years of age or older to address the court regarding custody or visitation, unless the court determines it is not in the best interests of the child.[13]

- Legislation currently under consideration to extend the statute of limitations in cases of child sexual abuse.[14]

Advocates believe that although California now has excellent laws on the books to ensure due process and child safety in family (divorce) court, judges have wide discretion with no effective oversight. This, in addition to the power of the divorce industry, which we address in the next chapter, essentially nullifies any positive impact of protective legislation.

Litigation

Appeals

Because of the wide discretion given to judges in family court cases, it is very difficult to successfully argue that a judge has abused his or her discretion, which is the basis for most appeals. Furthermore, very few protective parents have the resources to take their cases to the appellate level, unless they have pro bono attorneys, or unless they manage to file their appeals pro se. Nevertheless, there are some cases that we are aware of in which appeals have been successful. In 2001, Professor Joan Meier conducted a survey of appellate state court decisions concerning custody and DV. In 36 out of 38 cases that she identified, trial courts had awarded joint or sole custody to alleged and adjudicated batterers. Two thirds of these decisions were reversed on appeal.[15] Meier has noted, however, that it has become increasingly difficult to win appeals when gender-biased labels such as "parental alienation" are attached to battered mothers. Thus she sought and obtained a grant from the National Institute of Justice to study this problem more closely. At the time of writing, this study is still in progress.

Civil rights actions

Many protective parents and their advocates believe that the inhumane treatment of battered mothers and their children in family court amounts to violations of their civil rights, and some have attempted to sue the government under civil rights statutes. These lawsuits have typically invoked the equal protection clause of the Fourteenth Amendment, which states that states shall not *"deprive any person of life, liberty, or property, without due process; nor deny to any person in its jurisdiction the equal protection of the laws."* Protective parents have generally not fared well in the civil rights arena. Two precedent-setting cases that went all they way to the U.S. Supreme Court convey the shameful message that the government is not responsible for the harm that comes to children that the government itself has knowingly placed in harm's way (DeShaney v Winnebago), or for refusing to protect endangered children when the law requires them to do so (Castle-Rock v Gonzales).

DeShaney v Winnebago County. Joshua DeShaney, born in Wyoming in 1979, was placed in the custody of his father, Randy DeShaney when he was a little over one year old. His mother, Melody DeShaney, had agreed to give up custody of him to his father thinking that this would give him a "nice kid life" – the kind of life that she felt too poor and too alone to give him herself. Randy quickly moved from Wyoming to Winnebago County, Wisconsin and never disclosed his location to Melody. Melody DeShaney said she went to Wisconsin several times looking for Joshua, apparently unsuccessfully, and she did not have access to him again until after a fateful day in 1984 when she received a phone call to say that he was in the hospital undergoing surgery following a severe beating by his father, and that he might not survive the night.[16]

Joshua first came to the attention of the Wisconsin authorities in 1983, at the age of four, when a visit to the emergency room resulted in a physician's report of suspected child abuse to the county Department of Social Services (DSS).

A court order kept Joshua in the hospital temporarily, but three days later, it dismissed the case and returned the boy to his father's custody. Thereafter, DSS entered into an agreement with Randy DeShaney designed to maintain some level of surveillance on the child. Five times throughout 1983, DSS social workers visited the DeShaney home and recorded suspicion of child abuse and concerns that the father was not complying with the terms of the agreement. Still no action was taken. Again, in November 1983, a hospital reported child abuse suspicion to DSS. Visits to check up on Joshua in January and March 1984 were deflected and the social worker was told Joshua was too ill to see her. Again, no action was taken. Following the March 1984 visit, Randy DeShaney beat Joshua so severely that he fell into a life-threatening coma. Emergency brain surgery revealed a series of hemorrhages caused by traumatic injuries to the head inflicted over a long period of time. Although he did not die that night, Joshua suffered brain damage so severe that he was expected to spend the rest of his life in a total care institution.[17] Randy DeShaney was subsequently tried and convicted of child abuse, for which he received less than two years in prison.

Melody DeShaney, who was financially unable to provide Joshua with the care that he needed, filed a civil rights action against DSS for having allowed the permanent damage to her son's health and welfare, claiming they had violated Joshua's civil right to liberty without due process guaranteed to him by the Fourteenth Amendment to the U.S. Constitution. The suit made its way through the federal court system, which consistently ruled against Joshua. Judge Richard Posner wrote the opinion for the Seventh Circuit Court of Appeals affirming the lower court's ruling against Joshua, and noting the cost to the state of providing protective services to those in need, because failure of those efforts could result in a lawsuit. He also remarked on the difficulty courts face in "balancing the rights of the parents with those of the children," as well as the danger to social service agencies of exposure to lawsuits by parents whose rights they had terminated.[18] The case finally reached the Supreme Court, which ruled against Joshua in

February 1989. The majority opinion, written by Chief Justice Renquist, made it clear that Joshua had no rights he was entitled to enforce against his government. The damage was not done to him by the government, but by a "third party" for whose conduct the government had no responsibility. In fact it was noted that Joshua could not prevail because he sued for his liberty interest, which would only have been protected if DSS had a "special relationship" with him, which by its own choice it did not, since it did not take custody of him away from his abuser. The only actionable "special relationship" existing with Joshua was his "special relationship" with his custodial father, Randy. The court also noted that, had Joshua alleged that he was treated badly by DSS because he was a minority, he would possibly have had a claim. Since he did not even seek to prove that DSS would have treated him any better had he belonged to a different race or group, he had no case against the agency. In his famous dissent, Justice Blackmun stated:

> "Poor Joshua! Victim of repeated attacks by an irresponsible, bullying, cowardly, and intemperate father, and abandoned by respondents who placed him in a dangerous predicament and who knew or learned what was going on, and yet did essentially nothing except, as the Court revealingly observes, ante, at 193, "dutifully recorded these incidents in [their] files." It is a sad commentary upon American life, and constitutional principles - so full of late of patriotic fervor and proud proclamations about "liberty and justice for all" - that this child, Joshua DeShaney, now is assigned to live out the remainder of his life profoundly retarded. Joshua and his mother, as petitioners here, deserve - but now are denied by this Court - the opportunity to have the facts of their case considered in the light of the constitutional protection that 42 U.S.C. 1983 [the civil rights act] is meant to provide." [19]

At the age of 12, Joshua was adopted by Richard and Ginger Braam, who cared for him for the rest of his life. He passed away in November 2015 at the age of 36.[20]

Castle-Rock vs. Gonzales. In June, 1999, a Colorado judge issued a restraining order against Simon Gonzalez, preventing him from coming within 100 feet of the home of his ex-wife, Jessica, and commanding him not to "molest or disturb the peace " of Jessica and her children.[21] That order was later modified to allow Simon to spend time with his three daughters, ages 10, 9 and 7, on alternative weekends, for two weeks in the summer and for a mid-week dinner visit arranged by the parties and "upon reasonable notice." Later that month, Simon took his three daughters while they were playing outside the house, without advance arrangement. When Jessica noticed that the girls were missing, she suspected that Simon had taken them and contacted the Castle Rock Police Department, which dispatched two officers to her house. Jessica showed them the restraining order, but they told her there was nothing they could do, and suggested that she call the police department again if the children did not return home by 10:00 PM.

Shortly after that, Jessica reached Simon on his cell phone and he informed her that he had taken the three children to an amusement park in Denver. She called the police department again and asked them to have someone check on her husband or his vehicle at the amusement park, and put out an "all points bulletin" for her husband, but again an officer refused her request. Jessica called the police again at 10:00 PM when the children were still missing, but was now told to wait until midnight. At about 12:10 AM she went to Simon's apartment and, finding no one there, called the police again. She was told to wait for an officer to arrive. When the police failed to show up, she went to the police department herself and filed an incident report. Still, no action was taken. The officer went to dinner. At about 3:20 AM, Simon arrived at the police station and opened fire with a semi-automatic handgun. Police shot back, killing him. Inside the cab of his pickup truck they found the bodies of his three daughters, each killed by multiple bullet wounds.

Jessica sued the Castle Rock Police Department for failing to enforce the restraining order, alleging that the actions were taken either willfully, recklessly or with such gross negligence as to indicate wanton disregard and deliberate indifference to Jessica's civil rights. A federal district court rejected the claim, but the Tenth Circuit Court of Appeals found that Jessica had a "protected property interest" in the enforcement of the terms of her restraining order, and that the town had deprived her of due process because the police did not seriously entertain her request for enforcement. The case then moved to the Supreme Court, which rendered its decision in 2005.

In a seven-to-two decision, the Supreme Court found that the town of Castle Rock had not deprived Jessica of her property interest in the form of her entitlement to services, noting that this issue had not been settled in the DeShaney decision. The court argued that the mandatory language in the preprinted text of the restraining order that the Tenth Circuit Court had relied on to determine a legitimate expectation of entitlement, was not really mandatory, based on a well-established tradition of police discretion that has co-existed with other mandatory arrest statutes. Such statutes, said the court, could not be interpreted literally due to the sheer impracticality of enforcing every order, and lack of resources. Furthermore, it said, a mandatory duty had to be spelled out more specifically, and the Colorado statute was vague about the exact nature of the entitlement in question. Justice Stevens together with Justice Ginsburg challenged this assertion in their dissenting opinion, saying the Colorado statute was quite clear – either make an arrest or, if that is impractical, seek an arrest warrant. The court disagreed with the dissenters, saying that seeking an arrest warrant was procedural and could not be the basis of a property interest. The court went further to say that even if the Colorado statute could be said to make the enforcement of a restraining order mandatory, this did not create an entitlement for the protected person, since the enforcement of laws is for the benefit of the public, not individuals.

The dissenters argued that Colorado law has quite clearly eliminated police discretion to deny enforcement, and guaranteed the provision of certain services in certain defined circumstances to a certain class of beneficiaries. They pointed out that if Jessica had contracted with a security firm to provide protection to her and her daughters, she would clearly have a property interest in such a contract. Colorado had undertaken a comparable obligation, and Jessica was thus justified in relying on this restraining order as constitutionally protected property.

Jessica took her case to the Inter American Commission on Human Rights (IACHR), a body whose mission is to promote and protect human rights in the American hemisphere. The Commission, which was created in 1959, has its roots in the Inter American Human Rights System, established in Bogota, Columbia with the American Declaration of the Rights of Man. In its published findings on Jessica's case in 2011, the Commission established that the state' failure to protect Jessica and her daughters constituted a form of discrimination in violation of the American Declaration, since it took place in a context where there has been a historical problem with the enforcement of protection orders – a problem that disproportionately affects women.[22] The Commission also established that the state had failed to investigate the circumstances of the children's deaths, leaving the family with the uncertainty of who was responsible. The Commission encouraged the United States to conduct a serious, impartial, and exhaustive investigation into systematic failures that took place related to the enforcement of Jessica's protection order, to reinforce through legislative measures the mandatory nature of protection orders and other precautionary measures to protect women from imminent acts of violence and to create effective implementation mechanisms.

While the Commission's analysis did not deal with the scope of federal claims of action under national law – rather with the judicial responses at all levels – it reiterated an established principle in the inter-American system that it is not the formal existence of judicial remedies that fulfill the right to judicial protection, but rather that these remedies are available and effective. When the state fails to punish human rights violations, it has failed to comply with its positive duties under international human rights law. In 2014, the Commission gathered to review the steps the United States had taken to implement its recommendations. It found that the United States has failed to achieve full implementation citing the lack of investigation into the deaths of Jessica's daughters, and failure to pay her monetary reparations.

Nicholson v Scopetta. One notable exception to the failure of civil rights actions is the case of Nicholson v Scopetta.[23] This case was a class action civil rights suit brought against the New York City Administration for Children's Services (ACS) by a group of mothers whose children had been removed from their homes in child protection cases involving DV. These punitive practices faced by battered mothers in New York were similar to practices in other states, often referred to as "failure to protect" cases. In these cases, battered mothers were charged with failing to protect their children from the potential emotional or physical harm of being exposed to violence. In New York City a battered mother could be charged with neglect for "*engaging in domestic violence in the presence of her children,*" thus holding the victim liable for an assault against her. The City used this approach to justify removing children from victim-mothers in hundreds of cases similar to those of Nicholson and two other mothers who joined the lawsuit. The plaintiffs alleged that they were being deprived of both substantive and procedural due process, and that their children were being removed based on constitutionally inadequate investigations, without probable cause and absent training and supervision. Thus they alleged violation of their First and Fourteenth Amendment rights, with their children suffering additionally from a deprivation of their Fourth Amendment right to be free from unlawful search and seizure.

The case was filed in the U.S. District Court in January of 2001, and an expedited trial began in July of that year. In January 2002, the District Court issued a preliminary injunction against the City and its findings of fact were upheld on subsequent appeal. In finding for the plaintiffs, Judge Jack Weinstein of the U.S. District Court for the Eastern District of New York invoked the Thirteenth Amendment, which provides in part that *"neither slavery nor involuntary servitude shall exist in the United States except as punishment for a crime."* Weinstein noted that groups protected by the Thirteenth Amendment include at least those discriminated against in the past by religion and country of origin, and pointed out that the continued discrimination against females in the United States, particularly in the context of domestic abuse, was evident in ACS's practice of treating mothers unfairly as a group.

> "For purposes of the issues before the court, mothers are entitled to a particularly scrupulous protection of their rights to custody of their children in construing the Fourteenth Amendment in light of the Thirteenth. It hardly needs to be added that the exact language of the Thirteenth Amendment covers protection of the children's rights. They are continually forcibly removed from their abused mothers without court adjudication and placed in a forced state custody in either state or privately run institutions for long periods of time. There they are disciplined by those not their parents. This is a form of slavery.[24] While there is maybe disagreement in our society about whether the government has an obligation to assist those who suffer conditions of debilitating poverty, there is a consensus that even the most minimalist state has the responsibility of protecting its citizens from violence. At one time, it was thought that this responsibility did not extend to violence within the home, but that notion has long since been abandoned in the United States. Just as the government has a responsibility to protect children from an abusive parent, so too does the government have a responsibility to protect a victim of domestic violence from her partner, a responsibility not met by punishing her through forcible separation from her children. Yet the court finds as a matter of fact that the effect of the practice and policy of ACS is to punish the abused mother by separating her from her children and by not providing her and the children with adequate protection. "[25]

Weinstein's decision sustained two appeals, and the case was finally settled in 2004, with the City agreeing to pay the plaintiffs' attorney fees and to comply with the applicable law.

Michelle Etlin's "Life Interest" theory

Mothers' rights activist and co-author of *The Hostage Child*, Michelle Etlin, developed a novel theory explaining why federal courts have for the most part declined to address the due process violations that regularly occur in family court, especially with regard to the safety of children.[26] Etlin attributes these and other human rights violations in our society to a missing concept in our understanding of the Constitution. The Constitution, says Etlin, guarantees that we will not be deprived of life, liberty or property without "due process of law." To deprive somcone of liberty, the state must have a criminal charge, citing a certain criminal law, and then it must have a step-by-step procedure from probable cause to arrest, to arraignment to trial to sentencing to appeal and ultimately even, at times, to habeas corpus, all "by the book." But there is also a way to impinge on someone's liberty without arrest or imprisonment. A person's "liberty interest" is some quality less than actual physical liberty but that still restrains or limits the person in a way that is not permissible without due process. For example, the right to parent ones own child is considered a liberty interest, and this cannot be terminated without due process. There is also a way to take someone's property without removing money from his or her bank account. Access to services, including education, may be considered property interests.

So while there are "shadow interests" in property and liberty, the only interest you can presently rely on legally in your life, is your life itself. If you are deprived of your life without due process (such as being shot to death by police who have mistakenly come to your address in a drug raid gone wrong) your surviving family members may sue for damages based on the unconstitutional deprivation of your life. Other than that, our law recognizes only two meanings for the phrase "life interest." One is a term of art in probate law, meaning that someone has left you property in their will, but not to own outright, only to benefit from during your lifetime. The other use of "life interest" is the right, on the part of a convict on death row, not to be killed before the hour and minute written upon his death warrant.

Etlin defines the Life Interest as a person's interest in the natural continuation and development of her life, from the point of birth onwards, including but not limited to her interest in being provided with all the elements essential for natural development and continuation of life, so that within 18 years she can become fully functional in accessing her liberty and property interests along with all other citizens. Physical, sexual and emotional abuse deprives a person of her life interest and she should therefore have an inalienable right to be free from risk of abuse. A person's life interest is at its maximum at birth and continues to remain high throughout a child's period of dependency legally known as "minority," during which time, effective liberty or property interests are absent. A child's Life Interest remains the same regardless of whether or not her parents choose to exercise their liberty interests in parenting her, and if they are incapable of doing so, the state must take over.

The Life Interest versus the "best interests"

There are some who argue that the Life Interest is the same as "best interests," the standard that judges currently use to make custody decisions. We would argue against this. Wherever you go in the world, the elements needed to sustain life are the same. Best interest standards on the other hand, comprise laundry lists that vary from state to state, so that what is considered best for a child in one state may not be considered best in another. Thus statutes in Delaware, Massachusetts and Minnesota, say that its is not in a child's best interests to be placed in the joint or sole custody of a batterer, whereas in Rhode Island and Kentucky that arrangement is statutorily acceptable. However, in the end, as we have seen, statutes make little difference since even in states that have enacted the Model Code presumption, substantiated abuse gets factored into custody decisions only some of the time. Judges have wide discretion to override what the statutes consider best interests and substitute their own ideas. The Life Interest standard would require a mandatory hierarchy of items to be considered based on what is most essential to life and that would have to begin with safety in the home – safety of the child and safety of the primary caregiver. Since a child does not have the freedom to leave a home in which he is unsafe, there could be no balancing of the liberty interests of the parents with the child's right to safety. If the Life Interest were recognized, judges would not have the discretion to refuse to hear evidence of abuse, or to discount evidence of abuse, or to rely on non-scientific theories that discredit victims of abuse.

Application of the Life Interest in DeShaney, Castle Rock and Scopetta

The DeShaney court concluded that DSS did not violate Joshua's liberty interest to equal protection because that obligation rested solely in the hands of his father, with whom he had a "special relationship," a concept that denotes special responsibility. The Seventh Circuit Court even acknowledged that the government agency was within its rights to avoid this responsibility for a needy individual, because of concerns about a lawsuit if it failed. But more importantly, the court believed the agency appropriately "balanced" the rights of the father and of the child when it declined to interfere in any way in Randy DeShaney's liberty interest in parenting his child, even if the exercise of that liberty interest resulted in life-threatening injuries to the child. It is important to emphasize that in most cases, a parent's liberty interest to parent his or her child confers benefits on both the parent and the child. These benefits are primarily emotional for the parent, and undeniably further the Life Interest of the child. This concept is implicit in fatherhood programs that encourage single noncustodial fathers to pay child support as well as to engage with their children emotionally and develop positive relationships with them. Research has even shown that parents who fulfill their financial obligations to their children also tend to be more emotionally engaged with them. But where a parent is clearly dangerous to a child, his or her liberty interest to be a parent should be restricted, because the child's Life Interest should take precedence. Where a child's Life Interest is not articulated and is subsumed under the vague concept of "best interests," it is very easy for government agencies to ignore it and to focus solely on the parent's liberty interest, which was the case with Randy DeShaney. As far as Winnebago DSS was concerned, safe parenting was a suggestion, and Randy DeShaney was free to take it or leave it.

In the case of Castle Rock, despite the compelling property interest argument of the dissenters, we believe that the Life Interest should really be at the heart of the argument. The Colorado statute was enacted in order to protect women's and children's lives, specifically because of the risk of death in the absence of this statute and its enforcement. To treat it as just another entitlement that may or may not be a constitutionally protected property interest is to diminish the gravity of the circumstances that led to its enactment. The very concept of a protection order and the enactment of protection order statutes implicitly acknowledges the Life Interest and the existence of a vulnerable group of people whose Life Interest is at higher risk than other groups. The protection order itself establishes the existence of a "protected" group that should be recognized in the Constitution along with other protected groups such as persons with disabilities, the aged, and minorities who have historically been vulnerable to the violation of their civil rights.

One federal court's recognition of the Life Interest is also implicit in Judge Weinstein's decision in Nicholson v Scopetta, when he pointed out that the government has a responsibility to protect DV victims and children who have been abused by their parents. The most minimalist state, he said, has the responsibility to protect its citizens from violence, and this should extend to violence within the home. Judge Weinstein specifically stated that victims of violence within the home are an especially vulnerable group deserving of special protection together with other protected groups covered under the Thirteenth Amendment.

One could argue that coercive control, which is at the very heart of domestic abuse, places these victims in a category similar to that of slaves. Furthermore, domestic abuse, like slavery, is not just about liberty and property. It is about life itself. Without life, other rights have no meaning. While under the control of a domestic abuser or a slave owner, a person's life itself is constantly being threatened, and both mental and physical health are being diminished, which constitute injuries to the Life Interest. In the case of slavery, the victim's Life Interest was converted into the owner's property and liberty interests. The same is true at the present time of domestic abuse both of adult and child victims. Interestingly, some battered mothers who have sustained mental and emotional injuries as a result of the failure of family courts to protect them and their children, have begun to seek redress under the Americans with Disabilities Act (see Chapter 6.) Early indications are that they may fare better as disabled Americans than as battered mothers, even though their disabilities are the direct result of battering. The fact that these mothers are joining the ranks of the disabled is itself proof of the systemic violation of their Life Interests by state actors – a violation that is extremely difficult to address through civil rights action because of its invisibility in law.

According to Etlin, the lack of recognition of the Life Interest is the reason that American law has been able to ignore and deny – wholesale – the rights of children, and to camouflage and deny the rights of women, African Americans, and other hated, vulnerable classes. The common denominator of slavery, misogyny, and child oppression is the denial of the Life Interest in law and in real life. Indeed, says Etlin, this is why slavery was able to exist for 200 years simultaneously with law that provided for freedom and independence. For the last century of its existence, slavery was even able to coexist with the Bill of Rights. We can no longer think straight, she says, because we are living within this magnificent sleight of hand, and we cannot find the missing link because we are concerning ourselves more and more with tangles that form among the other links – the property and liberty links – in our hopelessly broken chain.

The Special Rapporteur to the United Nations on Violence Against Women filed a report in 2011, noting that in spite of the benefits to battered women from the Violence Against Women Act (VAWA), the Supreme Court rulings in DeShaney and Castle Rock left victims of gender-based violence with no federal level constitutional or statutory remedy.[27] One of her recommendations was the expansion of federal causes of action under VAWA in order to increase uniformity and accountability at the state and local levels. Thus, two respected international bodies have found that battered women in the United States remain vulnerable to the violation of their human rights by government entities. We believe that as long as the Life Interest is not recognized as a constitutionally protected right, these violations will remain invisible, undefined, and will persist.

Chapter 5

The Divorce Industry

While investigating the world of family law for a documentary film and book on divorce, Joseph Sorge and James Scurlock discovered what they describe as "the last vestige of lawlessness in America."

> "A dark corner of the judicial system where fiefdoms and tyrants still thrive, where the supreme law of the land is routinely ignored, where children are taken hostage for profit, and where lives are destroyed as a matter of course."[1]

Through a series of vignettes and personal histories, Sorge and Scurlock describe the $50 billion divorce "industry" – Divorce Corp. – as a system that enriches itself at the expense of troubled families, including price gauging by unscrupulous custody evaluators, attorneys who try to profit from divorce as much as they can by fanning the flames of conflict, cronyism, and conflicts of interest among judges and the attorneys who appear before them and contribute to their election campaigns. Judges, they say, can market the services of an attorney and then seize the litigant's property to pay the attorney's fees.[2] After retirement, judges may take up lucrative second careers as private judges in alternative dispute resolution practices, hired by the very attorneys they helped to enrich while practicing as family court judges.[3]

Protective parents' advocates are in agreement with the filmmakers on some of the critical issues that they address. One advocate likened it to a cottage industry of unregulated court appointees who charge resourced litigants whatever the market will bear. Anxious for their next lucrative appointment, she said, they tailor reports and testimony to meet judges' expectations. Advocates claim that money flows from litigants into court appointees' pockets at such a rate that corruption is inevitable. The result is that many litigants are reduced to bankruptcy and join the mass of unrepresented litigants who cannot afford attorneys, court reporters, or appeals. This view is consistent with the findings of a study conducted by the Battered Women's Justice Project described in the next chapter, which places most of the blame for family court failures on unregulated court appointees.

On the subject of DV, however, Sorge and Scurlock's characterization of the issues could not be more at odds with that of protective parents' advocates. To begin with, the filmmakers insist that the profit motive, which drives the divorce industry, results in equal victimization of men and women. Joseph Sorge – a multi-millionaire – had direct experience of this form of exploitation in his own divorce from his wife, Maryanne – also a multi-millionaire. At issue was Maryanne's demand for an increase in her child support for their 14-year-old son of whom the couple had joint custody. The litigation, which lasted for several years, resulted in a court-ordered increase of child support for Maryanne from $48,000 per year to $216,000 per year. In upholding the award, a California appeals court noted that California has a strong public policy favoring adequate child support, referring to "the best interests of the child" and "the child's needs." Harvard blogger, Phillip Greenspun remarked that the divorce industry was able to keep the Sorges as customers for 12 years to answer the question: "who will pay for a 14-year-old's T-shirts and skateboards?"[4]

Litigating financial disputes for the super-wealthy is certainly a lucrative service provided by the divorce industry, but it is hardly typical because most people don't have the resources to make prolonged litigation worthwhile for themselves or their attorneys. Yet divorce professionals manage to do well serving people with more limited resources.

Not all cases that come before family court involve rich people seeking to become richer. There are other cases involving matters of survival in which people seek safety from a variety of serious harms including physical, psychological and financial. These are the cases involving battered women and their children, and these are the cases in which divorce industry exploitation has the most devastating and life-shattering consequences.

Free-lance journalists who have spent years investigating family court dysfunction would agree that some cases involve male victims, and have reported on them in detail.[5] However the weight of the evidence suggests that battered mothers caught in the web of family court shenanigans far outnumber fathers.[6] But the filmmakers, feeling somehow compelled to promote their "gender equality" theme, attempt to minimize gender disparities in serious DV, and rely on the opinions of a handful of self-proclaimed "experts" who fuel the myth of widespread false allegations by women. The one true DV expert interviewed for the film – Judge Sol Gothard – later complained that his statements were presented out of context, and that the film erroneously portrayed him as agreeing with the its central message of "mandatory equal parenting." In a negation of the film's portrayal of his position, Judge Gothard wrote:

> "There is no question whatsoever that I participated in this 'documentary' to stress the point that it is women who primarily get mistreated in the family courts in America for a variety of reasons that I have been lecturing about for over 50 yrs [sic]. I am appalled that my remarks have been taken out of context to make it appear that I support the utterly insane concept that mandatory equal parenting is the solution to anything. The only answer to the problem of custody decisions is to place the child with the most capable parent. Period."[7]

He goes on to say:

"Contrary to their assertion that false allegations of abuse are common, one of the main problems in Family Court, with regard to custody, is that when a parent reports suspected abuse, as they are mandated by law to do, the courts, all too often, shift the paradigm by accusing the reporting parent of 'parental alienation syndrome.'"

The doctrine of mandatory equal parenting, contrary to the assertions of Sorge and Scurlock, is already one of the central tenets of the divorce industry. In fact, the filmmakers' argument that the divorce industry fuels conflict in order to profit is the exact opposite of how the industry presents itself, which is to resolve conflict and promote conciliation. So how are we to understand these contrasting views? Perhaps the explanation is that the divorce industry is adept at exploiting vulnerabilities wherever it may find them, and turning them into business opportunities. One way is to encourage litigation over money for the super-wealthy. Another is to promote conciliation where it is least appropriate – women trying to leave abusive relationships. Many of these women were stay-at-home moms or had low-paying part time work and few resources of their own. Many of them had experienced a variety of abuses including physical, financial, and emotional abuse, and coercive control. They may have experienced ongoing attacks on their self-esteem, efforts to undermine their parenting abilities, frequent put-downs in front of their children, isolation from sources of support, and worst of all – witnessed direct abuse of their children. Some may suffer from posttraumatic stress disorder as a result of these experiences, or have symptoms of depression and anxiety. In short, these survivors have experienced a diminution of their physical, emotional, psychological, financial and social wellbeing, all of which have been to the benefit of their abusers. When they try to leave, abusers are faced with the potential loss of these resources, and are highly motivated to find ways to maintain control over their victims, typically through the children. Abusers find willing partners in divorce professionals who will join the attacks against the survivors and force them to keep trying to defend themselves and their children, all to the financial benefit of the industry. These professionals will use the survivors' psychological injuries against them, attack their credibility, minimize the seriousness of the violence, and impose services on them that they are required to pay for and that only help to prolong the process of depleting their resources and often those of their extended families. In cases involving child abuse, state run child protective service agencies typically abdicate their investigative role to the divorce industry, or find themselves sidelined and ignored if the paid professionals have incentive to take over.

Three battered mothers have published personal memoirs offering us a glimpse into the insidiously destructive and profoundly misogynist operations of the divorce industry. Maralee McLean's daughter was two-and-a-half years old in 1989, when she complained of pain in her crotch, and indicated repeatedly both verbally and with explicit gestures that her father had touched her vaginal area. Over the following three years, the child made further disclosures of ongoing abuse to multiple mandated reporters, all of which were ignored, discounted and explained away by divorce professionals and child protective services.[8] A decade later, Wendy Titelman's daughters were about six and eight years old when they attempted to disclose to a psychologist that they were being molested by their father. Tapes of those sessions revealed that the psychologist changed the subject every time the children began to disclose the abuse, and instead tried to get them to speak negatively about their mother.[9] Both mothers were "diagnosed" with Parental Alienation Syndrome (PAS), and lost custody of their children. But even though PAS and botched child sexual abuse investigations are the most prominent manifestations of divorce industry malfeasance, they are simply one piece of a much larger system of deliberate case-rigging against battered mothers, involving suppression of real evidence, manufacture of fake evidence, and silencing of any voices of protest or dissent, as illustrated by Doreen Ludwig in her book *Motherless America*.[10]

Some battered mothers have tried "going public," by taking their stories to the media. Maralee McLean was successful in getting her story covered by local news media in Colorado as well as by CNN. However, the mainstream media's appetite for this type of story tends to evaporate following threats of or actual lawsuits, while judges are quick to issue gag orders, preventing mothers from talking about their cases to the media, or even posting information on their own websites.[11] Nevertheless, some dogged free-lance journalists have persisted in extensively documenting the divorce industry's abuse of power and corrupt practices. An exposé of Connecticut courts revealed that judges were ordering litigants to receive services from court affiliated service providers with questionable practices, who charged exorbitant fees.[12] Reporters have documented numerous cases in which mental health professionals ignored compelling evidence of child abuse or otherwise acted unprofessionally. In one example cited by the exposé, a mental health professional billed the state for a report evaluating children he had never met.[13] In another case, a mental health professional described his criteria for making diagnoses of mental illness which included whether the client was a Red Sox or Yankees fan, and the color of the skin in their face.[14] But even if some of these professionals are acting in good faith, survivors of DV find themselves in a system rigged against them, since its goal is conflict resolution, not long-term safety and security. In the light of this goal, survivors of DV who seek protection for themselves and their children are perceived as uncooperative, and this necessitates the piling on of numerous mandatory court-related services intended to force compliance with the court's goal of conciliation. Survivors are faced with a choice of either accepting ongoing risk to themselves and their children, or becoming bankrupted by the cost of these forced services that will leave them less safe than before. They may even end up completely cut off from their children.

In Connecticut many of the professionals who provide these services and the judges who appointed them are all members of the same trade organization – the Association of

Family and Conciliation Courts (AFCC) – which apparently operated for some time without being registered as a business in the state. A founding director, and past officers include Judicial Branch members, one of whom even sent an email from her state work account to 800 family court industry professionals soliciting business and donations.[15] These revelations possibly prompted the Connecticut Commission on Judicial Ethics to issue an informal opinion that it would be a violation of the judicial canon of ethics for court officers and their staff to serve on the board of directors of non-profit organizations that provide services to court-involved clients who appear before them and who receive the majority of their funding from contracts with the Judicial Branch.[16] Conflicts of interest are not unique to the Connecticut judiciary, and whether or not court-affiliated professionals are members of a particular organization, is not necessarily the problem in every family court system. At issue is the fact that AFCC is very influential nationally and internationally in that it sets standards, provides training, publishes a journal, and conducts annual meetings, which provide a forum for professionals to share and disseminate ideas and theories and promote their own particular band of practices, many of which have been adopted by federally-funded fatherhood programs.

History of AFCC

In 1955, a social worker, Meyer Elkin, founded the Los Angeles County Conciliation Court, a marriage counseling service located in the court for couples that were going through or contemplating divorce. His goal was to prevent couples from entering an adversarial system, filled with stigma, and lacking dignity and respect, and to resolve marital disputes and promote reconciliation. Born in 1915, Elkin was the son of Russian Jewish immigrants. His parents separated when he was five years old, and he grew up having no contact with his father, whom he described as "acculturated" to American life, and "too much" contact with his overprotective, mother, who adhered to the traditions of the old country.[17] His childhood background, which he acknowledged was filled with pain, inspired him to find ways to reach out to people who were going through difficult life experiences, leading him to establish the first marriage-counseling program in the Los Angeles courts, and paving the way for the professionalization of marriage counseling in California and elsewhere. Elkin's organization began publishing a newsletter in 1963, the *Conciliation Court Review*, which evolved into a journal, the *Family Court Review* currently associated with Hofstra University in New York.[18]

As the 1960s progressed, the organization moved beyond California, changing its name to the Conference of Conciliation Courts in 1965, and by 1968, 19 States had some court-connected counseling services. The focus on reconciliation changed in the 1970s, when no fault divorce became the law in most states beginning with California. The Conference's mission then began to shift from "reconciliation" to "divorce with dignity," the goal being to reduce the trauma of divorce for parents and children. Services focused on the resolution of custody disputes through mediation. In 1983, the Conference changed its name to the Association of Family and Conciliation Courts (AFCC) – the name by which it is known to this day, with a membership of 5,000 in 24 different countries.

In the 1980s the AFCC, with its historical roots in reconciliation and resolving disputes, found itself in conflict with the philosophy of the battered women's movement, which emphasized making it easier for women to leave abusive relationships. Divorce professionals associated with AFCC acknowledged the existence of DV but incorporated it into the general category of "high conflict" divorce, thus avoiding all distinction between perpetrator and victim. Supporting this approach was controversial research to be discussed later in this chapter, suggesting that women perpetrate relationship violence as frequently as men. It was in this decade that AFCC began to provide specialized training in custody evaluation for divorce professionals especially for those dealing with high conflict cases, and judges increasingly came to rely on their expertise in resolving complex custody disputes involving accusations and counter accusations. These professionals came from a variety of mental health backgrounds, mostly grounded in relationship theories, but typically lacked training and experience in dealing with and understanding the dynamics of DV.

Because joint custody seemed like an equitable solution to custody disputes, AFCC developed ties with the fathers' rights movement of the 1980s. Indeed, Meyer Elkin himself was a co-founder of the Children's Rights Council, the flagship organization of the fathers' rights movement of the late 20th and early 21st centuries. It is likely that his own painful childhood experience of being abandoned by his father at a young age inspired him to promote an organization that would prevent other children from losing contact with their fathers. In the context of DV, however, such contact could be dangerous both to the child and the mother. Thus custody evaluators, mediators, marriage counselors and other divorce professionals who fail to recognize DV, deny its significance, or subscribe to unsupported beliefs in widespread false allegations, pose an ongoing threat to the safety of survivors and their children through their influence on custody outcomes.

With the passage of the Violence Against Women Act (VAWA), and with the growing public recognition of DV as a problem, and the influence of the DV community in advocating for survivors, divorce professionals have begun to pay increased attention to DV. However, studies show discrepancies between theory and practice. In a 1996 survey, 38% of custody evaluators listed physical and sexual abuse as major factors to be considered in awarding sole custody to the survivor.[19] A similar study in 2008 found that 64% gave these reasons for recommending sole custody.[20] A 2003 survey of custody evaluators across the United States found that the vast majority recognized the importance of DV as a factor to be considered in custody evaluations, and claimed that they made differential custody and visitation recommendations when DV was identified.[21] In contrast to the results of surveys based on self-reports, studies of actual custody recommendations paint a different picture. A study of Kentucky family court documents found that DV was not a factor in custody recommendations,[22] consistent with a California study that found DV was not a factor in mediators' custody recommendations.[23] In order to understand these puzzling discrepancies, we need to explore two major sources of bias that guide the decision-making of divorce professionals – classifying DV, and so-called parental alienation.

Sources of bias I: Classifying DV

The hypothesis that there may be subtypes of DV arose as an explanation for discrepancies in research results. Population studies that primarily used an instrument known as the Conflict Tactics Scale found near equal rates of perpetration and victimization for both males and females.[24] Crime surveys, on the other hand, found a much higher rate of female victimization which was consistent with the fact that DV calls to police and requests for shelter services came predominantly from women.[25] Sociologist Michael P. Johnson proposed that these studies might be picking up distinct types of violence, which he labeled "common couple violence" (later renamed "situational couple violence") and "patriarchal terrorism" (later renamed "intimate terrorism").[26] According to this line of thinking, the former type, which was most likely to be reflected in populations surveys, arose out of relationship conflict, was typically less severe, possibly bidirectional, and was not associated with a pattern of coercive control. The latter type, which was more likely to surface in crime surveys, involved more severe violence, and was typically male perpetrated, and occurred in the context of ongoing coercive control of one partner by the other. Johnson also identified a third type of violence, which he termed "violent resistance," defined as a defensive response to intimate terrorism.[27]

In 2000, the National Institute of Justice convened a workshop comprising prominent researchers in the DV field, to discuss the issues of gender disparities and "gender symmetry" in intimate partner violence.[28] Proceedings of the workshop were posted online with the goal of stimulating research on little understood topics including women's use of violence, coercive control and the existence of possible DV subtypes. The studies that emerged following the workshop opened a window into the many complexities of violence perpetration and victimization, but none of them provided any real validation of Johnson's subtypes. Johnson himself continued to pursue his belief in his subtypes of DV, even when his own data analysis failed to support his position.   At the time of the workshop many of the participants warned that practitioners would not recognize the hypothetical nature of the typology and would treat it as proven fact, which would encourage them to "classify" DV, and make unsupportable assumptions about the seriousness (or lack thereof) of a particular act of violence. These concerns seem to have been borne out.

In a critique of Johnson's typology, Professor Joan Meier acknowledges that some relationship violence may occur outside the context of a wider tactic of control and may be the result of conflict run amok or even mental illness.[29] However, she notes that while Johnson's theory is appealing and probably captures a portion of the truth, it lacks empirical support with regard to critical elements, for example the notion that most violence between partners is not gendered and is simply a function of conflict rather than dominance or oppression. This element has fueled the widespread labeling of DV by divorce professionals as "situational" and therefore not of great concern, leading to custody determinations favoring the perpetrator over the victim. Meier points out that Johnson's empirical analysis is not based on original research, but rather a secondary analysis of existing data sets from studies that were not designed to test his theory, and which do not capture fundamental control behaviors. Johnson's re-analyses of two studies that did capture control behavior produced results that went contrary to his theory. Data from the National Violence Against Women Survey, which was a population survey, indicated a high representation (35%) of intimate terrorism among the violent men in the sample.[30] Data from a study of women seeking shelter or legal protection from violence indicated that half of them qualified as cases of situational couple violence.[31] This throws into question the validity of Johnson's categories, which are supposed to distinguish between population samples and shelter or legal samples. Meier considers a number of plausible explanations for the discrepant findings. First, situational couple violence may be as frightening, dangerous, and possibly gendered as intimate terrorism. Furthermore, when it induces fear and intimidation, control is implicit even without any other indicators. Second, Johnson may have mischaracterized cases as situational couple violence when they were actually intimate terrorism. Other research indicates that he has set the bar too high for determining control, and has missed controlling behaviors that could be serious and potential indicators of lethality.[32] Another important point is that coercive control may unfold over time, and one overt act of violence in a relationship at a particular point in time does not tell us if control will develop later or if it has already been a factor. The same argument applies to a third category of DV proposed by divorce professionals – separation violence, which is supposedly caused by the trauma of separation, in the absence of any previous violence or controlling behavior. This too could be the first indicator of control-based violence.[33]

Despite these deficits in Johnson's typology, divorce professionals have proclaimed it the "gold standard" for custody evaluations and have stressed that differentiating different types of violence is important in making recommendations based on the family's needs.[34] Yet it is not clear how well this message has been absorbed. One study found that responses to a vignette depicting conflict-based versus control-based violence did not result in different outcomes, with most evaluators recommending joint custody.[35] In another study, funded by the National Institute of Justice (NIJ), only 23% of custody evaluators focused on coercive controlling aspects of violence in their responses to a vignette.[36] These custody evaluators made recommendations that were more attentive to victim safety, compared to those that did not recognize coercive control. Overall, the most commonly recommended custody arrangement was joint legal custody and physical custody to the mother, which had an average likelihood of 47%. This was followed by sole legal and physical custody to the mother (40% likelihood) and joint legal and physical custody (30%).[37] Unsupervised visitation had the highest likelihood of being recommended (47%) followed by formal supervision (38%), and informal supervision (34%). Also, the evaluators reported on average a 40% likelihood that the couple would benefit from mediation.

A second study also funded by NIJ conducted in-depth examinations of 69 actual custody evaluations and found that strong safeguards for victims in the custody assessment were predicted by the custody evaluator's knowledge of DV and construction of DV as an issue of power and control.[38] The authors noted that the severity of the physical, emotional and social abuse in the couple's history did not predict the safety of the parenting plan. This finding confirmed the observation of the study's facilitators, that some evaluators, and courts, do not view a few incidents of physical abuse, no matter how severe, as constituting DV. Some evaluators view such incidents as merely "situational," driven by conflict between the parents, stress, or provocation by the victim.

Thus classification of DV, although well intentioned, may have contributed to the widespread misuse of labels that serve to minimize serious violence, and attribute it to relationship conflict. As we shall see later, this misapplication of labels provides a rationale for divorce professionals to recommend inappropriate services and parenting plans for families that have experienced DV, placing survivors and their children at risk of further abuse and ongoing coercive control.

Sources of bias II: Parental Alienation Syndrome and parental alienation

In the 1980s, Dr. Richard Gardner, a New York psychiatrist informally affiliated with Columbia University, proposed the existence of a psychiatric disorder, which he called Parental Alienation Syndrome or PAS.[39] He apparently developed a specialty counseling divorcing parents in the 1970s, and became convinced of the existence of this syndrome in the course of his clinical practice. According to Gardner, children suffering from PAS were victims of vengeful mothers who brainwashed, coached, or programmed them to make false allegations of sexual abuse against their fathers during the course of a custody dispute. Inducing PAS, according to Gardner, is a strategy that mothers employ as a means of gaining custody and punishing a hated ex-spouse. Gardner further claimed that child abuse allegations in custody disputes were rampant, and that while most allegations of child abuse were true, 95% of those occurring in custody disputes were false. PAS was quickly adopted by family courts throughout the country as an explanation for allegations of sexual abuse, obviating the need to investigate each claim on its merits, or examining corroborating evidence. PAS claims could not be refuted because they were based on tautological reasoning. A custody dispute involving sex abuse allegations was in itself all that was needed to prove PAS, and since PAS was diagnosed, the abuse allegations had to be false. Gardner's proposed measures for dealing with PAS were harsh in the extreme, and included switching custody to the hated parent, cutting off the child's contact with the aligned parent, and deprogramming the child to believe that he or she was not abused. At least one known case of suicide by a child has been attributed to Gardner's treatment.[40]

Scholarly criticism of Gardner's PAS theory raised serious doubts about its validity, which rested on nothing more than his own personal observations of patients in his private practice. Absent were any independent scientific studies supporting his theory, or even case studies that merited publication in peer-reviewed journals.[41] Gardner published all his PAS literature in his own vanity press, Creative Therapeutics. Indeed credible research tended to disprove the two major premises on which his theory rested – that sex abuse allegations in custody disputes were rampant (they are not),[42] and that allegations in that context had a high likelihood of being false (also untrue).[43] As of 2012, two published trial court opinions in New York and one in Connecticut found that PAS did not meet legal standards for admissibility.[44]   In addition, two appellate court decisions – one in California and one in Alabama – also ruled PAS inadmissible. Credible bodies such as the National Council of Juvenile and Family Court Judges, the National District Attorneys Association, and the American Psychiatric Association have also rejected PAS as a scientific theory.[45] Nevertheless most courts around the country have continued to accept its application in sex abuse cases, and have even permitted an expansion of its application to any kind of abuse allegations where the mother seeks to restrict the visitation of the father. Family courts continued to rely on it even when provided with corroborating evidence of sexual abuse by credible experts. In addition to PAS's rejection on the basis of scientific criteria, scholars were questioning Gardner's motives for the development of his theory in the light of his bizarre beliefs about human sexuality.[46] Gardner viewed pedophilia as a normal variant of human sexuality together with other deviant sexual behaviors such as sadism, necrophilia and zoophilia – all of which he claimed served the purpose of species survival. He argued that adult-child sex was not intrinsically harmful, since it had been practiced by most ancient societies except for the Jews, who had an excessively punitive attitude towards it, and who passed this on to the Christians. Gardner was against mandatory reporting of child sexual abuse, and wrote that his advice to pedophiles would be to tell them that unfortunately they were born in the wrong century, and that what they did was not inherently wrong. In 2003, Gardner committed suicide by stabbing himself multiple times in the chest.

With ongoing attacks on the validity of PAS, two respected divorce researchers proposed a new approach to the same phenomenon, dropping the term "syndrome" and referring simply to parental alienation. The new theory developed by Joan Kelly and Janet Johnston – both prominent members of AFCC – defines the alienated child as one who expresses unreasonable negative feelings towards a parent that are significantly disproportionate to the child's actual experience with the parent.[47] Kelly and Johnston propose multiple sources for the hostility, including behavior of both parents and the child's own vulnerabilities. They also distinguish between children who have become estranged from a parent as a result of physical or emotional abuse or witnessing DV of the other parent, and those who exhibit unreasonable anger or fear towards the hated parent. Curiously, the authors make the confusing claim that children who have been abused or who have witnessed DV could also be alienated, but that this can only be determined after they have been treated for posttraumatic stress disorder caused by the trauma of the abuse.

A small number of children in divorcing families, according to Kelly and Johnston, reject a parent for no reason, express intense hostility towards that parent without any ambivalence and resist contact. This type of alienation, they say, occurs in high conflict divorces, and involves an interaction of the parents' and the children's psychological responses to the conflict.[48] Parents may encourage the children to take sides, and pull them into the conflict, which is often characterized by unsubstantiated allegations and counter-allegations of violence, abuse, neglect and poor parenting. While this characterization of some marital conflicts seems reasonable, the authors make a disturbing notation that the aligned parent often fervently believes that the rejected parent is dangerous to the child in terms of physical or sexual abuse, and therefore takes steps to block the rejected parent's access to the child, mounting a campaign on several fronts involving attorneys, therapists and other professionals, and seeking restraining orders and supervised visitation.[49] They even go so far as to say that it is not normal for a parent to completely reject the other parent even when there is a history of abuse or if the child's safety is endangered.

The authors discuss possible behaviors by the rejected parent that may contribute to the alienation, but state that these behaviors do not warrant a disproportionately angry response of the child or refusal to have contact.[50] They also criticize therapists who support children's allegations as being "polarized" and "rigid" and lacking in understanding of child alienation.

While the new approach is perceived as less demonizing of mothers than that of Gardner,[51] it nevertheless preserves the core elements of Gardner's theory that mothers in high conflict divorces often falsely believe that their children are at risk of harm by the other parent and take concerted steps to protect them. Kelly and Johnston have softened the theory to make it appear more realistic by including multiple reasons why a child may reject a parent – including abuse. But they dismiss the idea that any parental behavior should reasonably justify rejection of a parent by a child, and they pathologize any steps that a mother may take to protect her child even if there has been abuse. In a later article, Johnston promotes the idea that alienating behaviors can even occur unconsciously or subconsciously, and while they may not be deliberate, their effects are pernicious and destructive. Surprisingly, these alienating behaviors can include "warm involved parenting."[52] Thus according to Johnston, a child who has been abused by one parent and has received warm loving parenting from the other parent, could still be pathologically alienated from the abusive parent as a result of the warm loving support received from the protective parent.

Parental alienation is actually more pernicious than Parental Alienation Syndrome because it posits that abuse and alienation can coexist. Thus proof of abuse is not a defense against accusations of alienation. Also, failing to prove that a mother has engaged in alienating behaviors is not required, since the process could be operating at an unconscious level. Alienating behaviors that can be proven include warm supportive parenting that normal people would consider appropriate for any mother particularly one whose children have been abused. The "alienation" label is thus inescapable since it requires no proof of actual negative behaviors, and may be applied even in cases where there has been proven abuse. There have hitherto been no systematic studies assessing the harms caused by the use of parental alienation theory. Qualitative, pilot and anecdotal studies documenting the

impact of the parental alienation label in custody determinations are presented in Table 4. At the time of writing,
Professor Joan Meier of George Washington University School
of Law is conducting a definitive national study on parental
alienation, custody and abuse in family court decisions.

AFCC on intimate partner violence

How does AFCC address these known biases? AFCC recently
produced guidelines for custody evaluators regarding how to
address DV.[53] Some of the issues raised in these guidelines
have been welcomed by DV experts as representing a good
understanding of DV, its many facets, dynamics, and its impact
on survivors. These include the need for high standards in
information gathering and for specialized training, recognition
of coercive control, sensitivity to victim's fears, emphasis on
evidence-based assessment, and explicit rejection of
psychological testing as a means to validate or discount
allegations of abuse. However, the guidelines do a poor job of
integrating this important information about DV with
recommended considerations for assessing parenting and they
send contradictory messages that have the potential to
undermine a DV evaluation. For example, the guidelines list
characteristics of DV that are known indicators of risk, danger
and potential lethality such as attempted strangulation, forced
sex, threats, willingness and means for lethal violence,
excessive control, jealousy or obsession, unwillingness to
accept responsibility, psychological and substance problems,
and recent separation. However, the guidelines preface this
list with a statement that these risk factors do not conclusively
establish that harm will occur in the future, and that their
absence does not guarantee that future harm will not occur.
This statement is disingenuous because it states the obvious
fact that evaluators are not fortune-tellers. All they can do is
make recommendations based on known risk factors. If 100%
certainty of future harm is required in order to take violence
seriously, the guidelines have little relevance to custody
recommendations. Yet the same guidelines discuss the

importance of the context of DV, suggesting that some violence could be a reaction to the stress of separation or divorce *"without any history of violence or propensity to future violence."* In other words, while rejecting the notion that future violence can be reliably predicted, they invite the evaluator to classify violence on the basis of a future prediction they have just said cannot be made. Elsewhere, the guidelines state: *"Past violence is a significant predictor of future violence."* These confusing contradictions suggest that the guidelines want it both ways. They permit evaluators to minimize serious violence, if they want to, but at the same time they have said things that are factually correct.

References to the impact of DV on children provide another example of factual statements followed by conclusions that steer the evaluator towards minimizing the potential impact of violence. The guidelines state that the impact of DV on children and on parenting differ from case to case, that children have unique experiences of and reactions to DV, and that it affects them in different ways. They then conclude that *"the presence or absence of a particular form or context of aggression does not in itself, dictate a particular outcome. A deeper individualized analysis is required to determine the impact of the aggression and its context on children, parenting and co-parenting."* While it is true that many children are resilient, the guidelines avoid any discussion of the long-term impact of trauma on children, the fact that abusers are terrible role models, and that one of the most insidious tactics of abusers is the undermining of the survivor's parenting role and of the children's relationship with her.[54] Furthermore, while the guidelines include questions about the types of exposures that children may have had to DV, whether directly or indirectly, surprisingly, they pay little attention to whether the child may have been directly abused, except for one brief item referencing *"physical, sexual, emotional, and/or economic abuse."* Specifically, the guidelines do not mention the well-established literature that 30% to 60% of children exposed to DV have also been direct targets of abuse.[55] In a critique of a draft of the guidelines, Evan Stark, an experienced forensic evaluator with expertise in DV, questioned the guidelines' focus on the threat of lethal violence (which has a low statistical probability) as a reason to limit access, to the detriment of nonlethal violence. Thus he asks:

> "If [the evaluator] established that the target parent was strangled, sexually assaulted and frequently pushed and shoved around in front of the children...why isn't that sufficient in itself to establish the case for limited or no access?"[56]

Although the AFCC guidelines do warn custody evaluators to be aware of their biases, and to avoid allowing these biases to interfere with their evaluations, they describe these biases in very general terms – for example "*gender stereotypes*" rather than specifying the actual biases that have come to light in recent literature. For example, in a study of 465 custody evaluators Saunders and colleagues found a constellation of false assumptions and beliefs that predicted recommendations of sole or joint custody to abusive fathers. These include the belief that women make false allegations of DV, that survivors make false allegations of child physical and sexual abuse, that DV is not important in custody decisions, that DV survivors alienate their children from the other parent and that children are hurt when survivors are reluctant to co-parent. Evaluators' actual recommendations of conditions that favored the offender over the victim were significantly related to these core beliefs, as well as to a more general set of beliefs supporting patriarchal norms and discrimination against women.[57] Another source of bias was identified regarding victims' demeanor. In a study of custody evaluators' responses to a vignette depicting DV, Hardesty and colleagues found that custody evaluators were five times more likely to recommend custody to the abuser if the victim was characterized as hostile.[58] As Evan Stark pointed out in his critique, the whole section on biases is simplistic since it proceeds behind the expectation that evaluators recognize their bias – if they did, they wouldn't be biased. Many of these biases are viewed as reasoned principled norms of practice that are widely shared and accepted by the family bar, judges, and fathers' rights groups that promote legislative mandates making joint custody the default.

> "We live in a system rife with sexism and face a family court system whose legitimacy derives from fostering the illusion of equity in the context of systematic sexual inequality. This status will not be changed by confronting bias."[59]

While the guidelines mention that DV offenders may deny or minimize their behavior, evaluators are told to seek information on an offender's demonstration of willingness and capacity to change, without warning them about the likelihood of manipulative responses, and the complexity and lack of reliability of predicting change in any individual case.[60] Most importantly, evaluators are not warned about DV offenders' capacity to charm, and to appear normal, rational and composed.[61] Finally, evaluators are instructed to conduct separate analyses of DV and other parenting factors such as "alienation" – as if it is possible to separate DV from other parenting factors. Although the problems identified in these guidelines are subtle, they pave the way for evaluators to find that while there may be DV, it is not serious, is not likely to recur, does not affect parenting and has nothing to do with "alienating" behavior by the non-offending parent.

Triage

Since custody evaluations are prohibitively expensive, and not affordable for many families, and since family court judges are eager to have cases settled in a timely, cost-effective manner by pre-court interventions, divorce professionals have proposed alternative solutions to settling custody disputes through a system of triage. In the past, most family court systems provided services using a linear model following the pyramid design described by Maccoby and Mnookin referenced in Chapter 3. Under this system, families would begin with services that are the least intrusive and time-consuming, and if this did not resolve the dispute, the family would move to the next available service. Such a progression might begin with a divorce education program followed by mediation, a child custody evaluation, a moderated settlement conference, and finally, a trial. The triage system, which was pioneered by AFCC affiliated divorce professionals in Connecticut, begins with an intake assessment of families, which then determines referral to the appropriate service for that family.[62] The Connecticut group developed a family intake screening questionnaire that comprised six domains: (1) general information (background issues such as demographics); (2) level of conflict (where they are in the litigation process); (3) ability to cooperate and communicate (parents' perceptions of how well they communicate and cooperate); (4) complexity of issues (child abuse, DV and mental health issues); (5) level of dangerousness (fears, police involvement, protective orders); and (6) disparity of facts/need for corroborating information (the extent to which the couple agree in their answers).[63] The screening begins after a short calendar negotiation meeting, which is an information gathering stage of the process. Screenings are then conducted by family relations counselors either conjointly or separately in face-to-face interviews. At relatively low levels of conflict couples may be referred to mediation. At moderate or mildly chronic levels of conflict, a conflict resolution conference would be considered appropriate. Where complex issues such as violence, substance abuse and mental health issues are involved, a comprehensive custody evaluation might be the appropriate avenue.[64]

Of specific interest to us is the way this system handles allegations of abuse. The developers of the triage system recommend careful screening for DV, which they assess on the basis of two instruments – the Domestic Violence Screening Instrument (DVSI) which evaluates imminent risk of violence toward a partner and toward others, and the Conflict Tactics Scale which asks about the frequency of specific acts of physical violence. While the triage authors emphasize the need to distinguish subtypes of DV, loosely referring to "common couple violence" and "abusive relationships," they provide no definition of these categories and propose no criteria that should be used to distinguish them. Johnson's classification, regardless of its validity, would require an assessment of controlling behavior, which is not addressed in the triage instrument or even mentioned in the report. Also absent from the triage instrument and the report is any mention of psychological, emotional or economic abuse. This is a good example of how divorce professionals are encouraged to attach labels to families experiencing DV using seat-of-the-pants methods that are guaranteed to result in biased assessments.

The DVSI places a great deal of emphasis on the temporal proximity of the violence and whether or not the offender is in treatment and/or acknowledges the impact of violence on the parenting relationship. Indicators of abuse that occurred prior to the past 12 months are accorded lower status than those occurring within the past 12 months. For example, a protective order that was in place more than a year ago would indicate a low level of dangerousness, and for such a family, mediation would be regarded as the appropriate level of intervention. A restraining order filed within the past 12 months would indicate a moderate level of dangerousness and for this family conflict resolution would be regarded as the appropriate intervention. The same would apply to a case in which one parent had been kicked, slapped, hit or bitten several times in the past year or choked or beaten up only once. Only if there had been frequent beatings, injuries, or use of weapons in the past 12 months would a focused evaluation or a comprehensive evaluation be considered necessary. Some readers might wonder what the purpose of an evaluation would be in such cases. Surely, if the violence were substantiated, or credibly alleged, why not take protective measures immediately? I would remind such readers that even an evaluation at this stage would not necessarily find that the perpetrator was an unfit parent, and could result in a recommendation of joint custody or worse. This in fact has been the experience of many battered mothers in Connecticut.

Pennsylvania is another state that has adopted the triage system similar to the Connecticut model. At the request of the Supreme Court in 2005, a committee was established under the direction of the Pennsylvania Bar Association to develop recommendations on *"changing the culture of custody in Pennsylvania."*[65] The recommendations, published in 2007, were based on the premise that *"the traditional approach of parents litigating and involving masters and judges to resolve conflicts has only served to intensify the wounds left with both parents and all of the children, and to cause inordinate delay in getting the fractured family back on a stable footing."* The Committee also considered the circumstances of those with limited resources and without legal representation, and noted how few public resources were devoted to helping parents resolve custody disputes.

The Committee developed a "multi-door" approach, spear-headed by a family relations counselor who would be the initial point of contact for families entering the system. The family relations counselor would conduct interviews with the parties using a screening instrument, make a swift assessment of the family's needs, and refer the parties to the appropriate services. Pennsylvania offers a larger variety of services to divorcing families including the family intake screen, court literature, comprehensive evaluations, issue focused evaluations, parenting mediation, parenting facilitation, parent-child education, domestic violence focused parent education, batterers' intervention, conflict resolution conferences, parenting capacity evaluations, treatment programs, counselors or guardians ad litem for children, and supervised visitation. The triage report emphasizes that these services are not offered on a continuum, but are based on the family's needs. However, mandatory education classes for parents and children are required within 30 days of filing a custody petition. These classes provide general information regarding separation and legal procedures for resolving parenting and child support disputes. Programs for children are tailored to meet their developmental needs, incorporate games, and teach coping skills. High conflict parents are provided with intensive instructional and experiential learning activities in group settings. These sessions are longer and may be offered weekly for a period of six to eight weeks.

The Pennsylvania triage report states that when a parent alleges that DV has occurred, unless a protective order is in place, the family relations counselor will conduct an assessment using an instrument that is said to be more comprehensive than the one used in Connecticut.[66] If either party is not satisfied with the results of the assessment, they may go before a judge, who will make the final decision as to whether or not DV took place. If it has been established that DV has occurred, whether by the existence of a protective order, or as a result of a decision by the family relations counselor or the court, the family then qualifies to receive "domestic violence intervention." But what exactly is DV intervention? All this ensures is that the parties are separated during the procedures and programmatic interventions that follow, and typically a temporary parenting arrangement is put in place based on the one that existed prior to the separation "*if it is deemed safe for the children.*" This scenario raises some confusion. Surely, the parenting arrangement that existed before the separation is the one in which the substantiated violence took place. While this violence may be considered serious enough to separate the two parties during the court proceedings, and delivery of services, it is not considered serious enough to protect the victim from returning to the conditions in which the violence occurred in the first place.

The Pennsylvania triage system does provide special accommodations for parents that have experienced DV. They are not required to submit parenting plans to the court within 30 days of filing the custody petition, as is the normal procedure, and while they are still required to attend mandatory education classes, DV parents are offered special consideration for these classes such as different times and locations for each parent to attend separately and safely. The triage report seems to promise unrealistically optimistic results for parent education programs that address DV noting:

"Any parenting program made available at this early stage will address domestic violence, prioritize safety, stop violence and protect children and advise parents that where there is domestic violence, parallel rather than cooperative parenting may be recommended."[67]

In a footnote, the report explains "parallel parenting":

"Parallel parenting is recommended and is appropriate when high conflict or issues of safety are present as, for example, when parents cannot resolve conflict on their own and repeatedly resort to the courts for resolution. Parallel parenting is characterized by each parent assuming total responsibility for the child during the time in his/her care with no expectation of flexibility in the schedule in order to prevent confrontation. Each parent remains part of the child's life while reducing opportunities for conflict. There is little or no face-to-face communication and e-mail, a third party or parenting notebook is used to communicate. There are separate households in which each parent makes decisions about the children when they are in his/her household. Additionally, the value of having a written parenting plan and following it or strictly adhering to the court order or judgment is emphasized."

Notice how the conflict and safety issues are blended together seamlessly in this definition as though they were one and the same. This despite the warning of an expert on DV who writes:

"Parallel parenting may be an option in high-conflict cases without domestic violence issues or a limited number of domestic violence cases where the abuse is minor, historical, and does not represent a pattern of behavior."[68]

The triage report acknowledges that some batterers use time with their children as an opportunity to inflict additional physical, emotional and/or psychological abuse on survivors and their children. In such cases, supervised access and exchange programs may be necessary.[69] But the report does not explain how one would determine which survivors and children would be at risk, and when to implement supervised visitation. The report notes that mediation in cases of DV is prohibited by statute in Pennsylvania, unless the survivor agrees, and the mediator believes that it can be done safely. The report says nothing about what alternatives to mediation might be considered appropriate in cases of DV. The triage experts seem to have overcome this problem by going directly to parallel parenting which is essentially a form of forced joint custody, and is almost guaranteed to continue patterns of abuse and coercive control through children.

Some critics of the triage system have raised concerns about whether the programs are equipped to conduct adequate evaluations of cases involving DV. Ver Steegh and colleagues point out that a one-time interview or administration of a screening instrument is unlikely to yield the information needed for a triage professional to predict what, if any, dispute resolution process will be safe and productive for a given family.[70] DV survivors are often reluctant to disclose the violence especially since disclosure to a triage professional is unlikely to be privileged, and might be discoverable. The authors recommend that where DV is an issue survivors would be better able to make informed decisions after confidential discussion – preferably with a lawyer – concerning the characteristics and implications of the violence, a realistic assessment of the processes and services available, the strategic consequences of choices in light of the party's interests, and how to prepare for participation in any processes selected. This would support the twin goals of safety and informed decision-making, while maintaining confidentiality.[71] Ver Steegh and colleagues do not address the question of what to do in DV cases where dispute resolution is deemed inappropriate. The cases they are referring to involve mostly self-represented litigants who would at best be offered one or two counseling sessions with an attorney. But what if the barriers to legal representation were removed, and battered mothers had full access to attorneys? Would they have better outcomes in family court than those who did not?

This was a question addressed by Mary Kernic, who conducted a study of child custody outcomes among DV survivors with and without legal representation.[72] Surprisingly, she found that survivors represented by legal aid attorneys had significantly safer outcomes that those represented by attorneys in private practice. Kernic surmises that private attorneys are likely to have adopted the dominant philosophy of the family court system, which is to encourage settlement. Legal aid attorneys, many of whom have received special training in the representation of DV survivors, are more likely to fight for their clients and secure the best outcomes. What this underscores is that where settlement is the goal, DV survivors do not do particularly well, even when represented by attorneys.

Conclusion

Evan Stark has proposed a new framework for understanding individual acts of victimization as part of a broad range of harms that diminish women's personhood and rights as citizens. These liberty harms, says Stark, are not recognized by the justice system, which is still governed by paternalistic stereotypes. They are also not fully recognized by advocacy groups, which still adhere to a narrow understanding of DV, yet they add up to tangible forms of discrimination including medical expenses, lost wages, the cost of deferred education or career opportunities, or degradation and dependence due to isolation, intimidation and control.[73] To this list of harms we could add the widespread loss of their children to their abusers through the efforts of a divorce industry that profits from their victimization. The divorce industry is thus a major instrument of their oppression. This is typically not accomplished through open expressions of sexism and gender bias, but rather – to borrow an expression from civil rights advocates – through "dog whistles."

Expressions of open bigotry are easily identifiable, and may take the form of using derogatory, offensive language, discriminatory and harmful behaviors including violence, and policies that are openly and explicitly disadvantageous to a particular group. Dog-whistles are subtle expressions of discrimination that use coded messages to achieve the same result as open bigotry without inviting the same public opprobrium. The term "common couple violence" or "situational couple violence" is dog-whistle for "the victim brought this on herself," or "they are both to blame," or "the violence isn't serious enough to require attention." Parental alienation is dog whistle for "women are manipulative liars" or "women are mentally unstable." Parental Alienation Syndrome, with its grotesquely exaggerated stereotypes and bizarre claims about sexuality, is more aptly described as open bigotry.

Parental alienation (with or without the "syndrome") must eventually take its place on the trash heap of pseudo-scientific theories that justify gender oppression, inequality and victimization. Chief among these was Freud's Oedipal theory, which posited that reports of childhood sexual abuse by his adult female patients were not memories of actual abuse, but rather reflected unconscious childhood fantasies of sex with their fathers. An examination of Freud's archives led to the revelation in 1984, that he actually believed his patients' allegations of incest, but reformulated his findings into the Oedipal theory after he was threatened with ouster from a prestigious position because of reactions of outrage from his colleagues who could not believe that so many upstanding citizens would abuse their daughters.[74] The same dynamics of denial and appeasement are still alive today among many practitioners in the divorce industry.

Table 4: Parental alienation and custody

Study 1

Author and date: Sheila Heim, et al. (2002)[75]
Institution: California National Organization for Women
Study name: Family Court Report 2002
Sample: 212 California women with cases in family court who responded to an online questionnaire, and 80 women who were interviewed by phone
Results: Mothers alleged DV in 86% of cases and child abuse in 76% of cases. In 69% of cases where child abuse was alleged, the offender received custody or unsupervised contact. In 53% of cases alleging child abuse the mother was labeled with Parental Alienation Syndrome.

Study 2

Author and date: Dianne Post (2003)[76]
Institution: Arizona Coalition Against Domestic Violence
Study name: Arizona Battered Women's Custody Project
Sample: 57 battered mothers who had gone through a custody battle in the Arizona family courts
Results: In 56% to 74% of cases, batterers won sole or joint custody depending on the county. The parental alienation label was used against 49% of mothers. In Maricopa County 67% of custody evaluators do parental alienation therapy.

Table 4 continued:

Study 3

Author and date: Rita Berg(2011)[77]
Institution: University of St. Thomas School of Law
Study name: Minnesota Study of Gender Bias in the Use of Parental Alienation
Sample: Minnesota Court of Appeals decisions mentioning parental alienation from 1987 to 2011(N=18)
Results: All mothers who were not able to substantiate their claims of DV (6 out of 11) lost custody. One mother with a substantiated claim also lost custody and one with a partially substantiated claim was awarded joint custody. Thus 7 out of 11 mothers claiming DV lost custody completely, and one received joint custody.

Study 4

Author and date: Keith Harmon Snow(2013)[78]
Institution: The Conscious Being Alliance
Study name: Connecticut Database on Family Court Abuses
Sample: 75 Connecticut family court cases covering a 20 year period obtained from published court cases, news articles and blogs
Results: All cases involved children whose safety and well-being were put at risk by unethical court professionals. Mothers were accused of parental alienation in 36 of those cases. Fathers were awarded sole custody in 28 of the 36 cases, and joint custody was awarded in 4 cases. The few mothers who retained custody were punished financially.

Table 4 continued:

Study 5

Author and date: Joyanna Silberg et. al. (2013)[79]
Institution: Leadership Council on Child Abuse and Interpersonal Violence
Study name: Family Court "Turned Around" Cases
Sample: 28 "turned around" custody cases from around the country involving abuse allegations
Results: All 28 cases involved mothers who initially lost custody because judges did not believe their allegations of abuse against the father. Later, these mothers regained custody after a different court credited their allegations. The study analyzed the reasons for the initial denial of custody. In 10 of the 28 cases, parental alienation by the mother was one of the reasons judges gave for awarding custody to the father.

Study 6

Author and date: Joan Meier (2013)[80]
Institution: Domestic Violence Legal Empowerment and Appeals Project
Study name: Pilot Study on Published Cases Involving Parental Alienation
Sample: 240 electronically available judicial opinions on cases involving custody and parental alienation over a 10 year period
Results: Primary custody was switched to the father in 88% of cases alleging sexual abuse, 80% of cases alleging child abuse, and 47% of cases alleging DV. In all 7 cases where paternal child abuse was credited, the father still won custody.

Chapter 6

Federal Action

Federal action to address the plight of battered mothers in family court predates the Violence Against Women Act (VAWA). We noted in Chapter 4 that as early as 1990, Congress passed a resolution calling on the states to review their policies with regards to DV and custody. The Model Code initiative was promoted and funded by federal agencies including the Department of Justice. In 1994, the same year that VAWA was passed, a group of advocates prevailed upon Congress to schedule separate hearings on the custody issue, but these were cancelled because of the death of President Nixon, and to date, they have not been rescheduled.

The battered women's movement that pushed for VAWA was aware that batterer manipulation of children and threats to remove children from their mothers was part of the power and control wheel that guided theoretical thinking on wife battering, but political action to address child custody was not on their radar. With its focus on law enforcement and the criminal justice system, the original VAWA did not recognize the special needs that battered mothers would face in family court when trying to protect their children in custody and visitation litigation. Over time there has been increased attention to this issue, increased resources to assist battered mothers in custody litigation, and new programs and new legislation designed to better protect battered mothers facing custody litigation. In this chapter we will discuss the gradual recognition of the protective parent problem as it became incorporated into the battered women's movement, and the different types of federal action that have addressed the custody issue over the past two decades.

Federal legislative efforts to address custody

The Violence Against Women Act

The Violence Against Women Act (VAWA), Title IV, sec. 40001-40703 of the Crime Control and Law Enforcement Act of 1994, known as Public Law 103-322, became law on September 13, 1994.[1] The Act allocated $1.6 billion over six years (from 1994 to 2000) to the U.S. Department of Justice (DOJ) toward investigation and prosecution of violent crimes against women, and $600 million to the U.S. Department of Health and Human Services (DHHS) for victim services, particularly shelters. Other provisions of the Act included imposing automatic and mandatory restitution on those convicted, and allowed civil redress in cases prosecutors declined to prosecute. The reauthorization of VAWA in 2000 allocated $3.33 billion over five years from 2001 to 2005; $565 million were allocated in 2005, and in 2006, $3.935 billion were allocated for another five-year period from 2007 to 2011. Most of these funds were allocated to grant programs to states and territories for the improvement of the criminal justice system's response to violence against women defined as DV, sexual assault and stalking. For example, the Grants to Encourage Arrest Policies and Enforcement of Protection Orders Program facilitates collaboration among law enforcement agencies, prosecutors' offices, courts and community partners to develop and implement programs strengthening the community response to violence against women through investigation, arrest, prosecution and judicial scrutiny and management of offender behavior. These grants were to be administered through the newly established Violence Against Women Office within the DOJ, later named the Office on Violence Against Women (OVW). The Act also provided funds for shelter services and the national domestic violence hotline to be administered through DHHS.

Half of the funds ($800,000 from 1994 to 2000) were allocated to the STOP (Services Training Officers Prosecutors) Formula Grants, which award funding to states and territories to develop partnerships among criminal justice practitioners and community stakeholders, provide training to law enforcement personnel, and implement comprehensive strategies that addressed victim safety and offender accountability. While STOP funds allowed for the legal representation of victims with regard to the victim's safety, the program was not intended to pay the fees charged by attorneys for divorces, legal separations, and other actions falling outside the scope of the statute. Support for legal services, such as custody or visitation, were only allowable in limited circumstances directly related to enhancing a victim's safety. For example, if a protection order specified "no contact" with the children, then attorney's fees related to a visitation case could be covered if resolution of the visitation case was necessary for the continued enforcement of the protection order. Thus VAWA funding provided the resources for DV victims to leave their abusers and obtain protective orders, but this resulted in an anomalous outcome described in the testimony of Joan Pennington on March 6, 1998 in a hearing of the New Jersey legislature regarding problems using VAWA funding for civil legal assistance .

> "There's a lot of money around for domestic violence programs and for implementing ways to help victims of domestic violence in court. We applied for some of that VAWA money for our program. Could not touch it because we do divorce and custody. We do not do just domestic violence. Okay. So when a woman goes into court and she has representation to get a restraining order, and immediately – because this is the real world – immediately, the abuser files for custody or divorce and custody to retaliate. And she's left swinging in the wind because nobody will represent her in that divorce or in that custody

or in that contested visitation case because she doesn't have any money."[2]

At the time of Pennington's remarks, Congress was attempting to rectify the problem by including in its appropriations for 1998, $12 million for legal assistance to DV survivors, that would become available later that year, and that would cover legal representation in custody cases. This amount was increased in subsequent years. But legal assistance alone could not address the entrenched biases in family court against battered mothers, which by the mid 1990s was becoming increasingly obvious.

The Morella Resolution

On October 30th, 1997 the House of Representatives introduced a resolution demonstrating Congress' understanding of key elements of the custody issue that are as problematic today as they were 20 years ago. The resolution was sponsored by Congresswoman Connie Morella (R Maryland), with co-sponsors that included Chuck Schumer (D New York) and Tom Davis (R Virginia).[3]

The Morella Resolution debunked the myths that women frequently make false accusations of abuse and that fathers are discriminated against in custody proceedings, noting that widespread belief in these myths results in failure of relevant agencies to conduct appropriate investigations when abuse allegations arise in custody cases. The Resolution also noted the absence of reliable data to support the phenomenon of Parent Alienation Syndrome and the lack of DV training on the part of mental health professionals who inappropriately blame mothers for their children's reasonable fear or anger towards violent fathers.

The Conyers Bill

Although the Morella Resolution did not become law, it was influential in inspiring other lawmakers to propose legislative remedies. Approximately five months after the introduction of the Morella Resolution, on March 19, 1998 Congressman John Conyers (D Michigan) of the House of Representative introduced a Bill, H.R. 3514 (105th): Violence Against Women Act of 1998, which reflected many of the same elements as the Morella Resolution.[4] This Bill died in committee, was introduced again the following year, and again died in committee, although some aspects were adopted in later versions of VAWA. Two key provisions of the Conyers Bill were incorporated into later VAWA legislation – namely the Safe Havens for Children Act, and the full faith and credit provision for custody and visitation orders contained within protective orders.

The Safe Haven for Children Act

A key provision of the Conyers Bill that was incorporated into VAWA 2000 appropriated $15 million per year, later increased to $20 million, for supervised visitation centers.[5] The first awards were made in 2002, and reauthorized in 2005 for $20 million. The idea was that if more supervised visitation centers were available, judges would be more likely to order supervised visitation rather than unsupervised visitation in cases of DV. Supervised visitation centers were already funded under the Access and Visitation Program administered by the Department of Health and Human Services, but the goal of that program was to motivate noncustodial parents to pay child support, and in exchange, to facilitate their access to their children. The goals of the Safe Havens Program were:

1) Provision of supervised visitation and safe exchange of children by and between parents in situations involving DV, dating violence, child abuse, sexual assault, or stalking;

2) Protection of children from the trauma of witnessing domestic or dating violence or experiencing abduction,

injury, or death during parent and child visitation exchanges;

3) Protection of parents or caretakers who are victims of DV and dating violence from experiencing further violence, abuse, and threats during child visitation exchanges;

4) Protection of children from the trauma of experiencing sexual assault or other forms of physical assault or abuse during parent and child visitation and visitation exchanges.

Custody stipulations in protective orders

VAWA 2000 incorporated another key provision of the Conyers Bill – the full-faith-and credit amendment to the Parental Kidnapping Prevention Act (PKPA).[6] This amendment afforded greater protection to battered mothers who crossed state lines with their children to escape from violence by requiring that states give full faith and credit to custody and visitation stipulations involving minor children that were incorporated into protection orders.

Defense for parental kidnapping

The Conyers Bill proposed several other changes to the PKPA including the establishment of a defense to custodial inter-ference for DV victims. The Bill proposed that flight to escape DV should serve as a positive defense for victims who left the state with their children, and who had valid custody or visitation orders before leaving. It also proposed that the U.S. Attorney General issue guidance to assist the U.S. Attorneys and the FBI in determining when to decline to initiate or to terminate an investigation or prosecution of custodial interference due to the potential availability of the defense. Although this part of the Bill was never enacted, VAWA 2000 commissioned a study on how the PKPA affected battered mothers. The results of this study will be discussed later in Chapter 8.

Training for professionals

The Conyers Bill proposed another resolution, which was in many ways similar to the Morella Resolution. In addition to reiterating much of what was in the Morella Resolution, the Conyers Resolution also proposed that states should provide training in DV and sexual assault, as they impact custody, child support and visitation determinations, to all professionals who interact with children and parents (including judges, attorneys, guardians ad litem and other individuals appointed to represent children, therapists and mental health professionals, custody evaluators, child protective services personnel, and court appointed special advocates). The Bill also called for training of child welfare workers in DV and in the intersection of DV and child abuse, and for the updating of training manuals and policies to reflect this latest information.

The child welfare provision was never enacted, but DOJ in collaboration with other agencies developed the Greenbook Initiative, which was designed to facilitate the collaboration of DV advocates and child welfare professionals in cases where DV and child maltreatment co-occur. VAWA 2005 provided further funding for Greenbook type collaborations, appropriating $5 millions per year from 2007 to 2011 for programs designed to support efforts by child welfare agencies, DV or dating violence victim services providers, courts, law enforcement, and other related professionals and community organizations to develop collaborative responses and services and provide cross training to enhance community responses to families where there is both child maltreatment and DV. The Greenbook Initiative will be discussed in greater detail below. The current VAWA reauthorization of 2013 provides grants to states to improve DV training for court personnel and mental health professionals who deal with child custody in DV cases.[7]

VAWA reauthorization of 2013

VAWA 2013 greatly expanded and enhanced the Safe Havens for Children Program. This program was to be combined with a court program intended to provide comprehensive support to victims of DV and child sexual abuse in family law matters in the civil system, with an annual budget of $22 million from 2014 through 2018. This was the first time that legislation acknowledged protective parents and sexually abused children and defined them as eligible for inclusion in VAWA program funding.

Executive branch awareness of the custody issue

The Office on Violence Against Women

At its inception in 1995, it appears that the Office on Violence Against Women (OVW) was not aware of the problems battered women were facing with regard to custody and visitation. Director Bonnie Campbell was soon briefed on the problem shortly after she took office, and over the next three years frequently heard from DV survivors. In May 1998, Bonnie stated in a memo to Noel Brennan, Deputy Assistant Attorney General for the Office of Justice Programs (OJP):

> "As you know, I am on the road quite a bit, and I am constantly approached by women whose children have allegedly been placed in custody of perpetrators of child abuse. Many of the calls and letters that I receive at my office are from women in this situation as well. I feel very strongly that we at the Department of Justice must take some action – not only because this is a domestic violence issue, but because it is endangering many children in this country. I am asking for your assistance in determining whether the Department can play a role in combating this problem."[8]

The memo then goes on to present summaries of five case histories from around the country, and concludes:

> "This is a serious problem, and one that deserves immediate attention. While I encourage people in the Department to search for federal jurisdiction in these cases, I also realize that we must search for longer-term solutions, in the form of judicial education, grant programs and outreach."

In late 1998 and early 1999, OJP scheduled two workshops to discuss the problem of DV and custody. The first workshop, held in Washington, D.C., dealt with the challenges and dangers of using mediation to resolve custody and visitation disputes in cases involving DV. The second workshop held in Reno, Nevada, and co-sponsored by the National Council of Juvenile and Family Court Judges, focused more broadly on all custody and visitation issues facing battered mothers in family court. Federal employees from OVW and other relevant federal agencies attended the workshop, as did researchers, practitioners, and DV advocates from nongovernmental agencies. There was consensus among workshop attendees that federally funded research was needed to document the impact on battered mothers of court-ordered mediation and to examine how judges were dealing with DV in contested custody and visitation cases.

The Greenbook Initiative

An important but little recognized project that attempted to deal with the intersection of DV and child maltreatment was the Greenbook Initiative, begun in 1998 under the leadership of the National Council of Juvenile and Family Court Judges, and with the support of the Departments of Justice, Health and Human Services, and private foundations. Impetus for the project came from the growing recognition that child maltreatment and DV often overlap.[9] The premise for Greenbook was that historically, two distinct intervention systems were created – each with its own law enforcement and judicial mandates, institutions, and funding. One offered DV services and legal protections and the other provided assistance and protections for abused children and their families. Confronted with a new set of facts that adult DV and child maltreatment often occur together, Greenbook proposed that communities required new responses if violence within families is to stop. Thus the purpose of the project was to develop guidelines for practice and policy in cases where DV and child maltreatment overlap. Led by Susan Schechter and Jeffrey Edelson, the advisory committee for the project comprised a diverse group of professionals from the courts, child welfare and DV services, federal agencies, the academic community, and judges. The National Council offered a framework for developing interventions and measuring progress by addressing the following questions:

1) How can child protection services work together with DV service providers to enhance the safety of multiple victims in violent homes?

2) How can juvenile courts protect children when their mothers are being battered without re-victimizing the mother?

3) How can communities protect battered mothers and their children and hold batterers accountable for their violence?

The final report included recommendations for the child protection system, the network of DV service providers, and the juvenile or other trial courts with jurisdiction over child maltreatment cases. The following were among the major recommendations:

- Child protection services, DV agencies, juvenile courts, and community-based services should design inter- ventions to achieve three outcomes: to create safety, enhance wellbeing, and provide stability for children and families.

- As a way to ensure stability and permanency for children, child welfare administrators and juvenile court personnel should try to keep children affected by maltreatment and DV in the care of their non-offending parent (or parents), whenever possible. Making adult victims safer and stopping batterers' assaults are two important ways to remove risk and thereby create permanency for children.

- Communities should design service systems that entitle any adult or child victim of violence to receive help with or without the opening of a child protection case. Families with less serious cases of child maltreatment and DV should be able to gain access to help without the initiation of a child protection investigation or the substantiation of a finding of maltreatment.

- Because DV encompasses a wide range of behaviors – from the extremely dangerous to the less serious – families require a range of interventions, some of them voluntary and some mandated. Creating safety and stability for families requires careful assessment of risk and the capacity to make differential responses.[10]

Soon after publication of the Greenbook guiding principles, DOJ and DHHS partnered to develop a demonstration project to support implementation of the Greenbook recommendations. In 2000 grants were awarded to six sites: El Paso County, Colorado; Grafton County, New Hampshire; Lane County, Oregon; San Francisco County, California; Santa Clara County, California; and St. Louis County, Missouri. These demonstration sites received federal grants, technical assistance, and other support to implement the Greenbook principles and recommendations over a five-year demon-stration period. During that time, the sites were expected to form collaborations that would plan and implement infrastructure changes within and across several family-serving systems to better meet the needs of victims of child maltreatment and DV.[11]

Most of the systems change activities centered on child welfare agencies, focusing for example on improving identification of co-occurrence through means such as revised intake and screening protocols and staff training. Child welfare agencies undertook additional training for caseworkers on DV, co-occurrence, and the impact of DV on children, and also expanded their use of collocated advocates, multidisciplinary case review, and other arrangements for sharing resources and expertise to address cases involving DV.

Although some positive changes were noted in certain areas, these were not necessarily sustained over time. For example, while there was evidence of active screening for DV in the earlier period, this diminished or even decreased over time. Revised tools were not always used routinely, and the project's evaluators suggested that frequent training and reinforcement would have been necessary to ensure the continued implementation of best practices. This was not always done, and the problem of sustaining practice was made more difficult by the high turnover among child welfare caseworkers, and the additional demands of their work. Reasons for variations in success across sites included differences in the availability of resources, a history of collaboration among agencies, and existing practices that could be expanded and developed. Experimentation with new processes, not all of which worked or were continued, was part of the Greenbook Initiative.

A major gap in the Greenbook experiment was the lack of involvement of judges, and lack of change in court practices. Although several judges and other court personnel from multiple sites spoke positively during interviews about Greenbook training, overall relatively little change in practice was found among the courts in the Greenbook sites. One judge reported, "*I have been in criminal law for 30 years, and I am still learning through Greenbook! Some judges say it's the best training they've ever had and that it helps them move forward with their work."*[12] Another judge said of Greenbook training, *"My eyes have been opened. I've gained new perspectives about domestic violence and how insensitive [judges] can be."* Unfortunately, collaboration among courts to address problems of families with co-occurrence did not become a major focus of efforts in the Greenbook demonstration sites, and the data do not show change in collaboration among different courts in the sites. The authors of the Greenbook report suggest that the organizational structure of the dependency court and the role of judges appear to have been barriers to change. Judges were bound by law and legal precedent, and there was no hierarchical structure or mandatory training to incorporate systemic changes into the courts. As a result, although court staff was responsive to training opportunities, and some courts implemented practice changes, there was limited overall change.

Although Greenbook did not deal with child custody per se, it addressed an important issue that has significant implications for battered mothers seeking custody in cases where DV and child maltreatment co-occur. Greenbook attempted to implement many of the changes in child welfare practice and policy that Congressman Conyers had attempted to introduce through legislation in the child welfare component of his Violence Against Women Act of 1998 and 1999. Greenbook was able to accomplish some of these changes voluntarily, without being compelled by legislation, albeit for a short period of time. Studying the lessons learned and examining some of the pitfalls that Greenbook experienced in achieving its goals may inform future legislative efforts to effect changes in the child welfare system's approach to the overlap between DV and child maltreatment. Greenbook demonstrated that child welfare workers and DV advocates could work together under the right circumstances. However, Greenbook's lack of success in engaging judges and courts in their program of change may be an indication that training alone cannot overcome barriers to change where courts are concerned, and that something more is required.

The Greenbook project continues to provide articles, documents, tools and training materials to help reform child welfare practice and assist communities in improving their response to the overlap of DV and child maltreatment.

Other federally funded projects related to custody

In 2009 OVW entered into a two-year cooperative agreement with the Battered Women's Justice Project (BWJP) to develop a framework to help family court practitioners better identify, understand and account for the context and implications of DV in child custody cases.[13] BWJP conducted an institutional analysis of the Henry County Family Court system in Ohio, and used their findings for the development of a roadmap to improve the institutional response to DV in family court. The study identified two major problem areas: (1) flawed decision-making, and (2) lack of accountability and due process. The first problem was blamed not only on judges, but all divorce industry professionals, including lawyers, mediators, custody evaluators and guardians ad litem, who were basing their decisions on misinformation, speculation and false assumptions. To address this problem, BWJP developed a conceptual framework for guiding practice to help parties gather, synthesize and analyze critical information about the context and implications of DV to improve informed decision-making across disciplines and court settings. Interestingly, when project personnel began vetting and testing their practice aids, they found that battered mothers and their advocates were more interested in the utility of the project materials than were many of the practitioners, who were reluctant to change their everyday practice.

The second major problem identified by the project was the inadequacy of the system of accountability and due process, largely attributed to the outsourcing of court functions to practitioners who are non-state employees. The project authors attribute the lack of accountability of court auxiliaries to the fact that they do not function as an arm of the state, but are private, independent actors not constrained by statutory limits to their actions, not accountable to a chain of command, and not required to do their jobs in any standardized fashion. These practitioners were described as having almost unfettered freedom to re-invent their jobs as they went along, deciding for themselves how they would approach each case, what information they would deem important, and what information they would prefer to ignore. Since much of what happens in family court occurs "off the record" – in the dark, behind closed doors – and because non-judicial court professionals are not constrained by rules of evidence and rules of civil procedure, it is extremely difficult, say the authors, for parties to put on a case, or challenge unreliable or misleading information. There is also no way to effectively challenge the process, correct misinformation, or complain about the result, since while judicial error can be appealed, the same is not true for a decision by a non-judicial actor.

The BWJP is careful not to blame judges too much, preferring to view the problem as structural, distinguishing between the rigorous observance of proper procedure in criminal court compared to the more relaxed approach in family court. They also do not address the problem of the almost unfettered discretion that judges have in custody cases in deciding on "best interests", and they also do not address gender bias in the selective way court auxiliaries view information and make their decisions.

Congressional Hearings

The Elizabeth Morgan case

Congress never rescheduled the hearing on abuse and custody as a national problem that had been slated to take place in April 1994. It did, however, schedule a hearing for one child, who at the time was under the protection of the New Zealand Government. On August 4th, 1995, the House of Represen-tatives Subcommittee on the District of Columbia, Committee on Government Reform and Oversight, held a hearing regarding a proposed amendment to Title 11 of the District of Columbia Code. The amendment proposed to restrict the authority of the D.C. Superior Court over certain pending cases involving child custody and visitation rights. Present at the hearing were Representatives Tom Davis (R Virginia), Frank Wolf (R Virginia), Connie Morella (R Maryland) and Susan Molinari (R New York). In a prepared statement, Congress-woman Morella stated:

"H.R. 1855 represents an opportunity to put an end to one of the most contentious and highly publicized child custody cases in recent times. In the summer of 1987, Dr. Elizabeth Morgan was jailed by the Superior Court of the District of Columbia for contempt of court. She had refused to abide by a court order directing her to present her five-year-old daughter Hilary to Dr. Eric Foretich, Hilary's father, for unsupervised visitation.

Dr. Morgan was convinced that Dr. Foretich had sexually abused their daughter. Hilary confirmed this. Doctors found evidence indicating such abuse, but could not determine who was responsible. Dr. Morgan took the only recourse available to her, to do what she had to as a responsible parent to protect her child in any way possible – she arranged transportation for Hilary out of the country, out of the reach of the court and, more importantly, out of the reach of an abusive father. And she faced the consequences of her actions, spending more than two years in jail in contempt of the court order. Dr. Morgan was freed in September 1989 when Congress passed legislation limiting to twelve months the time which one may serve for civil contempt. I was a composer of that legislation, which was introduced by our colleague from Virginia, Mr. Wolf.

Mr. Chairman, Dr. Morgan has now joined Hilary in New Zealand, where they have been living for the past five years. But while they are no longer bound by the Court, they not really free, either. They may not travel abroad without the permission of the New Zealand Government, which is holding their passports. New Zealand has become the Morgan's Elba.

We can go around and around debating the evidence in

this case, the personalities involved, the charges and the counter-charges, and we still wouldn't be able to convincingly determine the truth."[14]

Morella went on to say that for the purpose of the legislation under consideration, the truth did not matter. Seven years had passed since the original court order, and Hilary was now old enough to be an active participant in the decisions about her life. While she wished to come back to the United States, she was absolutely adamant that she did not want to see Dr. Foretich. The legislation under question would vacate the penalties arising from the original court order, thereby allowing Hilary, who now called herself Ellen, to return to the United States with her mother.

According to the Chairman of the Subcommittee, the proposed bill would *"permit Ellen Morgan to be and to feel free to return to the United States with no cloud of legal intervention over her head,"* and *"reflected the common sense basic principle that the law ought not to compel one who has reached the age of reason into being forced to be unsupervised with someone whom that person asserts has been sexually abusive."* Although members of the Subcommittee disclaimed retrying the case, the clear focus of the hearing was on the Morgan-Foretich custody dispute, and discussion during the hearing emphasized the need to vacate the orders of the D.C. Superior Court so that Dr. Morgan and Hilary would be free to return to the United States. Members also spoke of the need to "correct an injustice" and to protect Hilary's best interests by facilitating her "safe return" to the United States.

The Subcommittee heard testimony from Dr. Foretich, as well as from Dr. Morgan's mother and brother. Dr. Morgan and Hilary each submitted written statements expressing their desire to return to the United States without Hilary being forced to see her father. During Dr. Foretich's testimony, members of the Subcommittee repeatedly attempted to broker a deal with him. If he would give up his parental rights and voluntarily seek vacatur of the Superior Court visitation orders, the Subcommittee would withdraw the proposed legislation. No agreement could be reached, however, and having failed to negotiate a deal with Dr. Foretich, Congress passed the Elizabeth Morgan Act on September 30, 1996. The Act was signed into law on October 2, 1996. Dr. Morgan successfully petitioned the New Zealand Family Court for permission to leave the country and, in May 1997, she returned to the United States with Hilary, who was 14 years old at the time. Dr. Foretich informed the Superior Court of their return and indicated his intent to seek enforcement of that court's prior orders. To that end, Dr. Foretich filed a motion in Superior Court in June 1997 to compel Dr. Morgan to disclose Hilary's location and to reappoint a guardian ad litem. Dr. Morgan opposed the motion on the grounds that the D.C. Superior Court lacked jurisdiction over the matter, in part because of the Elizabeth Morgan Act.[15]

Fallout and consequences of the Elizabeth Morgan Act

Dr. Foretich and his parents filed suit on June 19, 1997, against the United States and the District of Columbia, seeking declaratory and injunctive relief. Dr. Foretich challenged the Elizabeth Morgan Act as an unconstitutional bill of attainder, a violation of his substantive and procedural due process rights, and a violation of separation of powers and D.C. home rule. While Dr. Foretich's parents also participated as plaintiffs in the action before the District Court, the claims principally focused on injuries suffered by Dr. Foretich.

The Foretichs' appeal resulted in the overturning of the Act by the U.S. Supreme Court in 2003.[16] At that time Ellen Morgan was 21 years old and could not be forced into visitation with her father. Professor Jonathan Turley of George Washington University, who filed and argued the brief for the accused father, suggested that Congress could have enacted legislation to cover similar cases around the country, but chose not to do so. He wrote:

> "After sponsors defended this bill as an effort to assist women in such circumstances, I located the names and

court cases of women around the country with similar cases and submitted them to Congress. If this is not an effort to assist one individual with leverage in Congress, the law can easily be extended to cover these other cases. No member, however, has come forward for these women and sponsors have confined the bill to benefit only Dr. Morgan and penalize her ex-husband."[17]

Wake up call or snooze button?

Congress was in a unique position with regard to the Elizabeth Morgan case compared to other cases around the country, in that only Congress had the authority to amend Title 11 of the District of Columbia Code, which deals with the organization and jurisdiction of the courts. While Congress could not have passed this type of legislation anywhere else in the country, members were aware that similar cases existed elsewhere. Representative Susan Molinari made the following statement at the Elizabeth Morgan hearing:

> "This is not a unique case. It is one case that's been brought to our attention, and perhaps in bringing justice to this family, we can send an inspiring wake-up call to judges all over the country to take more into account – the rights and wishes of children in the areas of their decisions; and that not all grown-ups are always right, particularly when they are professionals and respected members of the community."[18]

Unfortunately, the Elizabeth Morgan Act was more like a snooze button than a wake-up call for judges. It proved that Congress would only enact legislation for one child, and only at one time. Everyone else could go back to business as usual. Meanwhile, at the very same time it passed the Elizabeth Morgan Act, in response to intensive lobbying by fathers' rights activists, Congress did enact legislation affecting all children in the District of Columbia – mandating joint custody.

Other Initiatives

Richard Ducote's Protective Parent Reform Act

Around the turn of the millennium, a promising legislative proposal was initiated by a women's rights activist and author, inspired by what she heard at a the Fourth World Conference on Women in Beijing in 1995. Talia Carner learned about the protective mother problem in the United States while attending the Beijing Conference, and continued to gather information about it when she returned home to New York. What she learned inspired her to write a novel, *Puppet Child*, which she published in 2002.[19] Shortly after the publication of *Puppet Child*, Carner met Congressman Steve Israel (D New York) at a Democratic Party fundraiser in New York, and was able to interest him in seeking a possible legislative remedy for the problem that she addressed in her novel.

Carner continued her research, gathering information through meetings and conversations with leading protective mothers' advocates. She prevailed upon Richard Ducote, a highly respected attorney who had represented protective mothers for decades, to write the legislation, which became known as the *Protective Parent Reform Act.* This Act would have required states to ensure that they had in place statutes and procedures for protecting children in custody cases, in order to receive federal funding under the Child Abuse Prevention and Treatment Act (CAPTA).[20] These stipulations included: (1) statutory prohibitions in custody and visitation cases of *ex parte* contacts between the judge and other parties such as guardians ad litem, mental health professionals and custody evaluators; (2) limiting the role of guardians ad litem and minor's counsel to representing the wishes of the child involved; (3) excluding testimony based on unscientific theories that discredit victims; (4) requiring appropriate training and expertise from custody evaluators dealing with DV and child abuse, and (5) not depriving a parent of custody or visitation because of the reasonable belief that his or her child has been abused.

In 2003, Congressman Israel's press secretary, Jack Pratt, told *Forward Magazine* that they were in the early stages of working on a bill that would "meet muster in the court,"[21] but a year later Israel's office told the same magazine they were no longer seeking a legislative solution.[22] According to Carner, this sudden turnaround came as a result of the publication of the first *Forward* article, which resulted in an outpouring of outrage from fathers' rights advocates, and intense lobbying that convinced the Congressman to abandon this initiative.

The Rape Survivor Custody Act

Approximately 25,000 women become pregnant through rape each year, and in response, many states have passed special laws and devised streamlined procedures either to increase access to abortion for pregnant raped women, or to help them in placing their rape-conceived children for adoptions. However, few states have passed laws to aid women who choose to raise their rape-conceived children. In most states a man who fathers a child through rape has the same rights to custody and visitation as any other father.[23] According to the National Conference of State Legislatures, 22 states allow for the termination of parental rights if the parent was convicted of a sexual assault that resulted in a the birth of a child. Another 12 states and the District of Columbia deny or restrict custody or visitation if the child was conceived as a result of rape or sexual assault.[24] In May 2015, Congress passed the *Rape Survivor Custody Act* as part of the *Victims of Trafficking Act*, which would provide grants to states that have laws permitting mothers of children conceived through rape to seek termination of the parental rights of the rapist.[25] Advocates have noted that the standards for termination of parental rights of rapists, where they existed, were based on conviction, meaning proof beyond a reasonable doubt. This is a higher standard of proof than that normally required for termination of parental rights, which is the "clear and convincing" standard of proof. The federal law was modeled on one that had been enacted by the Florida State Legislature in 2014 spurred by the efforts of a rape survivor, Analyn Megison, whose attacker had challenged her for custody of the child that he had fathered through rape. As of March 2016, the Rape Abuse Incest National Network (RAINN) reported that currently eight states allow for the full termination of rapists' parental rights without requiring a conviction (see Table 5.)[26]

Some states seem to be going in the opposite direction. Massachusetts passed a law in 2014 that gives convicted rapists a pathway to visitation with the children they fathered through rape, based on the child' age, consent to the visitation, and "best interests."[27] Maryland is one of the states that does not provide for the termination of parental rights even of convicted impregnation rapists. A Bill to allow for termination of parental rights of impregnation rapists based on the clear and convincing standard, has been proposed repeatedly in the Maryland State Legislature since 2007, but the Maryland State Bar Association (MSBA) has argued vigorously against it, and as of March 2016, the Bill has failed. The MSBA has criticized the Bill for being too vague on a number of issues related to basic due process protections that are necessary in terminating parental rights. The MSBA also argues that it is unconstitutional to use a "preponderance of the evidence" standard in any step of the process that leads to the termination of parental rights. Even though the "clear and convincing" standard would be applied to determine whether or not the child was conceived as a result of rape, this finding would then be used to terminate parental rights "in the child's best interest" which requires a lower standard of proof. The MSBA rejects the notion that contact between a child and his or her rapist father would be harmful, since the assault that caused the pregnancy was against the child's mother, not the actual child.[28]

This view is symptomatic of a prevalent belief found in legal circles and among family court practitioners, that a father's violent behavior towards his child's mother does not make him a bad father. State legislators persuaded by this argument are unlikely to change the law even if this would qualify the state to apply for a few million dollars in federal grants. But there are other ways in which the federal government could facilitate change without necessarily requiring states to change their laws. That way would be to stop funding programs that encourage and facilitate violent fathers' access to their children, which is the topic of our next chapter.

Table 5: State statutes on parental rights of impregnation rapists

Type of statute	States meeting these criteria
Statutes allow for full terminations of parental rights without prerequisite of a conviction.	Alaska, Florida*, Idaho, Illinois*, Louisiana, Oklahoma, Pennsylvania, Vermont* (N=8)
Statutes allow for full termination of parental rights upon conviction for the rape that resulted in the pregnancy.	Colorado, Kansas, Maine, Missouri, Montana, Nebraska, North Carolina, Oregon, South Carolina, Tennessee Texas, Washington (N=12)
Statutes allow for partial termination of parental rights for the rape that resulted in the pregnancy.	Arkansas, California, Connecticut, Delaware, Iowa, Indiana**, Michigan, Nevada, New Jersey, South Dakota**, Utah (N=11)
Statutes allow for full termination of parental rights upon conviction or after a fact finding hearing.	New Hampshire, Wisconsin (N=2)

* These states specify the clear and convincing standard
** These states do not require convictions

The Americans With Disabilities Act

The Americans With Disabilities Act was not specifically enacted to assist battered mothers in family court, but a creative and insightful advocate for people with disabilities has found a way to make it work for battered mothers in some circumstances. The Americans With Disabilities Act (ADA) of 1990 is a civil rights law addressing the needs of people with disabilities, prohibiting discrimination in employment (Title I), public services (Title II), public accommodations (Title III), and telecommunications (Title IV).[29] The ADA defines a covered disability as a physical or mental impairment that substantially limits one or more major life activities, a history of having such an impairment, or being regarded as having such an impairment. In 2008, the ADA was amended to broaden the definition of impairment, thereby protecting a greater number of people. The amendment also added examples of "major life activities" including, but not limited to, "*caring for oneself, performing manual tasks, seeing, hearing, eating, sleeping, walking, standing, lifting, bending, speaking, breathing, learning, reading, concentrating, thinking, communicating, and working*" as well as the operation of several specified major bodily functions.[30]

The application of ADA to battered women emerged from the work of marriage and family therapist Karin Huffer. While working with clients in the 1980s, Huffer recognized and described Legal Abuse Syndrome, a form of PTSD, which develops in victims of ethical violations, betrayal of trust, abuse of power, or fraud within the legal system.[31] She also recognized that this type of PTSD affects many battered mothers, who like other victims of PTSD, often experience a double whammy. They may have PTSD as a result of the abuse/traumatic experience itself, and then when they come to court they find that their injuries are used against them, for example to impeach their credibility or prove them unfit for custody. Their stress is compounded by the betrayal of the legal system, which in the case of battered women includes attacks by divorce industry professionals.

Huffer has drawn attention to the fact that as a form of PTSD, LAS is eligible for accommodation under Title II and Title III of the Americans with Disabilities Act. This allows for the presence in the courtroom of an ADA advocate who may sit with the battered woman at her counsel's table, and may intervene if the procedures take on a tone of harassment and bullying. Huffer says that as an ADA advocate she has been able to prevent or mitigate the following problems:

1) Misuse of the courtroom as a weapon or tool of theft;

2) Use of slander, lies and misinformation to create extreme stress;

3) Purposeful creation of stress for strategic advantage;

4) Forced losses of assets, children, and the products of life's work;

5) Victims losing by attrition instead of a fair adjudication of evidence;

6) Lawyers fearing the stigma of using the ADA for themselves or their clients.[32]

She provides the following example:

> "....Carolyn, who suffers PTSD from domestic violence, used to be questioned by her abuser in court until an advocate obtained accommodations for her. She now appears in a sequestered room and questions from her abuser must be written for her to answer in her own time, not under intimidation, threat, and coercive control."[33]

Huffer was instrumental in promoting a program at the John Jay College of Criminal Justice for certifying ADA advocates by using a syllabus she developed through her organization, Equal Access Advocates. The first certified advocates graduated in September 2016. Huffer is aware of 27 cases involving battered women that used ADA accommodations in family court in the past nearly two years. She says cases generally settle once the advocates bring the federal mandate into the picture, but establishing case law is difficult, since it would require litigants to keep fighting all the way up to the Supreme Court.

Ultimately, the effectiveness of ADA depends on the willingness of the Civil Rights Division of the U.S. Department of Justice to hold accountable those state entities that violate its provisions. Numerous battered women from Connecticut say that their Judicial Branch routinely refuses to comply with ADA requirements, and that the federal authorities consistently ignore complaints, or inform litigants that they do not intend to take action. Advocates say that complaints about ADA violations filed in federal court are generally thrown out on frivolous grounds. However, on the positive side, innovative ideas often take a while to catch on, and what may seem absurd and outlandish at one time, may come to be regarded as obvious at another time. With the tenacity and perseverance of the ADA advocacy movement, that time must surely come.

Congressman Ted Poe's Resolution

Recognition that the unregulated custody evaluator system poses a risk to victims of DV and child abuse is implicit in a Bill introduced in the House of Representatives on September 9, 2016.[34] The Bill, sponsored by Congressman Ted Poe (R Texas) expresses the sense of Congress that child safety is the first priority of custody and visitation adjudications and that courts should resolve safety risks and claims of family violence before assessing other best interest factors. The Bill goes on to require that evidence admitted into court meet admissibility standards, and that expert testimony about abuse allegations be considered only when the professional witness possesses documented expertise and experience in the relevant types of abuse, trauma, and the behaviors of victims and perpetrators. The Bill also requires that states set standards of expertise and experience for professionals who provide evidence on these issues, and that states require courts to ensure that any appointed professionals meet those standards. Finally, the Bill addresses fair and equitable standards for the payment of court-appointed professionals and proposes that Congress schedule hearings on family courts' practices with regard to children's safety and civil rights. This Bill is a welcome ray of light in an otherwise bleak landscape for victims of abuse facing custody litigation in family court.

Chapter 7

Fatherhood Initiatives

Family law has traditionally fallen under the purview of the states, and pertains to such matters as marriage, divorce, adoption, child welfare, and child support obligations.[1] Since the 1930s however, Congress has increasingly enacted federal statutes to address family law problems that the states have been unable to resolve notably in the areas of child welfare and with regard to inter-jurisdictional or full faith and credit issues. The Social Security Act of 1935 established Aid to Families with Dependent Children (AFDC), which provided support to children from single parent homes. The growth of the welfare rolls, which doubled from the late 1960s to the early 1970s, spurred Congress to pass legislation that would reduce dependence on the government of children who have been financially abandoned by a non-resident parent. This legislation created the Title IV-D amendment of the Social Security Act, establishing a federal-state partnership designed to recover the costs of public assistance paid out to AFDC families. Another goal of the legislation was to help families on welfare leave the public assistance rolls, and to help families not yet on welfare avoid having to turn to public assistance. The 1974 Act stated the mission of the IV-D program as:

> "enforcing the support obligations owed by absent parents to their children and the spouse (or former spouse) with whom such children are living, locating absent parents, establishing paternity, obtaining child and spousal support, and assuring that assistance in obtaining support will be available . . . to all children (whether or not eligible for aid

under [the AFDC program]) for whom such assistance is requested."[2]

Title IV-D required families receiving or applying for public assistance to accept IV-D services and to cooperate with the state IV-D program absent a finding of "good cause" for non-cooperation, which included physical or emotional harm to the parent or child.[3] Congress also made IV-D services available to families not receiving public assistance on a voluntary basis in order to limit the growth of the public assistance rolls. Title IV-D also established different sets of obligations for the federal government and for the states. On the federal side, the Secretary of Health, Education and Welfare, (now Health and Human Services), was required to establish a separate organizational unit to oversee the operation of the Child Support Enforcement Program. Both the federal government and the states were required to establish parent locator services. In addition, the federal government's assistance to states included: (1) setting standards for state program organization; (2) reviewing and approving state plans for the program; (3) evaluating state programs' operations by conducting audits; (4) providing technical assistance; and (5) referring cases to the federal courts for enforcement, and to the IRS for support collection. States in turn, were required to: (1) designate a separate organizational unit to administer the program; (2) establish paternity and secure support for families receiving welfare; (3) cooperate with law enforcement and other states in locating parents; and (4) maintain records of collections and disbursements made under the plan. Title IV-D required Congress to reimburse states for two-thirds of their administrative costs, and later amendments provided additional incentive payments based on certain performance indicators such as paternity establishment levels, and support payment levels.[4]

Beginning with Title IV-D, and continuing over the next two decades Congress enacted legislation requiring states to establish and strengthen procedures for enforcing child support obligations for all families, not just those receiving welfare. Thus Title IV-D allowed for the withholding of child support from paychecks of federal employees and members of the Armed Services. The Family Support Act of 1988 required all employers to withhold child support from wages of employees in compliance with their child support obligations. The Child Support Recovery Act of 1992, and the Full Faith and Credit for Child Support Orders Act of 1994 regulated interstate child support enforcement and withstood legal challenges on the basis of the Commerce Clause of the U.S. Constitution, which gives Congress the power to regulate interstate commerce.[5]

The Personal Responsibility and Work Opportunity Reconciliation Act of 1996 (PRWORA) further extended the federal government's reach into the way states manage child welfare. PRWORA ended the AFDC program and replaced it with TANF – Temporary Assistance to Needy Families, which required welfare recipients to seek work and limited the amount of time that they could receive welfare. PRWORA also required that states enact a uniform law establishing exclusive home state jurisdiction for issuing and modifying child support orders and also laws creating tougher enforcement procedures. This requirement withstood legal challenges on the basis of "pursuit of the public welfare" clause of the Constitution, which allows Congress to condition federal funds upon the state's enactment of laws or regulations as long as the condition is in pursuit of the general welfare.[6]

Child access programs

Federal legislation related to improving compliance with child support payments went beyond simple enforcement and extended into the area of motivation. There was a perception that noncustodial parents would be more likely to pay child support if they were emotionally involved with their children, and that such involvement would also benefit children in a number of important ways. Thus another clearly stated goal of PRWORA was to increase noncustodial parents' access to their children.

Even before PRWORA, in the early 1990s, federal legislation provided financial support for demonstration projects to develop, improve or expand activities designed to increase compliance with child access provisions of court orders for noncustodial parents' access to and visitation of their children. In order to establish the efficacy of such activities, the legislation also required an evaluation of these projects and a report to Congress on the findings. In October 1996, the Department of Health and Human Services transmitted to Congress the report entitled, *Evaluation of the Child Access Demonstration Projects.*[7] The report indicated that when both parents attend mediation sessions parenting plans could be arrived at in 65% to 70% of cases with child access problems, and concluded that the program was successful for cases without extensive long-term problems. The report strongly endorsed additional emphases at all government levels, especially state and local levels, to ensure that each child from a divorced or unwed family has a parenting plan which encourages and enables both parents to stay emotionally involved with their children. Increasingly the federal government was becoming involved in funding family engineering programs that went well beyond the original stated goal of preventing dependency on welfare.

It was under PRWORA that these family engineering programs became established with dedicated funding streams. Thus, section 391 of PRWORA added a provision to award funds annually to states to establish and administer programs to support and facilitate noncustodial parents' (fathers or mothers) access to, and visitation of their children by means of activities including mediation (both voluntary and mandatory), counseling, education, development of parenting plans, visitation enforcement (including monitoring, supervision and neutral drop-off and pickup), and development of guidelines for visitation and alternative custody arrangements. States could administer programs directly or through contracts or grants with courts, local public agencies, or private nonprofit entities. This became known as the Access and Visitation (AV) Grant Program – a formula grant program for which Congress has appropriated $10 million each year since 1997. While the grant program supports various types of programmatic activities, the use of the funds and they way in which they are administered vary from state to state and are governed by state law. States are required to match the federal contribution with a minimum of 10% of state funds. While allotments are made to each state based on the number of children living with one biological parent, each state is assured of an allotment of at least $100,000. States have been permitted to supplement the AV allotment with other federal funds such as leftover TANF money.

States have broad discretion regarding the services that they choose to implement, the populations that they choose to serve, and even their definitions of success. The enabling federal legislation and the agency's rules established in 1999, limit the federal government's involvement to "guidance" and "technical assistance." According to a recent report, the program served 104,674 people in 2013 – up from 69,000 in 2003.[8] The report stated that 36% of those served were noncustodial fathers, 34% were custodial mothers, 15% were noncustodial mothers, and 11% were custodial fathers. Services were also provided to grandparents and legal guardians (4%). The most common service provided was education (41%), followed by mediation (34%), parenting planning (18%), counseling (5%), supervised visitation (9%), neutral drop off and pick up (2%), and visitation monitoring (1%). A majority of the clients had never married (55%). The report claimed that the program had succeeded in increasing parenting time for 64% of noncustodial fathers and 47% of noncustodial mothers. Unfortunately, lack of consistency in program implementation and definitions of outcome make it impossible to interpret reported statistics.

Preliminary program evaluation

After the AV program had been running for several years, the Office of the Inspector General (OIG) commissioned a study to determine the extent to which the AV grants increased access rights, visitation, and child support payment compliance for parents in five states. *The Effectiveness of Access and Visitation Grant Programs* report, published in 2001, specifically address-ed the extent to which mediation programs – one of the most popular services offered through the AV program – facilitated and increased access rights for participants.[9] The OIG Effectiveness study methodology included a review of mediat-ion case files, court files and child support payments, a telephone survey of parents, and interviews with program administrators. Two sets of analyses were conducted on case files. One set was on information from 190 case files in four states (Nevada, Connecticut, Oklahoma, and Illinois), and a second analysis was conducted on 64 case files in Georgia, which had different program goals compared to the other states. The following is a summary of the results for the four states:

1) Seventy-six percent of cases examined in the case file review resulted in a mediated agreement.

2) In 86% of these cases, access rights were increased for the noncustodial parent through mutually agreed upon visitation plans.

3) For all of the cases in the sample, regardless of whether or not an agreement was reached, 66% gained increased access rights through mediation.

4) According to a review of child support files, 61% of noncustodial parents increased the percent of current child support they paid after mediation.

Unlike the four other states, Georgia's mediation programs focused primarily on increasing immediate visitation, as opposed to longer-term access rights. Case file reviews found that at least 60% of cases that successfully completed program goals saw an increase in visits, and 55% of all program participants increased the percentage of current child support paid. The study concluded that the mediation programs successfully increased access rights for noncustodial parents in the four states, and increased visits for noncustodial parents in all the states. The study further concluded that participation in mediation programs was most likely associated with improved child support payment compliance.

While this study would qualify as a pilot study, its methodology falls far short of the requirements considered acceptable for a program evaluation by modern scientific standards. Studies that compare outcomes before and after the introduction of the program do not meet these standards. There was no random assignment of subjects to experimental and control conditions and no long-term follow up. Furthermore, the AV program encompasses numerous services, and this study examined only one. To our knowledge no further studies have examined the efficacy of the AV program.

Addressing concerns about DV in child access programs

Even before the AV program went into effect, DV advocates were concerned about its lack of protection for victims. The final rule for the program was published in the Federal Register on March 30, 1999 and included public comments on the legislation and the agency's responses to those comments.[10] Several of the comments raised concerns about DV. For example, there was a concern that the regulation contained no requirement to monitor whether states were screening potential clients for DV (spousal or child abuse) to ensure that the battered spouse was not put at further risk.

One comment-writer suggested that the final rule should acknowledge that DV occurs in many of the access and visitation cases before the family court and, therefore, the statement that involvement by noncustodial parents is desirable for children should be dropped or amended. In response, the agency claimed to share these concerns for safety and said that its intent was to encourage states to ensure safety when necessary in implementing grants under this program. In fact, in response to this comment, the agency added a new requirement to the regulation, namely that states should monitor programs to safeguard against DV. This requirement, however, left the methods of compliance entirely to the states.

Several comment-writers raised concerns about the safety of DV victims with regard to specific program elements such as mandated mediation and supervised transfer and visitation with children. The agency responded that they had not required specific approaches to dealing with the issue of DV since they wished to provide maximum flexibility to the states, and simply stated:

> "We recognize that in some cases, mediation may be dangerous for the victim of abuse. There is also evidence that in some cases involving partner abuse, mediation has been effective. This is a service that warrants careful monitoring by States to ensure that safety assessments are conducted. When it is determined not to be warranted, alternative forms of conflict resolution should be used. States may choose to use their grants to fund supervised transfer and visitation of children by noncustodial parents. Neutral drop-off or pickup of children (supervised transfer) is designed to provide for the transfer of children without danger for the abused parent or hostile actions between the parents when domestic violence or other situations involving acrimony between parents exist. Supervised visitation is designed to promote and protect the safety of the visited child. States should monitor such programs when funded by this authority (as discussed above) to ensure that adequate and appropriate procedures are in place and being used to ensure safety."

Other comment-writer suggested that grantees be required to consult local DV agencies about appropriate procedures for identifying and assisting battered parents, and some even suggested that those with DV training should run the programs. Side-stepping these issues, the agency stated:

> "Based on our experience with other service sectors that have addressed domestic violence, consultation with community based domestic violence experts is often very

useful. While requiring such consultation would go beyond the scope of this regulation, we do believe domestic violence experts have important experience and knowledge that can be useful to Access and Visitation Programs. We encourage all Access and Visitation grantees to hold consultations with experts in the field of domestic violence."

Perhaps most revealing about the agency's perspective on DV was its response to a comment suggesting that DV be included as a category of participant data to be reported. The agency, represented by Commissioner David Gray Ross, responded as follows:

"We have not included domestic violence as a category of participant data reported because the quality of information collected is not likely to be consistent or useful. It would be difficult to reach any agreement for reporting responses on how domestic violence should be defined or how the determination would be made that domestic violence had occurred. Additionally, services and targeted clientele will vary widely from State to State, and even within States, making comparisons even more inappropriate. We do encourage States to use their own State protocols and definitions of domestic violence to monitor and evaluate how their programs are protecting the safety of parents and children."

Commissioner David Gray Ross appeared to be saying that there is no meaningful way to determine if DV has occurred. It therefore stands to reason that there could be no meaningful definition of safety, rendering the rule about monitoring participant safety vague, amorphous and possibly meaningless.

Influence of fathers' rights advocacy

From the inception of the idea for AV programs, fathers' rights groups rapidly moved to take a share of this federal funding stream, and indeed claimed that they had lobbied for it. In an open letter to fathers' rights leaders in 1989, Dick Woods, a fathers' rights advocate representing the National Congress for Men announced that Congress had just appropriated $7.6 million for three projects including "access and visitation enforcement."[11] In the letter, Woods claimed to have met with a top government official heading the division that would be administering the grants (the Deputy Assistant Secretary for Program Operations, Administration for Children and Families, Department of Health and Human Services). He further claimed to have received assurances from the said secretary that a fair share of the money would be devoted to what he referred to as *"access enforcement"* grants, and that preference would be given to sub-grantees with demonstrated expertise at enforcing visitation rights – in other words – father's rights organizations. Woods went on to encourage fathers' rights organizations to apply for these grants, offering them assistance in preparing their grant applications, and also offering to provide accounting services that would be paid for by the grants. For fathers' rights groups that were not formally incorporated, Woods offered to prepare articles of incorporation, and to assist in the application for non-profit status.

In December 1992, Woods, now serving as director of a fathers' rights group based in Iowa, announced in a letter to Iowa State Representative Minette Doderer, that his organization was the only advocacy organization out of seven sub-contractors to be placed in control of an AV grant – worth $300,000 – after signing a contract with the Iowa Department of Human Services.[12] He claimed, furthermore, that the grant covered a much broader area than merely enforcing visitation rights, and included promoting shared legal guardianship and decision-making for the child, shared time and responsibility, shared authority over medical decisions and religious education, and shared attendance at in-school and out-of-school activities. Services included referrals to attorneys for "low-adversarial" litigation. Woods' letter to Representative Doderer plainly acknowledged that he planned to use the grant to promote shared custody – an agenda that went way beyond the federal government's intention for the grant program. His open letter to fathers' rights groups also revealed a disturbing pattern involving close ties between fathers' rights leaders and government officials sympathetic to the fathers' rights cause. For example, David Gray Ross, the OCSE Commissioner who oversaw the AV grant program from its inception until his retirement in 2001, was on the Board of Directors of the leading fathers' rights organization, the Children's Rights Council (CRC), according to his obituary in 2013.[13] Another former government official with close ties to CRC is Ron Haskins, previously Staff Director of the Human Resources Subcommittee of the House Ways and Means Committee in the mid 1990s, and one of the principle architects of the welfare reform legislation that funded AV and other fatherhood programs.[14] Haskins is now on the CRC family advisory board.[15]

Fathers' rights influence on the AV program

Fathers' rights principles were firmly embedded in the AV program by the "founding fathers", and this influence was evident in a document that was circulated as recently as 2009 in the form of a memo providing guidance to grantees on the kinds of services that were eligible for AV program funding. The memo, which was issued under the signature of AV program Specialist, Debra Pontisso, stated that the program would only pay for counseling that led to noncustodial parents' increased access to their children. Counselors were advised to "not focus on" DV, batterer intervention, anger management or substance abuse issues. They were also instructed that if they provided counseling for children, they should not focus on "sexual abuse" or "various reasons why that child may have been removed from their parents' custody." The memo did not address whether it was even appropriate for counselors to attempt to increase access to a child after a disclosure of sexual abuse, and made no mention of the necessity to refer such a case to other services or to law enforcement. In short, the memo clearly conveyed the message that DV, child sexual abuse and substance abuse were not issues that should be considered a barrier to increasing noncustodial parents' access to children. Although, according to OCSE, the memo was rescinded a year after it was issued because it had not been appropriately reviewed, the content is still indicative, at the very least, of the views of the staff members who were running the program at that time.

AV program elements that pose risks for DV victims

Several early reports describing the operation of the AV program mentioned principles and/or practices that could be harmful to DV victims. These include the following:

1) *Conflating DV and conflict.* A series of reports on the AV program included numerous references to dealing with "high conflict" families including those in which physical violence takes place. There were even passing references to "domestic violence," but no indication anywhere that the programs understood the dynamics of DV or had strategies to protect victims.[16] Yet research has shown that at least 50% of high conflict divorces or failed mediation cases involve DV.

2) *Psycho-education used to treat DV.* Some AV programs specialize in providing services for high conflict families, which encompass families that have experienced DV. The focus of these programs is primarily on education, although some may include a brief investigation by trained court personnel when parents have exhibited high conflict behavior. One report mentions multi-session programs targeting never-married, separated, or divorced parents for whom DV has been an issue with the objective of helping them to parent apart by educating them on the dynamics of DV. An example of this was a 12-week curriculum developed in California.[17] Another report describes a New Jersey program for high conflict families, which offered six weekly sessions, addressing a panoply of issues such as anger management, communication skills,

mental health, substance abuse, issues associated with nonpayment of child support, withholding of visitation rights, DV, and child abuse and neglect.[18] These programs bear similarities to some of those promoted by the divorce industry as described in Chapter 5. The Pennsylvania triage report, for example, considers parenting apart or parallel parenting as an appropriate arrangement for families that have experienced DV, ignoring the dangers it poses of ongoing coercion and manipulation of victims through children.

3) *Using AV services as a cheap form of custody evaluation.* Many mediation programs funded with AV money are located in the courts, and this allows them to use resources provided by the court including mediators, administrative personnel, and facilities, thus stretching the AV program resources. The disturbing aspect of AV mediation is that when couples fail to reach an agreement, many AV programs may require the mediator or some other court official to make a written recommendation to the court regarding custody/visitation, and this may become an enforceable court order. In South Carolina, for example, failed mediation may result in the mediator assisting the noncustodial parent in filing a pro se petition or submitting a recommendation to the court which could become a court order if the custodial parent fails to comply.[19] Mediation failure is most likely to occur in high conflict cases which often include DV, and this is of particularly concern when mediation programs target high conflict cases. Other services provided by some AV programs have a similar function to custody evaluations at a fraction of the cost. Such programs serve investigatory purposes, gathering information about families where there have been allegations of misconduct, and making recommendations to the court. For example, according to the 2004 report, Idaho was offering this type of service through an "alternative dispute resolution screening process," while Colorado was offering it through a "special advocate

program."[20] Training and licensing requirements for these services and the manner of their delivery are determined by the state, which in turn is largely influenced by divorce industry standards. In short, the AV program provides funding for a critical component of court-related profess-ional services that reflect the philosophy and principles of the divorce industry. This includes the rules about "victim safety" which tends to be narrowly defined as avoidance of physical assaults during participation in the program.

4) *Legal services.* Some AV programs provide litigation support for noncustodial parents seeking custody or visitation in a variety of ways. These include assistance with pro se filing, payment of court fees, and in some cases actual legal representation. In North Carolina, for example, the AV program provides funding for pro se clinics that are offered in five of the six districts with the program.[21] Pro se clinics are educational settings where attorneys volunteer their time to offer detailed instructions on com-pleting necessary paperwork to file a lawsuit and answer legal questions. In these clinics, noncustodial parents learn how to complete the documents that are required in order to file a lawsuit or motion for custody or visitation without having to retain an attorney. The North Carolina AV website provides no indication that cases are screened for DV. The same concerns about safety pertaining to custody evaluation, also apply to legal services, especially if these are provided by "fathers' rights" attorneys, as occurred in the case of Beltway Sniper, John Allen Muhammad. Muhammad's attorney, John Mills, was serving as contract attorney to the AV funded Devoted Dads Program, when he advised Muhammad to go and find his ex-wife so that she could be served with court papers. Apparently Mills paid no mind to the fact that his client had previously kidnapped his children, and that a judge had given his ex-wife permission to leave the state and go into hiding for her safety.[22]

5) *Parental alienation.* Reliance on parental alienation theory by some AV services is another disturbing example of divorce industry influence. For example, AV contracts obtained from certain grantees in the State of Texas listed parental alienation as one of the acceptable services allowed by the AV program, and claimed that that parental alienation was in fact endorsed by the enabling federal legislation. When I brought these contracts to the attention of OSCE officials, the language was removed. OCSE acknowledged that the contracts had misquoted federal legislation. Yet these contracts had been in existence for years. How many other contracts are out there that misquote federal legislation? Another reference to parental alienation was found in a description of an Arizona program in which parents who fail to comply with court-ordered visitation may be required to attend a four-hour class dealing with parental alienation.[23] However, this class is also referred to as a "parent conflict resolution class," which according to the report is offered in several jurisdictions and may also simply be referred to as "parent education." In fact parent education is the most commonly offered service accounting for 41% of all AV services according to the 2013 report.[24] The Arizona program was viewed as a necessary intervention, because *"judges needed to know that mothers were being educated before they put them in jail for contempt"* [author's emphasis].[25] It is therefore possible that many parental conflict resolution programs and many parent education programs offered by the AV program are based on parental alienation theory. Such theories may also find their way into reports by mediators and other professionals in their role as custody evaluator, when they make recommendations to the court about custody and visitation in DV cases, as we discussed above.

Proposed changes to family violence safeguards in the AV program

OCSE is currently considering a series of recommendations for improving family violence safeguards in the AV program. The following are some of the elements being considered:

- Requiring programs to develop partnerships and collaborations with DV agencies.

- Requiring programs to screen participants for DV, and to provide opportunities for disclosing DV throughout the program.

- Developing protocols for handling DV once it is disclosed including a system for referring clients to DV services, and establishing guidelines on how DV will affect eligibility for the program.

- Educating clients about DV and promoting safe parenting.

These are positive and welcome developments, but they cannot be fully implemented without amendments to the current legislation and to the current rules that were established in 1999. Without such amendments, the recommendations do not have the force of law, and are simply guidelines or suggestions. Critical considerations such as the definition of DV, choice of which screening instruments to use, decisions about which services are appropriate in cases of DV and numerous other details that affect victim safety are left entirely to the grantee. OCSE officials believe that a great deal of change can be accomplished using the "consultative collaborative approach", but they also acknowledge that the original rules need to be updated. Later in this chapter, we will discuss possible legislative and rule changes for the AV program that would enhance protections for DV survivors.

Responsible fatherhood and healthy marriage programs

The responsible fatherhood and healthy marriage programs like the AV program, received their impetus from the welfare reforms of the mid 1990s, motivated by growing concerns about the rising trend of out-of-wedlock births to poor single mothers, and the corresponding number of poor noncustodial fathers who were uninvolved in their children's lives, and often unable to pay child support. Underlying these reforms was the goal of ending dependency on welfare through the promotion of job preparation leading to work, the formation and maintenance of two parent families, and the involvement of noncustodial parents in their children's lives, both financially and emotionally.[26] The AV program is probably the oldest federally funded fatherhood program, and has had its own dedicated funding stream since 1997.

In addition, OCSE provided $2 million to fund Responsible Fatherhood Demonstration Projects from 1997 to 2002 under Section 1115 of the Social Security Act. Eight states (California, Colorado, Maryland, Massachusetts, Missouri, New Hampshire, Washington and Wisconsin) received waivers from OCSE allowing them to use child support enforcement funds to implement and test responsible fatherhood programs. The stated purpose of these programs was to improve the employment and earnings of underemployed and unemployed noncustodial parents and to motivate them to become more financially and emotionally involved in the lives of their children. An evaluation of these programs found that they experienced many serious challenges. Low-income non-custodial fathers were a difficult population to recruit and serve; child access problems were difficult to define and resolve, and while child support compliance rates increased significantly, especially for those who had not been paying previously, few participants were able to increase their earnings enough to meet their financial needs and those of their children.[27]

Additional sources of federal funding were made available for other responsible fatherhood programming. Thus in 2001,

Congress appropriated $4 million for two nongovernmental agencies – the National Fatherhood Initiative, and the Institute for Responsible Fatherhood and Family Revitalization.[28] Although Congress did not approve further funding for grant programs until 2005, other sources of federal funding for fatherhood programs existed and continue to exist. These include TANF welfare-to-work funds, and Social Security Block Grant (Title XX) funds. States may also use Maintenance of Effort (MOE) funds for fatherhood programs. These are the state's own funds which it must spend on needy families in order to continue receiving previous levels of TANF funding from the federal government.[29]

In 2005, Congress appropriated $50 millions per year for five years (from 2006 to 2010) for competitive responsible fatherhood grants to states, territories, tribes and nonprofit organizations. Ninety-nine grantees were awarded five-year contracts. In 2010 Congress began appropriating $75 million annually for responsible fatherhood grants, and another $75 million for a newcomer on the block – healthy marriage grants, intended to promote the formation and maintenance of two parent families. This grant program had its roots in concerns about the rising trend of out-of-wedlock births to poor young women, which prompted Congress to establish marriage promotion and the reduction of out-of-wedlock births as federal policy goals, with the enactment of welfare reform in 1996. In 2001, Congress began funding marriage education programs around the country,[30] but it was not until 2010 that an annual funding stream of $75 million was allocated to healthy marriage programming alongside that of responsible fatherhood programming. Currently, the two programs have been merged into one with a total annual budget of $150 million.

Fatherhood agendas

The Center for Law and Policy Research (CLASP) identified four distinct but overlapping strands within the fatherhood field: [31]

1) *Promoting fatherhood.* This refers to a broadly focused effort to help fathers become engaged, committed and responsible, and is led by a handful of national and state organizations that conduct media campaigns, public education, program training and technical assistance, and provide information to fathers themselves.

2) *Responsible fatherhood.* This is a more targeted effort to provide comprehensive services to low income, noncustodial and non-resident fathers – primarily urban African American and Latino fathers. Services include job training and referral, parent education, support groups and help with child support obligations.

3) *Father/male involvement.* This refers to programs designed to work with employers and early childhood welfare professionals and teachers to reach out to men and fathers and help them become more involved with their children.

4) *Fathers' rights groups.* These according to CLASP are the oldest, most vocal, and perhaps best financed fatherhood organizations, concerned primarily with divorced and separated fathers' rights and needs. They offer information and advocacy with regard to child support and visitation, and work vigorously for legal change promoting joint custody.

Few people could find fault with the worthwhile principles expressed by the first three strands within the fatherhood field, currently eligible for receiving fatherhood funding. Nor is there any objective reason why these principles should clash with the goals of the DV movement – victim safety and offender accountability. As regards the fourth fatherhood strand – fathers' rights organizations – according to CLASP, these groups are not currently receiving responsible fatherhood program funding. However, many of the groups that do receive these funds may be staffed by people who have been strongly influenced by the fathers' rights philosophy and may still be able to further an agenda that includes removing custody from battered mothers, or forcing children into unsafe visitation arrangements.

Fathers' rights principles and prejudices are evident in the hostility towards the DV movement and negative stereotypes of DV advocates, held by responsible fatherhood advocates. As a result of the outright antagonism between these camps, a meeting was held in 2006, in an attempt to "build bridges" between the responsible fatherhood, healthy marriage, and DV communities. The stereotypes discussed at this meeting are similar to those held by fathers' rights supporters. For example, fatherhood representatives grossly exaggerated the DV community's view of men as all being batterers or potential batterers. They also focused on the fact that some men are victims of DV, ignoring the overall much more serious nature of men's violence towards women. Finally, they minimized the abuser's responsibility for his behavior by claiming that "economic" and "systemic" problems contribute to battering.

There are clues to the source of these negative stereotypes. After the 2000 reauthorization of VAWA, which appropriated $15 million annually for two years to fund the Safe Havens Supervised Visitation Center Program, the Children's Rights Council (CRC) included an action alert in their periodic newsletter, *Speak Out for Children* calling upon fathers' rights' supporters to urge Congress to defund the program.[32] CRC, which already operated supervised visitation centers, could have applied for these funds, but this would have required them to work with local women's shelters and organizations designed to protect women from violence. The newsletter informed supporters that the new legislation would establish "police station type" environments for supervised visitation rather than neutral or family friendly settings. The newsletter also claimed that only 15% of families needing supervised visitation have experienced DV. Other reasons cited for requiring this service included parental substance abuse, "severe communication problems" between parents, and re-entry of a parent into a child's life after a long absence. The newsletter also claimed that 40% of the parents court-ordered to use these sites are women. Under the heading "Action Alert!" the newsletter said:

> "Write to Appropriations Committee Chairman Stevens (Senate) and Young (House) urging more funds for Family Friendly Programs and only $1 million a year for Police Station Type Supervised Access to Children."

The newsletter also advised supporters to claim that cooperation with DV programs had already proved unworkable because too many parents and children felt uncomfortable in such police station type settings. Since the DV supervised visitation programs were designed to protect DV survivors from further violence, one must assume that the complaints about these programs were not coming from DV survivors. It is impossible to interpret this newsletter in any way other than that CRC was advocating for the comfort of the alleged abusers. As to the 40% of women that CRC claimed to be in need of supervised visitation services, many of these were likely battered mothers who experienced custody switches following abuse allegations. According to these mothers, the supervised visitation settings they experience are anything but friendly, and often serve as a pathway to total loss of contact with their children. One mother had her visitation rights terminated for saying to her children: "Give me a hug" instead of saying: "May I have a hug?"[33]

Fortunately, Congress did not defund the Safe Havens Supervised Visitation Program. In fact, when Congress appropriated funds for the responsible fatherhood and healthy marriage grants, one of the stipulations was that grantees work with DV advocates and service providers to ensure the safety of the participants in these programs. Possibly fathers' rights organizations were excluded from these grants because they had already indicated their unwillingness to work with the DV community.

Importance of fathering

Proponents of fatherhood programs cite research indicating that children raised in single-parent families are more likely than children raised in two parent families, to do poorly in school, have emotional and behavioral problems, become teenage parents, and have poverty incomes as adults. Never do we hear the fact that while these outcomes refer to greater risk most children from father absent families do not experience these problems, and that most single mothers do a great job raising their children despite the added stress of being a single parent.[34] McLanahan and Sandefur, who have carefully analyzed data from various national surveys, and who firmly believe in the benefits of two-parent families have the following to say about single parenthood:

> "While living with just one parent increases the risk of these negative outcomes, it is not the only one, or even the major cause of them. Growing up with a single parent is just one among many factors that put children at risk of failure just as lack of exercise is one among many factors that put people at risk for heart disease. Many people who don't exercise never suffer a heart attack, and many children raised by single mothers grow up to be quite successful."[35]

Furthermore, fatherhood proponents rarely weigh the risks of single parenthood against the known noxious effects on children of exposure to abuse and DV and they assume that the benefits to the child of father contact are uniformly positive, regardless of the type of father making contact with the child.[36] This is not just a theoretical question. Even fatherhood programs that do not specifically target prisoners have found that criminal history among participants is the norm rather than the exception.[37] While a recent grant program targeting incarcerated fathers required grantees to work with DV service providers, there is no evidence that AV grants and other federally funded programs seeking to facilitate father-child contact, evaluate whether the participants pose a danger to their children, their children's mothers, or others.

A growing body of research is examining the impact of the quality of fathering on outcomes for children and adolescents. Consistently, these studies have found that children benefit from increased levels of father involvement except in cases where fathers manifest antisocial personality characteristics and coercive parenting techniques.[38] One recent study that relied on actual observation of father-child interaction found that antisocial fathers' contact with their children predicted worse outcomes, as did coercive parenting styles, which had an independent negative effect on children.[39] Antisocial personality has been documented in about 50% of correctional populations compared to 0.6% of the general population.[40] This should be of concern to responsible fatherhood initiatives focusing on prisoners and ex-prisoners. Such initiatives pose a problem not only to an offender's children, but also to the community at large as exemplified by the case of Joshua Komisarjevsky, notorious for the murder of a mother and her two daughters in Cheshire, Connecticut in 2007. Even though a criminal court judge had described Komisarjevsky as dangerous and calculating when he sentenced him to nine years in prison for a string of nighttime home invasions, Komisarjevsky was later "rebranded" as a Responsible Father in family court, and awarded custody of his five-year-old daughter. Connecticut prison-based programs for responsible fatherhood, funded with state and federal money, facilitated this rebranding, providing him with legal services, and apparently helping to hide his mental illness from the parole board to ensure lenient parole conditions so that he would look good in family court.[41]

Addressing DV: The MFS-IP Grant Programs

In 2006, the Office of Family Assistance (OFA) within the Administration for Children and Families provided $500,000 per year for five years to 12 grantees for the Responsible Fatherhood, Marriage and Family Strengthening Grants for Incarcerated and Reentering Fathers and Their Partners (MSF-IP).[42] The purpose of these grants was to reduce recidivism by strengthening families through diverse services including relationship and family counseling; parenting and co-parenting education; mentoring and coaching services; DV education; employment services; and financial literacy education. The programs targeted couples with children where the father was incarcerated or recently released. Grantees were all required to demonstrate plans to partner with a DV coalition or expert consultant even though DV services were not covered by the grant. In 2010, the Assistant Secretary for Planning and Evaluation contracted with Research Triangle Institute to conduct evaluations of the implementation of the programs and of the outcome of their efforts to build partnerships with DV service providers and agencies. Preliminary results were released in 2013.

The evaluation of DV partnerships found varying degrees of success.[43] Some grantees experienced difficulties building DV partnerships, and some DV agencies were extremely reluctant to enter into such collaborations. When successful partnership were built, grantees had sought and incorporated the guidance of DV partners in every aspect of the program, including training of staff, screening, recruitment, and delivery of services. Most sites developed formal screening procedures for DV, and consulted correctional databases for information on DV convictions or a current restraining order. Several sites conducted a separate screening for the female partner. At some sites, couples that were seen as being at elevated risk for DV were excluded from the program. Other sites required men identified as being at elevated risk for DV to participate in batterer intervention programs before beginning or resuming the MFS-IP program.

The DV partnership evaluation is a longitudinal study that will continue to collect data over a period of several years. At the baseline evaluation, the study found a large discrepancy between the high levels of self-reported DV among program participants in the previous six months, compared to the very low levels of DV detected in the program screening procedures. MFS-IP grantees noted that it was unrealistic to expect incarcerated or recently incarcerated men to reveal illegal, abusive behavior, especially at the beginning of the program before rapport had been established. They suggested other approaches to identifying DV, for example, examining risk factors such as power and control issues, or using recently developed tools that measure the propensity to abuse.

The MFS-IP study has already identified the importance of building stable collaborative partnerships between DV agencies and fatherhood or healthy marriage organizations. In fact the authors went further to say that grantees should be given more explicit guidance on developing DV protocols and partnerships, and that more investment is needed in developing stable, mutually trusting collaborations in order to better serve incarcerated and reentering fathers and their families. This study demonstrates that it is possible for fatherhood programs to work with DV service providers and advocates when this is made a condition of the grant. As more data on best practices emerge from this ongoing study, Congress and the federal government will have more information for determining how to frame grant requirements for future projects.

The implementation study found that grantees had a great deal of difficulty in keeping participants in the program particularly after they were released, and some did not attempt to deliver services to couples after release.[44] Those that were successful had three main characteristics: (1) rapport with the incarcerated father, his partner, and possibly other family members; (2) practical assistance with employment, housing, or child support issues; and (3) a focus on character development or religious faith. Some of the grantees found that many female partners of participating fathers were reluctant to enroll in relationship strengthening programs because they had strained or tenuous relationships with their children's fathers. Grantees tried to overcome these barriers by emphasizing the benefits of the program to the couples' children. But was this really honest salesmanship? What if the woman's partner was among the 50% of incarcerated prisoners with antisocial personality characteristics, and the woman feared that this would negatively influence her children? While positive involvement from grantees in assisting formerly incarcerated fathers in building healthy lives is commendable, it is important to ensure that this assistance is not given to the detriment of the partners and children of these men.

How other fatherhood programs have addressed DV

Studies that have catalogued, reviewed, or conducted interviews on other responsible fatherhood programs have produced very little information on how these programs address DV. A review of 17 responsible fatherhood programs by the National Responsible Fatherhood Clearinghouse published in 2009 revealed that only two of these programs mentioned services or referrals to services addressing DV. A third program, the John S. Martinez Fatherhood Initiative described in the next section, collected data on DV histories of participants, but did not mention offering DV services.[45] Also in 2009, a study commissioned by the State of Connecticut found that about 56% of fatherhood program clients in that state had engaged in coercive controlling behaviors at least "a few times."[46]

Only four of 63 responsible fatherhood programs reviewed by Mathematica Policy Research in 2011, mentioned screening potential participants for DV. Two of these programs excluded cases that screened positive for DV; one simply reported on DV as an outcome, and one did not address DV at all after the initial screening. In addition, two fatherhood programs, that neither screened for DV nor addressed DV, nevertheless reported recruiting some of their clients through *mandated court referrals of DV cases.*[47]

More recently, in 2015, Mathematica reported on the results of a qualitative component of an ongoing longitudinal study that includes a randomized controlled trial of four fatherhood programs.[48] The qualitative component involved interviews with 87 noncustodial fathers, providing a detailed portrait of their lives, their views on fathering, and their relationships with their children and the mothers of their children. Very few fathers raised the issue of DV, and when they did, it was mostly in the context of "mutual violence" or "false allegations." On the other hand, a recurrent problem described in these interviews was the contentious relation-ships that the fathers had with the mothers of their children, which they perceived as the cause of maternal "gate-keeping" – a term referring to mothers' restriction of fathers' access to their children. The authors of the report acknowledge that gate-keeping would be appropriate in cases of DV or child maltreatment, but they did not ask whether DV was a factor in gate-keeping, or obtain the mothers' perspectives on the reasons for the gate-keeping. What the authors do note is the fact that 95% of the fathers had contact with the criminal justice system, and many had problems with substance abuse. These problems, which are quite common in responsible fatherhood programs, could influence maternal gate-keeping behavior but this possibility is not given any consideration. The report nevertheless concludes with the recommendation that *responsible fatherhood programs should provide more referrals to legal services for noncustodial fathers to establish parenting time agreements, without mentioning the need to address DV.*

Custody switching

Author and activist Doreen Ludwig argues that fatherhood programs have a hidden agenda – to switch custody from mothers to fathers. While the overt goal of programs is to help fathers acquire job skills and employment so that they can pay child support, fathers are learning that the best way to reduce child support is to increase custody, and if they receive the majority of custody, they can become eligible for housing subsidies, food stamps, and even support payments from their children's mothers. Pointing to the 2011 Mathematica report, Ludwig noted that many of the programs reviewed in the report provide legal services to fathers related to child support and child custody, but very few programs resulted in income improvements.[49] While little direct proof of intentional custody switching will be found in these types of reports, reading between the lines, combining multiple sources, and paying close attention to detail can be revealing.

An example of this is the John S. Martinez Fatherhood Initiative of Connecticut – a broad-based multi-agency state-wide program led by the Department of Social Services, and funded through federal grants, state funds, and some private foundation money. The program's official website states that the initiative is focused on changing systems that can improve fathers' ability to be fully and positively involved in their children's lives and that the target population is men aged 16 to 65 who live in Connecticut.[50] But the National Responsible Fatherhood Clearinghouse's report specifies that the Martinez initiative targets noncustodial fathers whose children are or have been eligible for TANF assistance.[51] The report profiles three types of services that were offered at three different sites: (1) job assistance, (2) advocacy for court related issues such as custody and visitation, and (3) preparation of incarcerated fathers for reentry.

Thirty five percent of the fathers who received legal assistance with custody had a history of arrests for DV, 17% had protective orders against them that prevented them from seeing their children, and 52% reported having a strained relationship with the mothers of their children. If DV services were offered to these men, the report makes no mention of it, nor does it address DV at follow up. At the conclusion of the program there were modest improvements in employment and child support payments, but 65% of fathers still reported having either no income, or income below $15,000 after six months of service. Reports of strained relationships with their children's mothers were higher than at baseline, yet, miraculously father custody had increased from 5% to 20% – a fourfold "improvement"![52]

How do fathers with extensive histories of criminality and DV and with little or no income, manage to switch custody? This question is all the more puzzling in light of additional results from the Connecticut responsible fatherhood survey mentioned in the previous section. David Mandel, an expert on interventions with DV perpetrators, and author of the study, made recommendations that included comprehensive screening for past and current DV, ongoing lethality assessment, and developing behavioral goals for clients found to be engaging in coercive control. A key principle of his model known as "Safe Engagement" is that a safe and positive relationship with the children's mother is key to being a good father and that the promotion of fatherhood should never be at the expense of denigrating the role of the mother. Over 80% of service providers and stakeholders participating in his survey agreed with this principle, but subsequent data collection suggests this belief does not translate into programmatic practices.[53]

Poor financial oversight and lack of accountability for TANF spending

How are programs such as the one that rebranded Joshua Komisarjevsky being funded? The answers to this could help inform proposals for program and policy changes, but at the same time they are elusive because program funding does not necessarily come with a "responsible fatherhood" label. Some responsible fatherhood grants have come under criticism for poor financial oversight and management,[54] but these types of problems can be pinpointed and potentially fixed. Less accessible to critics are programs that are funded through other federal sources such as Social Security Block Grants, but the one source that has given the most cause for concern is TANF, because states do not have to provide a detailed account of how they spend the money. This is an unintended negative consequence of the welfare reform initiative of 1996, which gave states broad flexibility on how to use the TANF block grants. Under the earlier system known as AFDC, federal and matching state funds provided cash assistance to needy families. Policy makers believed that replacing this system with a block grant would provide the states with the flexibility to shift funds to other programs when families left welfare, for example, to child-care or other programs that would support work. But this is not what happened according to policy analysts.

In the early years of TANF when the economy was strong, welfare loads shrank, and states redirected the funding to other spending including filling state budget gaps.[55] But when the Great Recession hit, states did not return this spending to support needy families with the result that more families sank into poverty. In 2014 states were spending only 26% of their TANF funds on basic assistance compared to 70% when TANF was first implemented. By this date the number of children living in deep poverty had increased by 50% from 1.5 million to 2.2 million. States were also spending only 8% of their TANF budgets on work-related activities despite the central rationale for TANF, which was that cash assistance should provide temporary support while families engage in activities that help them prepare for work. So the question is where is all the money going?

Federal law specifies four broad purposes of TANF: (1) assisting needy families so children can be cared for in their own homes or the homes of relatives; (2) reducing the dependency of needy parents by promoting job preparation, work, and marriage; (3) preventing out-of-wedlock pregnancies; and (4) encouraging the formation and maintenance of two-parent families. Purpose 4 includes a range of initiatives such as healthy marriage promotion, parenting skills training, premarital and marriage counseling and initiatives to promote responsible fatherhood and help fathers provide emotional and financial support to their children through job placement and training services. In 2014, almost half the states reported spending under this purpose totaling $258 million and representing less than one percent of total TANF/MOE spending nationally. States also spent $2.6 billion on the third core TANF purpose – preventing out of wedlock pregnancies. Services under Purpose 3 and 4 can be provided without regard to income.

It is also important to be aware that states' spending across different categories varies widely. For example, state spending on basic assistance ranges from 6% to 61% of their total TANF/MOE funds. Non-assistance spending could be as high as 80%. Connecticut is a state that spends two thirds of its state and federal TANF dollars on other areas, mostly child welfare and early childhood education. Included in non-assistance spending in 2014, was $21 million that went to TANF Purpose 4 – encouraging the formation of two parent families.[56] Spending under this purpose included $19 million to the Department of Corrections for addiction services for noncustodial parents. Records show that this program was receiving TANF funding during most of the period of Komisarjevsky's earlier incarceration, and he was very likely a beneficiary of its services.[57]

Records also show that Connecticut spent over $60 million in 2014 on TANF Purpose 3 – prevention of out of wedlock pregnancies. Included under this purpose was $700,000 that went to Judicial Counseling Services for ancillary court services known to promote father custody, including mediation and custody evaluation. In addition, Connecticut spent 43% of its federal TANF dollars and 36% of state MOE funds on "other" areas outside the four core purpose areas. Most of this went to the Department of Children's Services for investigations ($55.9 million) and case management ($34.5 million). In fact most of Connecticut's non-assistance TANF dollars went to agencies that are partners in the John S. Martinez Fatherhood Initiative, and signatories to a Memorandum of Understanding in which they agree to use their resources for a wide range of activities and programs to promote responsible fatherhood.[58]

Recommendations

Reform child support policies

Child support policy at the federal level needs to be carefully re-examined, with attention to the unintended negative consequences of incentives to states to comply with Title IV-D goals, and with regard to policies that encourage shared parenting as a way to reduce child support rather than to promote the child's best interests. There appears to be consensus on this point, but for different reasons. Fatherhood and conservative groups have complained that Title IV-D incentives motivate judges to elevate the state's child support totals by ordering sole custody to one parent (usually the mother) thus increasing the amount of support owed by the noncustodial parent (usually the father). Mothers' advocates, on the other hand, argue that OCSE encourages shared parenting as a way to reduce the child support burden on fathers, shifting some or all of the responsibility onto mothers, who have been the primary caregivers, and who may have even less income generating potential than fathers. These advocates say that child support programs should focus on helping fathers to improve their economic standing rather than trying to achieve their goals through disrupting children's bonds with their primary caregivers. Mothers' rights advocate Doreen Ludwig proposes fair and reasonable standards for determining child support amounts, saying that child support should not be a lucrative source of income for one parent. She adds that the parent paying support should be able to request an accounting of expenses to ensure that the support payments are necessary, and benefitting the children, and that support payments should never leave either parent below the poverty line.[59]

Audit state fatherhood programs that use federal funds

It is absolutely imperative that the federal government obtain detailed information on how the states are spending TANF funds with specific reference to fatherhood programs. This may include a General Accounting Office (GAO) audit as well as commissioning a study that would require in depth interviews with program participants, and especially with the mothers of the program participants' children. We want to know how the expenditure of funds is affecting the mothers and their children. Most particularly, has it improved the children's quality of life?

Screen for DV and other negative behaviors

An innovative program developed by the Office of the Texas Attorney General proves that it is possible to conduct DV screenings of all cases that come through the state child support offices, and to develop strategies to help survivors obtain child support safely. It is therefore not unreasonable to suggest that all fatherhood programs receiving federal funding be required to screen for DV. This is especially true for the AV program, which currently does not mandate DV screening. Even though newly proposed guidelines encourage screening, they leave it to the grantee to decide on the tools to be used, and even on the definition of DV. New legislation should require OCSE to establish a definition of DV to be applied in the AV program, and to provide grantees with the appropriate tools and technical assistance to screen for DV. In addition to screening for DV, programs for incarcerated fathers should also screen for characteristics known to adversely affect children such as antisocial personality, and potential for coercive parenting.

Address DV once it is identified

Where DV or child abuse has been identified, these cases should be excluded from receiving routine access services unless programs have qualified dedicated personnel with expertise in addressing access issues in DV and child maltreatment cases. Partnering with DV agencies is not enough, especially when no part of the budget is dedicated to paying specialized personnel to provide services addressing complex access issues. If fatherhood programs do not have the resources to provide specialized DV access services, such cases should be referred to specialized DV programs such as the Safe Havens Program. It is also important for OCSE to clarify for AV grantees that parental alienation and similar theories are *not* endorsed by the federal enabling legislation and that the federal government will not fund services or referrals to services by providers guided by parental alienation theory. At the same time, more funding should be made available for the development, implementation and evaluation of parenting programs for DV offenders based on principles which incorporate victim safety and offender accountability and responsibility as priorities. Safe Engagement, developed by David Mandel, is such a program. It is based on the principle that a father's continued co-parenting with a child's mother is dependent on his willingness to safely engage in a positive alliance with the mother. The program includes periodic threat and lethality assessment for mother and child, and monitoring batterers' coercive controlling behavior by staff members who have been trained to recognize coercive control tactics. By recognizing danger signs, program staff can help to prevent DV before it occurs thus limiting the child's exposure to trauma. The program also recognizes that in some cases, where the threat assessment is too high, positive co-parenting may mean that the father is not involved in the child's life and safe co-parenting may mean no contact with the victim mother. An important feature of the Safe Engagement program is its recognition of gender-based prejudices on parenting that hold fathers to very low standards, but have unrealistically high expectations of mothers. Thus in addition to dealing with violence and safety issues, the program raises consciousness on gender-based prejudices that disadvantage mothers.

Reassign program funding

Some advocates have suggested that fatherhood funding should be used to enhance the parenting skills of both parents, or could be better put to use to improve the lives of currently targeted populations through focused and coordinated programs that include substance abuse treatment, batterer treatment, trauma treatment, non-violent parenting education, and personal improvement through character-building programs and mentoring. At the very least continued program funding should depend on rigorous outcome evaluations that examine short and long-term benefits to children (such as emotional development, educational achievement, overall health, avoidance of drugs and delinquency.) Outcomes should also include the safety and wellbeing of the child's primary caregiver.

Title IV-D as a force for change

By incorporating the abovementioned recommendations, Title IV-D could become a force for positive change in protecting parents and children affected by DV. Beyond routine DV screening and the development of safe parenting plans, child support offices could monitor courts' compliance with these plans, and keep a log of how often judges violate safety recommendations, placing parents and children at risk. Safety records could become another index of a state's compliance with federal OCSE standards together with child support collection and paternity establishment, and would therefore form another basis for monetary rewards and penalties.

Chapter 8

Unfinished Business

The purpose of this chapter is to discuss the Congressional mandate, which was part of the VAWA reauthorization of 2000, requiring the Attorney General to study the impact of federal parental kidnapping laws on DV survivors. The National Clearinghouse for the Defense of Battered Women (NCDBW) conducted the study, and submitted a report to Congress in 2006, including numerous recommendations for change.[1] None of these recommendations has been addressed. The subject dropped off the radar, and was never mentioned again. In order to understand the proposed changes and why they were ignored, it is necessary to provide a brief background on the history of state and federal legislation regarding parental kidnapping.

As divorce became more common, custody battles often took the form of unilateral abduction of children by the noncustodial parents from the state where the original custody determination was made to another state where the abducting parent would open a new custody proceeding. This resulted in multiple, conflicting custody and visitation orders, in the absence of effective judicial oversight and remedies. Thus, in order to overcome the confusion and unpredictability resulting from this method of custody determination, the National Conference of Commissioners on Uniform State Laws promulgated model legislation in 1968 known as the Uniform Child Custody Jurisdiction Act (UCCJA), which was adopted by all 50 states and the District of Columbia by 1981.[2] The purpose of this Act was to facilitate the enforcement of one state's custody order in other states by allowing only one state to exercise jurisdiction in original child custody determinations, as well as in subsequent modifications, and to prevent interstate jurisdictional competition and child abductions. This legislation was developed before the battered women's movement and the enactment of VAWA raised consciousness about the problem of DV survivors needing to sometimes flee across state lines to seek safety. As we noted in Chapter 6, even the original VAWA of 1994 was not fully cognizant of how custody issues affected victim safety, and subsequent reauthorizations attempted to deal with this issue. At the same time, improvements in parental kidnapping laws were taking battered women's safety issues into account in accordance with the updated VAWA legislation. But it was clear to battered women's advocates that serious inconsistencies continued to exist between the intent of the VAWA legislation and parental kidnapping laws, which continued to discriminate against battered mothers. At the present time, the efforts to address these inconsistencies have stalled and need to be revitalized. What follows is a brief account of the development of parental kidnapping legislation, and its relationship to VAWA.

Provisions of the UCCJA

The UCCJA provided four criteria for determining original jurisdiction:

1) *Home state.* The state must have been the child's home for the past six months.

2) *Significant connection.* The child and at least one parent must have "a significant connection" with the state, and there must be "substantial evidence" about the child available in the state.

3) *Emergencies.* Child is present in the state and has either been abandoned or has been subjected to or threatened with abuse, mistreatment, neglect or is dependent.

4) *Vacuum.* Either no other state would have jurisdiction to decide the case or a state that does have jurisdiction had expressly declined to exercise it.

The biggest problem with the UCCJA was that it provided two seemingly equal bases for exercising subject matter jurisdiction: "home state" and "significant connections." While "home state" was an objective standard, under which only one state could qualify, "significant connections" was far more subjective. The states of both parents could usually make reasonable findings regarding significant connections. In addition, lack of consistency in the legislative language across states meant that forum shopping and interstate abductions would continue.

The PKPA

In 1980, the federal government enacted the Federal Parental Kidnapping Prevention Act (PKPA), to address the interstate custody jurisdictional problems that continued to exist after the adoption of the UCCJA.[3] The PKPA mandates that state authorities give full faith and credit to other states' custody determinations, so long as those determinations were made in conformity with the provisions of the PKPA. While most of the legal provisions in the PKPA are similar to those in the UCCJA, there are, some significant differences. For example, the PKPA authorizes continuing exclusive jurisdiction in the original decree state so long as one parent or the child remains there and that state has continuing jurisdiction under its own law. The UCCJA did not directly address this issue. Inconsistencies between the UCCJA and the PKPA, as well as inconsistency of interpretation of the UCCJA across states further complicated interstate custody disputes. According to a study conducted by the American Bar Association, these problems could only be solved by certain amendments to the UCCJA.

The UCCJEA

In order to remedy the problems with the UCCJA noted above, the National Conference of Commissioners on Uniform State Laws promulgated new model legislation in 1997 – The Uniform Child Custody Jurisdiction and Enforcement Act (UCCJEA), which revised the jurisdictional aspects of the UCCJA eliminating the inconsistent state interpretations.[4] Like the PKPA, the UCCJEA prioritizes home state jurisdiction both for initial custody determinations as well as any subsequent modifications. In addition, it specifies that emergency jurisdiction may be exercised to protect the child only on a temporary basis until the court with appropriate jurisdiction issues a permanent order. While tightening the rules to prevent forum shopping, the UCCJEA nevertheless recognizes DV as a circumstance requiring special consideration, and incorporates this recognition into the model legislation.

Emergency jurisdiction

The UCCJEA allows that under certain circumstances, an emergency custody determination may become a final custody determination. For example, if there is no existing custody determination, and no custody proceeding is filed in a state with jurisdiction, an emergency custody determination may becomes a final determination, when the state that issues the order becomes the home state of the child (after six months). The UCCJEA is concerned with the temporary nature of the order when there exists a prior custody order that is entitled to be enforced under this Act or when a subsequent custody proceeding is filed in a state with jurisdiction. In such cases, the Act allows the temporary order to remain in effect only so long as is necessary for the person who obtained the determination to present a case and obtain an order from the state with jurisdiction.

The UCCJEA recognizes that a protective order proceeding will often be the basis for requesting that a court assume temporary emergency jurisdiction when the child's parent or sibling has been subjected to or threatened with mistreatment or abuse. While VAWA of 1994 did provide an independent basis for the granting of full faith and credit to protective orders, it expressly excluded "custody" orders from the definition of "protective order." This problem was remedied in the reauthorization of VAWA in 2000, and 2005, which specified that full faith and credit be granted to custody orders contained in protective orders. In order for a protective order that contains a custody determination to be enforceable in another state under the UCCJEA, it must comply with the provisions requiring that the opposing party receive notice and a reasonable opportunity to be heard. While some states authorize the issuance of protective orders in an emergency without notice and hearing, ex parte orders are not eligible for enforcement under the UCCJEA. However, the requirement that opposing parties receive notice and reasonable opportunity to be heard is solely for the purpose of determining the validity of the protective order; the court deciding emergency jurisdiction may not re-litigate the factual findings on which the order is based. A person seeking a temporary emergency custody determination is required to inform the court of any proceeding concerning the child that has been commenced elsewhere. The person commencing the temporary custody proceeding is to inform the court about the temporary emergency proceeding. These requirements are to be strictly followed so that the courts are able to resolve the emergency, protect the safety of the parties and the child, and determine a period for the duration of the temporary order. If there is a concern that the person obtaining the temporary emergency determination would be in danger upon returning to the state with jurisdiction, the UCCJEA provides for interstate discovery mechanisms that allow victims to remain in a safe location while litigating custody. It also recognizes the danger of revealing the location of the survivor and children, and recommends that the court keep information about survivors' location confidential and sealed.

More convenient forum

The UCCJEA also authorizes courts to decide that another state is in a better position to make the custody determination, taking into consideration the relative circumstances of the parties. DV is the first factors that a court must consider in deciding more convenient jurisdiction. For example, the court with appropriate jurisdiction may decide that the court that entered an emergency order is in a better position to address the safety of the person who obtained the emergency order, or of the child, and decline jurisdiction. In addition, if it is determined that the parties are located in different states because one party is a survivor of DV or child abuse this authorizes the court to consider which state can best protect the survivor from further violence or abuse. Other factors that courts may consider include:

1) The length of time the child resided outside the state;

2) The distance between the state declining jurisdiction and the state that would assume jurisdiction;

3) The financial circumstances of the parties;

4) Any agreement of the parties as to which state should assume jurisdiction;

5) The nature and location of the evidence, including the testimony of the child;

6) The ability of the court in each state to decide the issue quickly and the procedures necessary to present the evidence;

7) The familiarity of the court of each state with the facts and issues in the pending litigation.

"Clean hands" provision

Another provision of the UCCJEA ensures that abducting parents will not receive an advantage for their unjustifiable conduct. If the conduct that creates the jurisdiction is unjustified, courts must decline to exercise jurisdiction that is inappropriately invoked by one of the parties. For example, if one parent abducts the child pre-decree and establishes a new home state, that jurisdiction will decline to hear the case. There are exceptions. If the other party has acquiesced in the court's jurisdiction, the court may hear the case. Such acquiescence may occur by filing a pleading submitting to the jurisdiction, or by not filing in the court that would otherwise have jurisdiction under this Act. Similarly, if the court that would have jurisdiction finds that the court of this state is a more appropriate forum, the court may hear the case. The focus in this section is on the unjustified conduct of the person who invokes the jurisdiction of the court. A technical illegality or wrong is insufficient to trigger the applicability of this section. This is particularly important in cases involving DV and child abuse. The UCCJEA specifies that DV survivors should not be charged with unjustifiable conduct for conduct that occurred in the process of fleeing DV, even if their conduct is technically illegal. Thus, if a parent flees with a child to escape DV and in the process violates a joint custody decree, the case should not be automatically dismissed. An inquiry must be made into whether the flight was justified under the circumstances of the case. However, an abusive parent who seizes the child and flees to another state to establish jurisdiction has engaged in unjustifiable conduct and the new state must decline to exercise jurisdiction under this section.

At the time of writing, all states except for Massachusetts have enacted some form of the UCCJEA. Massachusetts has held out because of concerns that the proposed legislation does not go far enough to protect battered women. Currently there is a bill before the legislature that purports to address these issues. In particular, the bill allows the state to decline jurisdiction if the court finds that a parent or person acting as a parent has engaged in a serious incident or pattern of abuse against the other parent or person acting as a parent or the child.

Battered women's advocate Joan Zorza believes that the UCCJEA does not go far enough in protecting battered women in interstate custody disputes.[5] In cases where DV is at issue, she recommends deleting the provision permitting the parties to agree where the case will be heard, and the provision permitting the use of judicial calendars to determine which state will hear a case in the most timely manner.[5] These provisions may defeat the purpose of the DV provision, which is to ensure victim safety. She also proposes that courts should be mandated to cede jurisdiction to the state where a survivor has fled with her children if they have safety issues. Currently, the ceding of jurisdiction in such cases is only discretionary. Zorza goes further to propose that this mandate to cede jurisdiction be extended to cases with a variety of other elements known to be prejudicial to DV survivors, for example, the use of parental alienation and other unscientific theories to explain allegations of DV.

Evaluation of the PKPA

The PKPA is a full faith and credit law, which tells state courts when to honor and enforce custody determinations issued in sister states. The PKPA is not a federal criminal statute. There is no federal criminal parental kidnapping offense. While there is a federal crime prohibiting international parental kidnapping, this offense does not include kidnapping across state lines within the United States. The enforcement of the PKPA takes place through another federal law known as UFAP (Unlawful Flight to Avoid Prosecution), which authorizes federal assistance to local law enforcement in apprehending fugitives from state justice. Thus when Congress enacted the PKPA, it declared that the federal UFAP law applied in cases involving interstate parental abduction as well as international parental abduction. While some state parental kidnapping laws as well as international kidnapping laws (see the Hague

Convention below) recognize DV as a defense, the same is not true for the PKPA and UFAP. Despite the fact that the PKPA, like the UCCJEA, recognizes DV as grounds for "emergency jurisdiction", there is nothing to prevent UFAP warrants from being issued against DV survivors. As a result, the FBI has been used to locate and arrest DV survivors who have sought refuge by crossing state lines with their children, in some cases tracking them down to DV shelters.

The NCDBW report to Congress adds that because there is no screening mechanism for DV, a survivor's profile may be posted as a missing person's notice on the FBI website tracking "parental kidnappers", or the children's description may be posted on the website of the National Center for Missing and exploited Children.[6] The report notes the dire impact of this federal process on survivors, who are often forced to return to dangerous jurisdictions where their children may be returned to the perpetrator. Even if the survivors are eventually acquitted of parental kidnapping charges, they may have to serve jail time after the arrest and usually lose custody of their children.

The NCDBW study examined state kidnapping laws, as well as exemptions and defenses for parental kidnapping across states. They found that state criminal statutes vary widely in their definition of parental kidnapping as well as the types of penalties that have been established. In addition, while some state laws include exemptions or defenses for DV, there are many states that do not include any exemptions or defenses for DV.[7] In states with exemptions survivors should not face criminal charges at all if they meet statutory criteria. Even state statutes that do not specifically mention DV may still be written in a way that would allow such evidence to be introduced, for example a showing of "good cause", but in other cases, such as Alaska, the statute does not require a specific intent, and evidence of DV may not be relevant or admissible.

While exemptions are reported to have been helpful to DV survivors in some cases, the system does not always work as intended. The exemption laws require survivors of DV to take certain steps to avail themselves of the exemptions, and thus only protect survivors who are aware of the requirements prior to flight. Many survivors, however, are unaware of these requirements, and do not have legal representation or assistance from advocates before they flee. Similarly, states that allow DV as a defense may also not be able to protect survivors. Many survivors do not have access to adequate legal representation, and many judges and juries do not understand the reality of DV, even when there is significant evidence of abuse, resulting in inappropriate decisions from courts.[8]

The NCDBW report includes numerous recommendations for improvement, both for state actors and for the federal government. The purpose of these recommendations is to enable states to pursue more arrests and prosecution in parental kidnapping cases without punishing survivors of DV who flee for safety with their children. Improvements at the state level would include providing training and resources to judges, prosecutors, and law enforcement personnel; the development of protocols that prevent prosecutors from charging survivors when there is evidence of DV; training defense attorneys and encouraging partnerships between advocates and prosecutors, defense attorneys and law enforcement so that local relationships are in place when cases arise. The report also includes recommendations for changes in state legislation to include legal protections for survivors.[9]

Most relevant to our discussion here are the report's recommendations for actions that could be taken by the federal government. For the most part parental kidnapping is handled by state and local law enforcement, and by district attorneys. But in some cases federal resources are used, and thus the NCDBW report recommends that protocols should be developed to prevent DV perpetrators from misusing federal resources to track down and harass their former victims when they have fled to safety.[10] This was the very intent of the legislation proposed by Congressman Conyers in 1998 and 1999 – a portion of which was incorporated into the VAWA reauthorization of 2000 in the form of the very requested study.

The report points out that federal authorities have previously had separate guidelines for the issuance of warrants in parental kidnapping cases, for example, requiring independent credible information that the child was seriously abused or neglected by the abducting parent. Furthermore, U.S. Attorneys are required to prevent the use of UFAP warrants in the enforcement of discriminatory state statutes or to compel discharge of civil obligations. Thus creating a specialized rule for the issuance of UFAP warrants in cases involving DV (an underlying factor in many parental kidnapping cases) is consistent with their historical use. The report goes on to propose that a screening tool be developed, and that a screening process be initiated at the state level prior to the involvement of federal authorities. In other words, the guidelines should be revised to prohibit the issuance of a UFAP warrant in parental kidnapping cases until state or local authorities investigate and determine whether there was a history of DV against the fleeing parent. The report recommends that those conducting such an investigation take following factors into account: [11]

1) Determining whether there is a history of DV-related convictions against the left-behind parent;

2) Determining whether the fleeing parent sought a protective order from local courts;

3) Asking if the fleeing parent sought medical treatment for injuries related to DV;

4) Determining if child protective services were aware of allegations of abuse against children or the fleeing parent;

5) Questioning family members, neighbors, friends and co-workers or other potential witnesses who may have been aware of a history of abuse;

6) Determining if the fleeing parent sought help from local victim advocacy organizations.

Not mentioned in the NCDBW report, but potentially also very helpful would be a review of the court file involving the custody case. Reviewers should look for red flags such as the use of the parental alienation label or similar prejudicial labels against the fleeing parent.

In addition to the development of a protocol for issuing UFAP warrants, the NCDBW report recommends DV training for staff posting cases on the parental kidnapping section of the FBI website. FBI staff responsible for these postings should be trained to spot red flags suggesting that the abducting parent was a survivor of DV and refrain from posting the profile. This would provide a supplemental measure in case state authorities failed to conduct a proper investigation and would provide an opportunity for the FBI to check on this. Training should also be conducted for staff of the National Center for Missing and Exploited Children as a special condition for receiving federal funding, and for Assistant U.S. Attorneys and FBI investigators about the impact of DV on parental kidnapping cases. The report concludes that at present parental kidnapping laws do not adequately protect many survivors of DV, but that these laws could be strengthened to protect communities and families and allow victims of abuse to escape from violence while ensuring that they do not suffer criminal sanctions.[12]

The Hague Convention

The Hague Convention on the Civil Aspects of International Child Abduction is a multilateral treaty developed by the Hague Conference on Private International Law that was concluded in October 1980.[13] The treaty was drafted to ensure the prompt return of children who have been abducted from their country of habitual residence or wrongfully retained in a contracting state not their country of habitual residence. It provides an expeditious method to return a child abducted by a parent from one member country to another. The primary intention of the treaty is to preserve whatever child custody arrangement existed immediately before an alleged wrongful removal or retention thereby deterring a parent from crossing international boundaries in search of a more sympathetic court. The Convention applies only to children under the age of 16. As of January 2014, 91 states had signed onto the treaty.

The International Child Abduction Remedies Act (ICARA), is a federal law that was enacted in 1988, establishing procedures to implement the Hague Convention treaty in the United States. An action under the Hague Convention begins with the filing of a petition in the jurisdiction where the child is presently located. Notice of a Hague Convention Petition must be given in accordance with the applicable law governing interstate child custody proceedings. In the United States, this would be the PKPA, UCCJA, or UCCJEA. The petitioner bears the initial burden of proving, by a preponderance of the evidence, that the removal or retention of the child was "wrongful". Once this has been demonstrated, the burden shifts to the respondent to prove an affirmative defense. Because the affirmative defenses are narrowly construed a trial court still retains the discretion to order the child's return, even where such a defense has been accredited. Unlike the UCCJEA, the Hague Convention and ICARA provide no specific guidance on the handling of DV cases. However, there are three potential affirmative defenses that could be applicable to DV survivors. The most common one is the "grave risk" defense, which allows that a child not be returned to the country of habitual residence, if such action would pose a grave risk to the child. Other defenses include "intolerable situation" and "human rights violation."

In 2012 the National Center for Missing and Exploited Children (NCMEC) published a training manual for attorneys litigating Hague Convention cases, and had this to say about DV and the "grave risk" defense:

> "Although a clear judicial consensus has not emerged, the issue of domestic and family violence as it relates to the

grave risk defense has been raised repeatedly in recent years. There are not yet any specific comprehensive statistics on how often respondents are fleeing domestic violence or raising allegations of domestic violence, but statistics indicate that the incidence of successful grave risk defenses has increased globally and in the United States. Scholars and advocates have highlighted the difference between the stereotypical abductor envisioned by the drafters of the Hague Convention and the reality that abductors are most commonly women who act as primary caretakers for the children. In alleging grave risk to the children, litigants are increasingly raising the issue of domestic abuse, in addition to emphasizing the decades of scholarship addressing the harmful effects of domestic violence on children in the home. Counsel on both sides of a case must be prepared to address this issue when litigating a Hague Convention case.

In assessing grave risk, some courts examine whether the country of habitual residence has the means to protect the child from potential abuse. However, in 2008, the Eleventh Circuit concluded that neither the Hague Convention, ICARA nor the Perez-Vera Report require a court to review evidence of whether the habitual residence can protect at-risk children. The court noted that such an analysis requires evidence of the habitual residence's "legal and social service systems" which can lead to 'difficult problems of proof' since the respondent left the habitual residence. Consequently, the Eleventh Circuit declined to 'impose on a responding parent a duty to prove that her child's country of habitual residence is unable or unwilling to ameliorate the grave risk of harm which would otherwise accompany the child's return.'"[14]

The manual acknowledges that no comprehensive statistics exist on how often respondents in Hague cases are fleeing DV, but a review of the current social science literature by Dr. Jeffrey Edelson, whose work is cited in the manual, indicates that a high proportion of parental kidnapping cases involve parent-to-parent violence with the focus being typically on the abductor. However, in one study, reviewed by Shetty and

Edelson, 30% of left behind parents either admitted to being violent towards the other parent or had been accused of it.[15] Edelson and his colleagues conducted an in-depth study of 22 mothers who had fled to the United States seeking refuge from DV that they had experienced in other countries.[16] These women, most of whom were U.S. citizens, sought but received little help from foreign authorities or social services, and also received little help from U.S. authorities. In most cases, the U.S. courts were unsympathetic to the safety issues concerning these children, and sent them back to the custody of the abusive fathers in the other country. Although Edleson's study dealt with incoming Hague cases, his findings and recommendations could be applicable to outgoing Hague cases in much the same way as the UCCJEA allows for the ceding of jurisdiction in cases involving DV. The first step in handling both incoming and out-going cases would be the recognition of DV and the need to assess it. Some of Edelson's key recommendations include the following:[17]

- All Hague cases should be assessed for the presence of DV, including patterns of coercive control and emotional terrorizing in addition to the presence of physical violence.

- The Hague Permanent Bureau should issue interpretive guidelines that clarify when a child's exposure to DV should be considered a form of grave risk or an intolerable situation.

- U.S. state and federal courts and attorneys should consider greater applicability of the "intolerable situation," and "human rights violation" exceptions, as these may be relevant to children's harm from exposure to DV.

- The level of evidence required to prove grave risk, intolerable situation or human rights violations should be changed from clear and convincing to preponderance.

- U.S. Embassies should provide emergency assistance to battered parents and children attempting to flee from abusive situations.

Other recommendations include the provision of legal and other resources to the fleeing parent, strengthening of legal and social services for DV survivors in all countries, and training for judges and attorneys on the relevance of DV in Hague cases.

Where things stand now

Both the PKPA study and the Hague study came up with similar recommendations – in summary – that parental kidnapping cases need to be screened for DV and that interventions be set in place to protect victims of abuse and not punish them or turn children over to the custody of abusers. Both studies recommend that the government should set clear policy standards that this is not permissible, particularly in any case where there has been abuse by the parent seeking enforcement to bring home the child. The possibility of implementing these recommendations seems highly unlikely, given the federal government's persistent failure to acknowledge or even collect data on the presence of DV in parental kidnapping cases and the fact that federal agents may be in the business of endangering children by turning them over to DV perpetrators and rapist.

A 2010 DOJ report on parental kidnapping acknowledges that DV and child abuse are among the reasons that a parent may kidnap a child. The report states the following as one of the reasons a parent may abduct a child:

"The abductor is removing the child from *real* physical and/or emotional threat or injury by the other parent."[18]

Other than mentioning this in one bullet, the DOJ report provides no further information on this matter – as if it were of little relevance. Most of the report is devoted to children's personal accounts regarding their experiences of being kidnapped, but not one of the stories deals with a child being returned to a violent parent. It is difficult to explain this omission other than by the term "cognitive dissonance." The DOJ is a law and order organization in which "justice" is a synonym for law and order. In this context, kidnappers are always "bad guys" who must be caught and brought to justice. The concept that the child was kidnapped for his or her own safety, and may be returned to an abuser or rapist is impossible to contemplate within this framework.

The fact is that some of our legislators in Congress were concerned enough to include a special provision in VAWA 2000, requiring that the Attorney General commission a study to evaluate the impact of the PKPA on DV survivors. Yet after the completion of the study and the report sat unnoticed and today, few people even know of its existence. In a recent conversation with the authors of the report I learned that the $200,000 authorized by Congress for the PKPA study, never actually went through appropriations. In the end, NCDBW only received one eighth of that amount to conduct the study and write the report. Perhaps in order for Congress to take action, it would need more proof that battered mothers are being hurt by the current status quo. In order to obtain reliable statistics on how often this occurs, a new study would have to be commissioned, and a suitable amount of money would have to be appropriated – not just authorized – for this purpose. However, it would still be possible to implement the recommendations of the NCDBW report, just as they are, without the need for any additional data collection.

Chapter 9

Fixing Family Court

Incest survivor and victims' rights activist Louise Armstrong struck a pessimistic tone in *Rocking the Cradle of Sexual Politics* in regard to the appropriate forum for dealing with incest:

> "So far, we have learned that incest/child sexual abuse does not really belong in the criminal justice system – for reasons of evidence, age of the children, and for an assortment of other proposed reasons beyond enumeration.
>
> It does not belong in the juvenile justice system – because mothers are punished there for having failed to protect, and because middle-class men will hit the ceiling at this invasion of their privacy and their property.
>
> It does not belong in custody/probate court – because this court is designed for compromise and for working out equitable solutions between separating adults. And it is dangerous because it's a court in which fathers are once again gaining overwhelming superiority – in the name of equality."[1]

Unfortunately, Armstrong passed away in 2008, without having been able to witness any positive changes in the systems that handle incest. But the voices of advocates for change have been growing louder, and in this chapter we describe various models that have been proposed by advocacy groups and professionals as alternatives to family court in dealing with custody and abuse cases. Implementation of these models would for the most part require prior legislative action. Changes in the family law system are up to state legislatures, and are not within the purview of the federal government – with one exception – the District of Columbia, which is still under the control of Congress, even in matters of family law. The section that follows describes promising models for change proposed by experts and advocates in the fields of DV and child abuse. In the final section we will present our own model for change based on a synthesis of other models and our original proposal described in *The Hostage Child: Sex Abuse Allegations in Custody Disputes.*[2]

Joan Zorza's abuse-custody laboratory

Battered women's advocate, Joan Zorza, has recommended the funding of an abuse-custody laboratory that would have a fact-finding function in cases where abuse allegations arise in custody cases. Zorza made the following recommendation later published in the Domestic Violence Reports:

> "Consider funding one or, ideally, more, model or exploratory trial abuse custody courts in jurisdictions which will apply the approaches, discussed at the Roundtable, and be willing to be analyzed and compared to traditional jurisdictions by experienced researchers knowledgeable in abuse areas. Specifically the court would first look to see if there are any abuse or safety issues, and only if none are found can the rest of the case be handled as usual. If any abuse or safety issues are found, all measures would be taken to provide safety for victims and children, including, as necessary, no visitation (or only visitation by photograph, or other safe way), and permission to relocate with the children."[3]

The Greenbook Project

Another proposal for dealing with custody and DV came from the Greenbook project, which is best known for its accomplishments in bridging the gap between child welfare workers and DV advocates in dealing with cases where DV overlaps with child maltreatment. Greenbook also made recommendations about best practices for juvenile courts, and about court powers and jurisdiction that currently do not exist. The authors of the Greenbook project recommended that juvenile courts should have specific powers to enable them to ensure the safety of all family members.[4] These powers should enable the court to do the following:

- Issue protection orders for adults and children, including the power to remove a perpetrator of DV from the home;

- Issue visitation orders;

- Issue custody orders when the dependency case is to be dismissed;

- Establish paternity;

- Make child support orders;

- Hold a non-parent accountable for violent or dangerous acts, after notice and an opportunity to be heard;

- Order protective services for children and DV victims;

- Enforce its orders.

According to Greenbook, juvenile courts should be empowered to address and resolve all of a family's problems before one court. Litigants should expect that their legal business could be conducted in one court setting. The Greenbook authors pointed out that it is poor practice and potentially dangerous to victims to require them to go to different courts to get the legal protection they need, and proposed following existing models of court coordination. Unfortunately, Greenbook was not successful in bringing about meaningful change in the operation of juvenile courts. Although some judges admitted benefitting from Greenbook training, most were reluctant to change. Greenbook attributed some of this reluctance to prevailing norms, case law, precedent, and legislative constraints. Juvenile courts operated under statutes and followed legal precedents that were not necessarily consistent with Greenbook principles. Thus the obvious next step would be to create a Greenbook-type juvenile court. Other experts in the field have suggested similar solutions.

California NOW's juvenile court proposal

California National Organization for Women (NOW) also proposed that abuse cases be handled by a court other than family court, and suggested that juvenile courts take jurisdiction in custody cases involving abuse allegations. Although California NOW acknowledged that the juvenile courts have many flaws, they liked the fact that the proceedings are non-adversarial and focus on the child. They noted that currently there are many problems with juvenile courts. For example in California, juvenile court findings cannot be used in family court.[5]

A juvenile court in Los Angeles is credited with protecting Alanna K, a California child who was the subject of a bitter custody battle between her parents in Marin County Family Court.[6] Alanna's father was awarded custody of her even though she alleged that he physically abused her. According to a report submitted to the Los Angeles Juvenile Courts, Alanna's therapist had had a "seemingly intimate" relationship with her father (which he denied), and both the court-appointed evaluator and her court-appointed attorney relied on the questionable theory of parental alienation in making their recommendations. Once he had custody, Mr. K checked Alanna into a locked residential treatment facility in Utah for five months, although she had no criminal history or evidence of mental health problems. When she returned to her father's care at age 13, she decided that she could not live with what she claimed were constant fights and the threat of physical confrontation, so she ran away to Los Angeles. A juvenile court there finally placed Alanna with her mother until she left for college.

The Los Angeles Juvenile Court ordered an independent psychological evaluation, which found that the father's allegations that the mother alienated the child were not credible, while the child's allegations of physical abuse by the father were credible. The report also gave weight to Alanna's wish to live with her mother, since she was getting older, and there was no evidence that the mother was a risk. The Los Angeles Department of Children's Services also submitted a report to the court in which it stated that it believed Alanna had suffered from physical abuse by her father on several occasions and that this had been substantiated by several sources. In addition, it accused the Marin County Child Protective Services of having been remiss in not responding to many of the referrals and simply dismissing them as "custody dispute issues." The report also mentioned that the Department was disturbed when it discovered the father had made arrangements for Alanna to receive treatment at a residential facility on the day of the juvenile court hearing, particularly as she did not exhibit any signs of psychotic behavior, and did not appear to be a danger to herself or others. The Department discounted evidence that Alanna needed treatment on the grounds that the practitioner who submitted this material appeared to have an intimate relationship with the father and was therefore likely biased.

The father eventually pleaded no contest to using inappropriate discipline, and custody automatically went to the mother. In an interview with the San Francisco Chronicle, Alanna told the reporter that while she saw the Marin Family Courts as her undoing, she saw the Los Angeles Juvenile Court as her savior.

"In the L.A. Juvenile Courts, that's where I got some faith in the system restored," Alanna adds. "Juvenile court is about kids, it's not family court. The [juvenile court] judge would say, 'OK, parents, I don't know what you guys are doing, but what's in the best interest of the kid?'"[6]

One of the most important aspects to the success of the Alanna K case was the willingness and ability of the juvenile court to obtain objective information from reliable evaluators. Family courts typically do not rely on the results of objective investigations. Thus any attempt to change court practice in abuse cases must be especially concerned with the source of the information that courts rely upon to make their decisions. There have been several proposals to require custody evaluators to undergo specialized DV training, and California has even incorporated some of these proposals into its legislation. But questions remain as to whether this can work in a system that is already biased against victims at its core.

California Protective Parents Association Model

The California Protective Parents Association, in collaboration with other organizations, is proposing that incest cases be processed through the criminal justice system, but without prosecution being the necessary outcome. They point out that children who report sexual abuse by a non-parent are treated differently by the criminal justice system compared to children who report sexual abuse by a parent. In child sex abuse cases where the accused is a non-parent, the crime is investigated by law enforcement. In cases of incest, social workers and mental health professionals are primarily the ones who conduct the investigations, and they do not treat these cases as real crimes. In child sex abuse cases where the accused is a non-parent, the victim witness is kept from any contact with the accused to prevent possible further harm and witness tampering. However, in incest cases, the accused frequently gains access to the victim witness through family court. Advocates regard this as a civil rights violation. Children who report sexual abuse should be treated alike by the criminal justice system regardless of the relationship to the accused. California advocates propose a four-pronged approach to ensuring equal protection for children who report a sexual crime to the multidisciplinary interview team (MDIT) and names a parent as the accused.

1) The child is presumed to be making a valid crime report in terms of victim witness protection (not guilt or innocence of the accused).

2) The child is assigned a victim witness advocate from the district attorney's office who obtains a restraining order for the child and facilitates victims of crime compensation for therapy.

3) The non-accused parent is enjoined not to speak to the child about the criminal procedure or to allow the child to have contact with the accused in advance of a criminal trial.

4) If the district attorney decides not to press charges at the time of the report, the child continues to be protected until the child is old enough to testify.

In California, the MDIT is run by law enforcement, not child protective services (CPS). The new proposal would require that if a case were first reported to CPS, the agency would be required to turn it over to law enforcement. A key to the success of such a program would require buy-in from the district attorney's office. This could be made possible if it involved funding opportunities in the form of federal grants and victim compensation money.

Barry Goldstein's "Safe Child Act" and the Quincy Solution

Attorney, author and advocate for protective parents, Barry Goldstein, has proposed model legislation for adoption by state legislatures known as the Safe Child Act.[7] This Act would make child safety the paramount concern of all custody decisions when determining the child's best interests. It covers the kinds of professional qualifications and training of experts who testify before the court in custody cases involving allegations of abuse, and addresses the scientific validity of research about abuse that informs the court's decisions. It requires the court to place a child with the safer parent based on a preponderance of the evidence, and requires that a child's visitation with a parent who poses a safety risk be supervised. The Act also addresses gender-biased practices, myths and stereotypes that are often characteristic of family courts, prohibiting the penalization of parents who make good faith allegations about DV or child abuse.[8]

The Safe Child Act is actually a recently added component to a broader scheme to address DV that Goldstein refers to as "The Quincy Solution" named after a program to address DV that was implemented in Quincy Massachusetts from 1975 to 1996.[9] The program was initiated by the district attorney, Bill Delahunt, and was based on strict enforcement of criminal laws pertaining to DV and protective orders. It required the cooperation of multiple components of the criminal justice system including police, prosecutors, probation and the judiciary. One component of the system that was not on board, was probate court where custody decisions are made. Delahunt noticed that victims who were challenged for custody, often chose not to pursue their cases. Since this problem happened only rarely, it was not addressed in the Quincy model. Goldstein believes that abusers were only just beginning to figure out how to use custody court to control their victims at the time the program was in operation. After Delahunt was elected to Congress in 1996, the program was taken over by other people, and soon unraveled. Any re-creation of the Quincy model, says Goldstein, must include courts where custody decisions are made.

Child At Risk Classification Office (CARCO)

In *The Hostage Child*, we proposed the establishment of a government office possibly within the U.S. Public Health Service called the Child at Risk Classification Office (CARCO), which would develop criteria for the assessment of a child's risk of exposure to violence or abuse after some initial indication was reported.[10] The purpose of this system would be to facilitate decision-making about the placement of children based on level of risk and available options. According to this system, after careful assessment using established criteria, a child would be assigned a risk level.

The federal CARCO would have two main functions – first, the establishment of risk criteria, methods for assessing risk, training materials and training methods for those who would carry out the investigative and risk assessment function, and second, the administration of grants to states to implement CARCO. Regarding the first function, we propose that the federal government appoint a CARCO Task Force comprised of leading professionals in the fields of psychology, medicine, and law enforcement with expertise in child abuse, child sexual abuse, DV and trauma, to begin drafting recommendations that would assist CARCO in developing its risk assessment tools and training manuals. Next we propose that the federal government offer grants to states that are willing and able to enact legislation that would facilitate the implementation of CARCO in that state. The grants would pay for the training and salaries of CARCO investigators, and also for victim services following the disposition of cases. The states in their turn, would have to demonstrate through legislation their recognition and acceptance of the fundamental CARCO principle – that a child at risk falls under the jurisdiction of CARCO and that his or her placement is based solely on risk and not the competing interests of other parties. CARCO is a holistic system incorporating five steps known as TRIAL – which stands for Training, Reporting, Investigation, Adjudi-cation, and Long-term planning and follow-up.

Training. The problem with custody evaluators in the family courts cannot be rectified by "reforming the professional curriculum" and "spot training," according to Evan Stark.[11] He argues that the current problem has less to do with ignorance and more to do with the political context in which evaluators work. He points out that not just evaluators, but the entire family court system lags behind the rest of the justice system in its understanding of and response to abuse, clinging to discredited attitudes and practices. Stark concludes that facing the true scope of abuse would threaten the paradigm on which the entire family court system is based – the belief that most family problems are interactive, reducible to family dynamics, and manageable through cooperation, counseling and court imposed constraints. Thus any proposal for a family court alternative must include a way to bypass the dysfunctional custody evaluator system. CARCO would provide an alternative to the evaluator system based on principles similar to those developed by David Mandel in his Safe Engagement study.[12] The definition of child safety would include the safety and security of the mother, with the focus on the behavior of the perpetrator of DV in all its forms, and not on the efforts made by the mother to protect herself and her children. While some custody evaluators do voluntarily adopt these principles, they are not required to do so, and furthermore they may come up against resistance from judges and lawyers who are mired in a system built on discrediting women and children. CARCO training would not just be for those conducting the investigative function. It is also for those performing the judicial function – judges who would be mandated by the enabling legislation to make decisions based on the Life Interest principle, discussed in Chapter 4.

Reporting. The enabling legislation would establish a reporting system requiring that all custody cases coming before family court judges should be screened for DV. Such cases would be referred to CARCO for triage. If CARCO establishes that abuse has occurred, the case remains within the CARCO system. Otherwise, it is referred back to family court. If allegations of abuse arise during custody proceedings after the original screening, the case is automatically referred to CARCO for triage. While judges, court personnel and custody evaluators would be required to report abuse allegations to CARCO, anyone may report a case to CARCO. In other words, if a report fell through the cracks, a victim or victims' advocate could make a referral. Another useful approach for identifying cases that should be referred to CARCO is the one developed by the

Texas Attorney General in which all child support applicants are screened for DV.

Investigation. A CARCO investigation would proceed after a case is opened. Cases that meet certain established criteria would proceed to the next step of an in-depth investigation. The purpose of the investigation would be fact finding, using established protocols developed by the federal CARCO office, and could be similar to systems used by MDITs. While the goal of the investigation would be fact-finding, the purpose would not be to bring criminal charges, but to establish level of risk for the victim. If the district attorney believed prosecution was appropriate, it would be up to him or her to proceed with filing criminal charges. The goal of CARCO, however, is first and foremost the safety and wellbeing of the victim. While the results of the investigation would be available to law enforcement, any outcome on the law enforcement side would have no effect on the CARCO outcome, for example, a decision not to prosecute, or an acquittal. While the investigation is ongoing, CARCO personnel may request a temporary restraining order for a victim and coordinate services with DV service providers. The CARCO investigation serves to establish risk, not probable cause. This is important because the CARCO system is non-adversarial. An important question is how CARCO triage would differ from the triage undertaken by divorce industry professionals in states such as Pennsylvania, described in Chapter 5. Aside from the strict qualifications, and rigorous training requirements for personnel conducting the triage, the goals of the two types of investigation are diametrically opposed. The divorce industry treats abuse as a dispute between two parties, and the goal of the triage is to determine which form of dispute resolution would be most appropriate to settle the dispute. A CARCO investigation would assess the level of risk to determine which custody arrangements and services would be most appropriate to keep victims safe. In addition, CARCO would define safety more broadly than just risk of immediate physical harm. This definition would include safety from psychological and emotional abuse, manipulation, intimidation, threats, under-mining of parenting, and other coercive controlling behaviors.

Adjudication. Once the investigation is complete, the case would be presented to a judge who would decide on the disposition of the case. Judges would be constrained by legislation to consider the child's risk level – as established by the investigation – as the primary factor in determining the disposition of the case.

Long-term planning and follow up. The CARCO system would not end with a placement decision. Victims would receive referrals to appropriate services such as therapy for children who have been traumatized, and services for DV survivors. The safety of the family would continue to be monitored, and further measures taken to protect them if necessary. In this regard, CARCO could work with fatherhood programs that adopt the Safe Engagement model, mentioned in Chapter 7, which is based on the principle that a father's continued co-parenting with a child's mother is dependent on his willingness to safely engage in a positive alliance with the mother. Such programs should include periodic threat and lethality assess-ments for the mother and child, which could be coordinated with the investigative component of the CARCO system. Case management would include ongoing monitoring of a perpetrator's continued use of coercive control, and screening for the likelihood of DV before the act has been committed. Waiting for documented incidences of abuse only increases childhood trauma and compromises the safety of the family. The Safe Engagement model is entirely consistent with CARCO principles and could work as a component of CARCO.

Doreen Ludwig's administrative unit solution

Advocate and author Doreen Ludwig has proposed that custody be taken out of the legal system and placed in an administrative environment that has accountability, oversight and correction of mistakes as its first priority.[13] This entity would treat abuse like the highly dysfunctional, detrimental behavior it is. It would perform a thorough investigation, and help to create stability for the family. While therapeutic services such as batterer intervention and counseling would be offered, the unit would be prohibited from ordering counseling, mediation, or co-parenting services. The services that would be offered would be low cost, and not above market value. Ludwig also proposes the development of a computerized template for assessing the many factors that contribute to custody determinations. The forms would use data gathered from parents, teachers, family, friends and neighbors. Level of care provided by each parent prior to the divorce would be an important criterion in the custody determination. Discrepancies in answers could be addressed through, further data collection, which would make it more difficult for abusers to manipulate the system. The computer program would integrate all the data, and create a factual record that could be disputed and verified. Child abuse would be addressed using a system similar to Child Abuse Solutions Inc., a California based organization that offers templates for assessing family abuse.[14] These templates form the basis of an investigative report with an emphasis on facts and how to ascertain the veracity of facts.

Ludwig's proposed solution has many of the same elements as CARCO, but without the adjudication component. It is interesting that in some states, child custody is dealt with administratively through child support offices, for example, in Texas where cases only go before a judge if the parties disagree. Ludwig's system, unlike the others proposed here, also addresses custody decisions in non-abuse cases. Ludwig's system shares with CARCO emphasis on fact-based investigation, and services geared towards helping families cope with trauma while recognizing that abusers should be held accountable.

All the systems described in this chapter place the safety of the child above all other considerations, which is as it should be. This is the very essence of the Life Interest principle, which must supersede all other considerations in any "best interest" analysis. The California Protective Parents Association proposal focuses narrowly on the urgent problem of child sexual abuse. Barry Goldstein envisions a broader approach calling for communities to develop a multi-system coordinated response to DV centered on law enforcement and prosecution as occurred in Quincy, Massachusetts. The Greenbook approach also calls for a multi-system response centering on child protective services. Overall there seems to be a broad consensus that the dysfunctional custody evaluation system must be torpedoed.

Chapter 10

A Problem With No Name

In her groundbreaking book, *The Feminine Mystique*, Betty Freidan immortalized the term "a problem that has no name."[1] She gave the problem a name and a definition. The feminine mystique was a set of largely fictional doctrines and fixed beliefs about what fulfillment means (or should mean) to women that restricted them to being housewives and mothers, while closing off all other career avenues to them. This concept resonated with women in the United States and across the world. It was the "Aha!" moment that led to the birth of modern day feminism. Today we have a different "problem with no name". It overlaps with DV and child abuse, but it is not either of those two problems. Parents who have lived through the problem with no name perceive it to be a systematic violation of their human rights perpetrated by state actors, but two Supreme Court rulings have said that the state is not responsible for violating any constitutionally protected rights in these cases. My goal in this chapter is to give the problem a name and a definition and suggest how our government can begin to help solve it.

The "friendly parent mystique"

A major obstacle in naming the problem is that it already has a variety of names assigned to it in family court: conflict, warring parties, bitter divorce, parental alienation, malicious mother, vengeful ex-wife – names that delegitimize it and remove any hope of redress for the injured parties. These names have created a mystique of their own – "the friendly parent mystique" – that prohibits divorcing parents (mostly mothers) from raising the topic of abuse in child custody disputes. Like the feminine mystique before it, the friendly parent mystique is based on a false set of ideals, fixed beliefs and assumptions that are primarily designed to keep abused women in their place, although of course it can impact men as well. The most pernicious aspect of this mystique is its blatantly sexist assumptions about women's credibility and the belief that women typically lie about abuse to gain an advantage over men. So strong is this mystique that it precludes the necessity of actually weighing the evidence. A mother who raises legitimate concerns about abuse in family court is often perceived by the court as leaving it with no option but to strip her of custody, and possibly cut her off completely from her children. In actual fact, the court is subjecting one parent to the coercive control of the other parent through its control of the child victim. By exploiting the protective parent's natural instinct to protect his or her child from harm, the court is legalizing coercive control. There is no escape for survivors – there is no shelter to which they can go – there is no "north" – because the system has a hostage. The feminine mystique barred women from seeking careers outside the home based on false beliefs about women's attributes. The friendly parent mystique bars divorcing mothers from objecting to DV and child abuse similarly based on false beliefs about women's attributes.

Court ordered child endangerment

The friendly parent mystique is the direct cause of court ordered child endangerment, which occurs when a court orders a child into unsafe contact with a violent or abusive parent or guardian. In cases of sexual abuse, Keith Harmon Snow put it best when he described the process as the *"trafficking of children and parents through U.S. family courts."*[2] This is no less than human trafficking, except that it is legal by virtue of having been defined as something else. In all these cases, the court failed to do due diligence by refusing to hear the evidence, or discounting the evidence, or relying on unscientific theories such as parental alienation. We must also name the human right that is being violated – the Life Interest. Family court-ordered endangerment and trafficking violate the Life Interest of children by placing them in harm's way. It also violates the Life Interest of the protective parents by subjecting them to the trauma of witnessing the abuse of their children or knowing that their children are being abused, and not being able to stop it, and by subjecting them to the *continued punishment and coercive control of the abuser.*

There is no agency in our government that addresses the problem of court-ordered child endangerment or trafficking. There is no systematic effort to conduct research into the problem or to alter policy in a meaningful way or to search for solutions. Nevertheless, our federal government is aware of the problem and has made some efforts to address it as we discussed earlier in this book. The Office on Violence Against Women (OVW) and the White House convened a Roundtable on March 22, 2011 in Washington, DC, at which they acknowledged that women and children are being badly hurt in custody cases in the nation's courts. Present at the meeting was attorney Joan Zorza, who provided the attendees with a document listing twenty solutions that the federal government as well as state governments could implement to improve outcomes for battered mothers and their children.[3] As a result of this meeting demonstration projects were implemented in various jurisdictions to develop strategies to improve family court practices.[4] These projects may produce helpful results, but the problem of court-ordered endangerment and trafficking of children is so pervasive, so grave, and so culturally entrenched that it requires a more comprehensive response, which must begin with a name and a visible presence in a prominent government agency.

Office on Children of Domestic Violence

Protective parents' advocates have long hoped to see the establishment of an office within a major federal agency that would focus exclusively on the endangerment and trafficking of children by family court. Conversations with ranking officials at OVW initially indicated support for this idea but some have raised concerns that the focus on children might be too far outside their mission unless it was limited to children witnessing DV. This view makes it clear that no government agency recognizes the unique discrimination and violations experienced by protective parents or gives them a voice. That is why an office is needed that will give visibility to protective parents, and to the problem of family court child endangerment and trafficking, and help search for solutions. Such a unit could be located within OVW as a subdivision, or it could be a stand-alone office within the Department of Justice. If legislation is needed to expand OVW's mission making it possible to incorporate this office, then that is what must happen.

The protective parents movement needs leadership at the federal level that will establish goals, develop strategies for achieving them and provide long-term stewardship if these goals are to be successfully attained. While multiple federal agencies should have a role in addressing this problem, their activities must be coordinated. The Office on Children of Domestic Violence (OCDV) would be the coordinator providing long-range vision and following through on the step-by-step requirements, ultimately leading to the changes sought by protective parents and their advocates for so long. Without such central leadership, energy becomes dissipated, focus is lost, and efforts put into important projects are wasted. In this final chapter of the book, we set out some ideas for the mission of OCDV. The mission of OCDV would be to provide federal leadership in developing the national capacity to reduce the legal endangerment and trafficking of children in family court and to administer justice for and strengthen services to adult and child victims of family court endangerment and trafficking. What follows are some specific actions that OCDV could take to accomplish its mission. Many of these ideas have been adapted from the list of 20 solutions that Joan Zorza presented at the OVW White House Round Table.

Sponsoring research and data collection

The most important function of OCDV would be to gather reliable information on family court-ordered child endangerment and trafficking. Thus far we have some information on the seven states discussed in Chapters 3 and 4, but more information is needed. These studies only addressed DV, and we have no comparable information on child sex abuse cases, which advocates believe have the worst outcomes. Zorza has pointed out the need for research on beliefs about women's lack of credibility that persist in judicial settings typified by such statements as *"a woman scorned..."* or *"women are forever making false allegations for tactical advantage..."* or *"mothers often coach their children to make false allegations."* There is already a body of research on false allegations in custody disputes showing that such allegations are rare. One fairly recent Canadian study found that where false allegations do occur, they are more likely to be brought by fathers rather than by mothers,[5] but these studies have been insufficient to persuade judges to discard their fixed beliefs that form part of the friendly parent mystique. Zorza has proposed that one way to deal with this would be for Congress to commission a definitive research study on men's and women's credibility, to publish and disseminate the results of such research, and to insist that the research be included in legislative findings or a joint Congressional resolution so that courts may take judicial notice of it without expert testimony on it, or use it to refute the typical statements used to discredit women.[6]

Education and information dissemination: federal agencies

OCDV would have a unique role in correcting misinformation and disseminating accurate information through producing published materials and conducting training. For example, training could be done on myths held by courts and administrative agencies that discriminate against DV survivors and their children, such as that women are less credible than men, that incest seldom happens, and that incest does not hurt children. OCDV could begin by correcting misinformation within federal agencies, and agencies supported by federal funding whose mission is relevant to this issue. These agencies would include the Department of Justice, the Department of Health and Human Services, the State Department, the National Center for Missing and Exploited Children, and the National Center on Child Abuse and Neglect.

Several years ago, at a seminar hosted by the Office of Juvenile Justice and Delinquency Prevention (OJJDP), one of the presenters, a manager of the Missing and Exploited Children's Program, described a peculiar pattern of parental abductions involving women from the former Soviet Union who came to the United States as mail order brides, and later kidnapped the children born from these marriages and returned with them to their countries of origin. The program manager was unaware of the extreme vulnerability of mail order brides to DV, and had not considered the possibility that these women could be fleeing DV. In fact she noted that all the husbands in these cases claimed *they* were the victims of DV perpetrated by their mail order brides. The program manager was also unaware of the biases against women alleging DV and child abuse in family court. An educational campaign among relevant federal agencies would increase awareness of the problem, with the potential to send up red flags when peculiar patterns were detected. This could lead to further investigation and to outreach and services to extremely vulnerable battered mothers who need protection for themselves and their children.[7]

Education and information dissemination: state agencies

OCDV could sponsor educational campaigns, as proposed by Zorza, to correct the misinformation about incest in state child protection and law enforcement agencies. She suggests that child protection agencies should be encouraged to conduct impartial investigations of incest crimes and protect child victims. Police and prosecutors should likewise be encouraged to treat these crimes seriously and charge offenders accordingly. It is also important to train child protection workers in the Greenbook principles dealing with the overlap of DV and child maltreatment. Incest should be understood as a form of battering based on power and control as proposed by Lundy Bancroft and Jay Silverman.[8] Understanding this dynamic would help to dispel the myths that mothers somehow allow these crimes to occur or are collusive.

Setting standards

Zorza suggests that the federal government should define "good" and "bad" laws and practices and should produce written materials and conduct trainings on them, ideally linking them to what will or will not be funded. This could be one of the functions of OCDV. The following are some of Zorza's suggestions for improving state statutes:

- *Reliance on unscientific syndromes*: Parental alienation syndrome and other scientifically invalid syndromes must be made inadmissible in court. Similarly, statutes must forbid the use of reunification counseling to overcome "parental alienation." Child protection agencies or courts may not refer children to reunification counseling or programs doing such counseling.

- *Presumptions about credibility:* Statutes must presume that abuse allegations made in custody disputes are just as credible as those made at other times or just as credible as those made against any other caretaker or stranger or non-family member, and as a result, such allegations must require as full, impartial and thorough an investigation as any other type of sex abuse allegation.

- *Application of friendly parent concept:* States must have clear statutory language that the friendly parent concept never applies in cases where there has been abuse. Ideally states should be encouraged to look at the course of conduct of an entire relationship in assessing abuse, and always assess for the predominant or primary aggressor when there are mutual allegations of abuse.

- *Immunity for ancillary court professionals:* States must abolish immunity for mediators, custody evaluators and others who urge/require a victim to drop a court ordered order of protection, or fail to investigate impartially and fully claims of abuse, or do so when they do not have the expertise to do so.

- *Admissibility of prior abuse history:* State statutes must make prior abuse history against this or another victim admissible in civil or criminal order of protection cases.

- *Consensual order:* State statutes must forbid courts to enter consensual orders without an admission of findings.

- *Giving victims useable DV findings:* Many state legislatures have passed laws to help DV survivors gain custody of their children. Courts, however, often get around these laws in a variety of ways, setting abuse victims up to not gain the custody that the legislatures intended for them. Some practices are particularly difficult to deal with because they involve judicial discretion, (for example, failure to find the victim credible) but many practices clearly violate rules against having offenders end up with findings or even offenses. These practices include vacating offenses after a batterer program is completed or after the passage of a certain amount of time, or making a finding of mutual abuse without specific findings of which party was the primary aggressor.

- *Custody evaluators:* There is widespread consensus among victim advocates backed by growing evidence that courts are using custody evaluators inappropriately in ways that are prejudicial against survivors of DV and incest. Zorza proposes that courts should stop using custody evaluators except when there are actual issues involving mental health, and specifically not use them to assess for DV, child abuse or incest. Others have proposed that courts should not use custody evaluators in abuse cases unless they have demonstrated expertise and qualifications in this area of specialty.

Developing a government litigation strategy

Zorza and others have described numerous abhorrent practices, used by family courts, to further victimize battered mothers and abused children. Some of these practices involve the exercise of "broad judicial discretion." For example, it is very common for custody courts to gag mothers, who have made allegations of abuse and to punish them by contempt, jail, fines, and/or loss of custody for alleging that the partner abused them or their children. At the same time, courts ignore the many assaults and indignities that men often do to their intimate partners (for example spitting on them, swearing at them, badmouthing them to the children and others), and indeed may treat a man's allegation that the mother was misbehaving as grounds for a custody transfer, often *ex parte*. As was reported at the Roundtable, even some indigent mothers and their pro bono attorneys, are being slapped with paying the attorney fees of their children's fathers. Zorza proposes that the federal government should file or appear in cases that challenge these unusually punitive measures.[9] She also suggests disciplinary actions against various court players who deprive mothers of due process, or do not practice up to ethical standards. She recommends that the Civil Rights Division of the Justice Department, OVW, or the Solicitor General's Office should weight in on such cases, either by bringing the cases themselves or by filing amicus briefs. Another way to deal with some of these practices would be for the government to file ethical complaints or malpractice cases against those in the court system (including custody evaluators, parent coordinators and others appointed by the courts) who are committing unethical and gender biased practices against protective parents, battered mothers, and their children. Government litigation on behalf of battered mothers should definitely include – or even give priority to ADA cases involving family court discrimination against DV survivors with psychological injuries. Even one success in such a case could radically alter the playing field for battered mothers in their struggle for justice. This too could be an area of involvement for OCDV.

Other Government Actions

Restrictions on funding eligibility under VAWA and CAPTA

Zorza has proposed that future reauthorizations of the Violence Against Women Act (VAWA) and the Child Abuse Prevention and Treatment Act (CAPTA) should specify that states are not eligible for funding under these programs if child custody statutes do not include certain provisions that protect battered mothers and abused children in custody litigation.[10] This approach is similar to that proposed in Richard Ducote's Protective Parent Reform Act (see Chapter 6.) There is precedent for such action. One of the provisions of the VAWA 2005 Reauthorization Act prohibited STOP grantees from using polygraph testing or other truth-telling devices on victims in sexual assault investigations.[11] Section 2013 stated that in order to be eligible for STOP grants, a state, Indian tribal government, or unit of local government would be required to certify within three years of enactment of VAWA 2005 that their laws, policies, or practices ensured that no law enforce-ment officer, prosecuting officer or other government official would ask or require an adult or child victim of a sex offense to submit to a polygraph examination or similar truth-telling device or method as a condition for proceeding with the investigation, charging or prosecution of such an offense. The Rape Survivor Custody Act has similarly established funding eligibility criteria for states that wish to apply for a newly created STOP grant program. These criteria require states to enact laws that allow rape survivors to apply for termination of the parental rights of the fathers of their rape-conceived children.

Restructuring fatherhood programs

In Chapter 7 we laid out a detailed plan of steps Congress can take requiring federally funded fatherhood programs to adopt the principle that mother and child safety is its highest priority. This includes introducing mandatory screening for DV, and a system for addressing DV once it is identified. Changes to the AV program are particularly important because this program currently funds services provided by court-related practitioners that have been identified as a major part of the court ordered child endangerment problem. This includes mediators, custody evaluators, and parenting coordinators. These service providers should not be involved in DV cases unless they have demonstrated expertise, experience and training in dealing with DV offenders. Referral of the victim to DV services as an add-on to routine access services is insufficient, and implies a narrow definition of safety that may not take into account DV offenders' ongoing coercive control through manipulation of inexperienced program staff. It does not provide for ongoing monitoring for threat and lethality after the program has ended. Finally, father access services, like the court-related services from which they are derived do not take into account gender-based prejudices on parenting that hold fathers to very low standards, but have unrealistically high expectations of mothers. Mothers are thus disadvantaged overall in the program's pursuit of its goals, and the mother's pivotal role in child rearing and in looking out for the safety of her children is minimized, ignored and even dismissed as irrelevant. Father access programs, and all fatherhood programs, must include promoting respect and support for mothers, as envisioned by the Safe Engagement program.

Revisiting federal laws that regulate interstate custody disputes

The National Conference of Commissioners on Uniform State Laws (NCCUSL) is an elite national organization that drafts proposed legislation to make state laws more uniform. Among these were laws affecting interstate child custody disputes – first the Uniform Child Custody Jurisdiction Act approved in the 1970s, and later the Uniform Child Custody Jurisdiction and Enforcement Act approved in the 1990s. Zorza has proposed that NCCUSL reopen these Acts, and include input from DV experts in reframing some of the provisions.[12] Some of these issues were discussed in Chapter 8, which deals with parental kidnapping laws and their impact on battered mothers. Meanwhile, Congress should consider adopting the recommendations of the NCDBW's report on parental kidnapping discussed in Chapter 8, and if necessary commission another study, which should be appropriately funded, to collect further information.

Expansion of legal services to battered mothers

Surprising results from a recent study conducted at the Harborview Medical Center in Seattle found that battered mothers represented by legal aid attorneys had better outcomes than those represented by private attorneys.[13] Ninety percent of legal aid attorneys achieved safe outcomes for their clients compared to 63% of private attorneys. The authors of the study attribute this to the fact that private attorneys operate more within the conflict resolution model favored in family court, and are thus more likely to urge their clients to settle and avoid appearing hostile and confrontational. On the other hand, legal aid attorneys have received training through OVW grants on how to zealously represent their clients. The problem for battered mothers is lack of availability of these legal services, and the fact that many of them would not qualify for these services because their incomes are too high. Instead, middle class battered mothers have become impoverished and have had to file for bankruptcy after spending their life savings and that of their families fighting for custody of their abused children, and still losing. One solution would be to expand the legal services program for battered mothers, making them accessible to higher income women who would pay for these services on a sliding scale based on the Community Health Center model. In this way, they would receive the same excellent services as poor women, and their payments would go back into the clinic to cover costs, thus maximizing the benefits for all battered mothers. The current legislation, which has strict income requirements for legal aid eligibility for battered mothers, would have to be changed to accommodate such a program.

Conclusion

This book has tracked the historical course and current status of a problem that has been in existence for at least three decades, and which centers on the failure of family courts to take seriously the safety of mothers and children when making child custody determinations. The problem has its roots in a false set of doctrines and fixed beliefs that women are not credible, and lie about abuse in order to hurt men and gain an advantage over them especially in child custody disputes. This phenomenon, which I call the friendly parent mystique is entrenched in sexist and gender biased attitudes and assumptions designed to keep abused women in their place, just as the feminine mystique described half a century ago was designed to keep all women in their place. The consequences of the friendly parent mystique are devastating. Children are being ordered into dangerous custodial conditions where they may be physically abused and even raped, and their protective parents punished with jail, fines, and often, total loss of contact with their abused children. While some men are also victimized in this system, most of the victims are women. Contributing to this problem is a cadre of court-related professionals that uphold the friendly parent mystique, and enshrine it through the practice of their professional services. Many of these service providers receive government funding through fatherhood programs, which further establishes their legitimacy and camouflages the terrible harm that they are doing. The time is long overdue to shatter the myths that continue to devastate the lives of abused women and children, to bring a halt to the unethical practices supported by these myths, to finally achieve justice for them, and to end their suffering.

Notes

Introduction

1. Leora Rosen and Michelle Etlin, *The Hostage Child: Sex Abuse Allegations in Custody Disputes,* (Bloomington, Indiana University Press, 1996).
2. Phyllis Chesler, *Mothers on Trial: The Battle for Children and Custody,* (Chicago, IL, Chicago Review Press, 1986, 1987, 2011)
3. Karen Winner, *Divorced from Justice: The Abuse of Women and Children by Divorce Lawyers and Judges.* (New York, New York, Harpercollins, 1996)
4. Nancy Thoennes and Patricia Tjaden, "The Extent, Nature, and Validity of Sexual Abuse Allegations in Custody and Visitation Disputes." *Child Abuse and Neglect* 14, (1990): 151-163.
5. Supra Note 1.
6. Jay G. Silverman et al., "Child Custody Determinations in Cases Involving Intimate Partner Violence: A Human Rights Analysis," *American Journal of Public Health,* 94, no. 6 (2004): 951-957
7. Dianne Post, *Battered Mothers' Testimony Project: A Human Rights Approach to Child Custody and Domestic Violence.* (Arizona Coalition Against Domestic Violence, Phoenix, AZ, 2003); Sheila Heim et al., *Family Court Report 2002,* (California National Organization for Women, Sacramento, CA, 2002).
8. The Washington Post, *Conference Shines Light on the Plight of Battered Mothers Seeking Custody,* (May 10, 2013), Available at:http://www.washingtonpost.com/opinions/conference-shines-light-on-plight-of-battered-mothers-seeking-custody/2013/05/10/8a2830fc-b8f1-11e2-92f3-f291801936b8_story.html (Accessed July 22, 2014)
9. Amy Neustein and Michael Lesher, *From Madness to Mutiny: Why Mothers Are Running from the Family Court and What Can Be Done about It.* (Boston, Northeastern University Press, 2005)
10. See Garland Waller Productions. Available at: www.garland wallerproductions.com/PastProjects.html (Accessed July 22, 2014)
11. Id

12. "Breaking The Silence: Children's Stories," Available at: www.pbs.org/aboutpbs/news/0051221_breakingthesilence.ht ml (Accessed July 22, 2014)

13. "Children Lost in the System," Available at: http://www. Myfoxla.com/story /19671733/children-lost-in-the-system-of-our-nations-family-courts (Accessed July 22, 2014).

14. See for example: Mary Moewe, http://www.dailykos.com/ blog/MCMoewe; Anne Stevenson, http://www.commdiginews. com/life/dying-for-custody-part-1-doj-announces-investigation -into-connecticut-court-programs-4659/; Keith Harmon Snow, *The Worst Interests of the Child: The Trafficking of Children and Parents Through U.S. Family Courts,* (Atlanta, Burning Sage, 2016).

15. See United States Department of State on Human Rights: http://www.state.gov/j/drl/hr/ (Accessed July 21, 2014).

Chapter 1

1. Marvin Timothy Gray, "Historical Legal Context in Domestic Violence Custody Cases," in Mo Therese Hannah and Barry Goldstein (Eds.) *Domestic Violence, Abuse, and Child Custody.* (Kingston, NJ, Civic Research Institute, 2010), Chapter 3

2. According to rabbinic tradition, Moses received the Oral Law at Mount Sinai, the same time as he received the written law (the Torah), in the year 1313 before the Common Era. From then, tradition holds that the Oral Law was passed from teacher to student in an unbroken chain until rabbinic leaders committed it to writing beginning around the year 200 of the Common Era and continuing until the year 475.

3. Rabbi Yisroel Simcha Schorr and Rabbi Chaim Malinowitz (Eds.) Tractate Kesubos Volumes II and III (Brooklyn, New York, Art Scroll, Mesorah Publications 2010).

4. Jewish Virtual Library, *Modern Jewish History: Tacitus on the Jews* (c.110 C. E.) http://www.jewishvirtuallibrary.org/jsource /History/tacitus.html

5. Ramsey Laing Klaff, "The Tender Years Doctrine: A Defense." California Law Review, 70, no. 2 (1982): 340

6. Pearce Stevenson, Esq. *A plain letter to the Lord Chancellor on the Infant Custody Bill.* London, James Ridgeway, Piccadilly, (1839): 3-4. Available at: http://webapp1.dlib.indiana.edu/ vwwp/view?docId=VAB7126 (Accessed July 7th 2014)

7. Diane Atkinson, The Criminal Conversation of Mrs. Norton. (Chicago, Chicago Review Press, 2013), 132.
8. Id at 12-16
9. Id at 301-303
10. Supra Note 6 at 61-68
11. Supra Note 7 at 207
12. British 19th century grounds for divorce. Available at: http://www.parliament.uk/about/livingheritage/transformingsociety/private-lives/relationships/overview/divorce/ (Accessed July 7, 2014).
13. Supra Note 6
14. Id at 14
15. Id at 25
16. Id at 41-42
17. Id at 43
18. Id at 46
19. Naomi R. Cahn, "Faithless Wives and Lazy Husbands: Gender Norms in Nineteenth Century Divorce Law." *University of Illinois Law Review*, (2002): 651: 23-26 Available at: http://scholarship.law.gwu.edu/faculty_publications (Accessed July 7, 2014).
20. Id
21. Id
22. U.S. Department of Health, Education, and Welfare, Public Health Service. *100 Years of Marriage and Divorce Statistics, 1867-1967.* (Health Resources Administration, National Center for Health Statistics, Rockville, MD, 1973).
23. Id at 19
24. Meyer H. Weinstein, "Mental Cruelty as Grounds for Divorce," *Marquette Law Review*, 17, no. 2 (1933) 101-113.
25. Alison Clarke-Stewart and Cornelia Brentano, *Divorce: Causes and Consequences.* (New Haven, CT, Yale University Press, 2007), 9.
26. Supra Note 22 at 19
27. Supra Note 19 at 49-53
28. Id at 74
29. Supra Note 6 at 251

Chapter 2

1. Supra Introduction Note 9 at xiv
2. History of the New York Society for the Prevention of Cruelty to

Children. Available at: http://www.nyspcc.org/nyspcc/history/ the response/ (Accessed July 1, 2014).

3. John E.B. Myers, "A Short History of Child Protection in the United States," *Family Law Quarterly*, 42(2008-2009): 452-453

4. The Children's Bureau Centennial: The Story of the Children's Bureau: Available at: https://cb100.acf.hhs.gov/Cb_ebrochure (Accessed July 1, 2014).

5. Supra Note 3

6. C. Henry Kempe, et al., "The Battered Child Syndrome," *Journal of the American Medical Association*, 181 (1962): 17- 24.

7. Supra Note 3 at 456

8. About CAPTA: A Legislative History. Available at: https://www.childwelfare.gov/pubs /factsheets/about.cfm (Accessed July 1, 2014)

9. Title XX are social service block grants created by the Social Security Act of 1975 (Public Law 93-647) and provided to States for a number of social policy goals included remedying abuse and neglect of children, and preserving, rehabilitating or reuniting families. Interestingly, Title XX provided the first federal funds for establishing shelters for battered women.

10. Description of the Adoption Assistance and Child Welfare Act of 1980. Available at: https://www.childwelfare.gov/systemwide /laws_policies/federal/index.cfm?event=federalLegislation.vie wLegis&id=22 (Accessed July 1, 2014)

11. Richard Gelles, *The Book of David: How Preserving Families Can Cost Children's Lives.* (New York, NY, Basic Books, 1977).

12. Adoption and Safe Families Act of 1997: Summary. Available at: http://www.cwla.org/advocacy/asfapl105-89summary.htm (Accessed July 1, 2014).

13. Susan Schechter, *Women and Male Violence: The Vision and Struggles of the Battered Women's Movement.* (Cambridge, MA., South End Press, 1982.)

14. Susan Brownmiller, *Against Our Will: Men, Women and Rape.* (New York, Fawcett, The Ballantine Publishing Group, 1975.)

15. Del Martin, *Battered Wives*, (Volcano, CA, Volcano Press, 1976)

16. J.E. Snell, R.J. Rosenwald and A. Robey, "The Wifebeater's Wife: A Study of Family Interaction. *Archives of General Psychiatry*, 11 (1964): 107-112

17. Supra Note 13 at 113-122

18. Supra Note 13 at 137

19. Supra Note 13 at 195, 198

20. Brief description of the Family Violence Prevention and Services Act. Available at: http://nnedv.org/policy/issues/fvpsa.html (Accessed July 1, 2014)

21. Murray A. Straus, Richard J. Gelles and Suzanne K. Steinmetz, *Behind Closed Doors: Violence in the American Family.* (Garden City, NY, Anchor Books, 1980)

22. See for example the "Gender Symmetry" debate in *Violence Against Women*, 12 (11) 2006

23. John Hamel, *Gender Inclusive Treatment of Intimate Partner Abuse.* (New York, NY: Springer Publishing Company 2005).

24. Supra Note 13 at 324

25. Evan Stark and Anne Flitcraft, "Women and Children at Risk: A Feminist Perspective on Child Abuse," *International Journal of Health Services*, 18 (1988): 97-118; L.H. Bowker, M. Arbitell, and J.R.McFerron, "On the Relationship Between Wife Beating and Child Abuse." In K. Yllo and M Bogards (Eds.) *Feminist Perspectives on Wife Abuse.* (Newsbury Park, CA: Sage, 1988) 158-174.

26. For a review of early studies see B.B. Robbie Rossman, "Longer Term Effects of Exposure to Domestic Violence." In Sandra A. Graham Berman and Jeffrey L. Edelson (Eds.) *Domestic Violence in the Lives of Children: The Future of Research, Intervention, and Social Policy.* (Washington, DC, American Psychological Association, 2002) 35-66.

27. Susan Schechter and Jeffrey L. Edelson, *Effective Intervention in Domestic Violence and Child Maltreatment Cases: Guidelines for Policy and Practice.* (Reno Nevada, National Council of Juvenile and Family Court Judges, 1999).

28. Linda Gordon, *Heroes of Their Own Lives: The Politics and History of Family Violence—Boston 1880-1960.* (New York: Viking, 1988) 22

29. Jeffrey Moussaieff Masson, *Assault on the Truth: Freud's Suppression of the Seduction Theory.* (New York, NY, Farrar, Straus and Giroux, 1984).

30. Florence Rush, "The Sexual Abuse of Children: A Feminist Point of View," in N. Connell and C. Wilson (Eds.) *Rape: The first Sourcebook for Women.* (New York, NY, New American Library, 1974) 64-75.

31. Supra Note 29

32. Louise Armstrong, *Rocking the Cradle of Sexual Politics: What Happened When Women Said Incest.* (London, The Women's

Press, 1996. First published in the United States by Addison-Wesley Publishing Company, 1994) 20-24

33. Id at 41
34. Id at 42
35. Louise Armstrong, *Kiss Daddy Goodnight*, (Pocket Books Publishing Company, 1978)
36. Judith Lewis Herman, "Father Daughter Incest", *Signs*, 2, no. 4 (1977): 735-757.
37. Sandra Butler, *Conspiracy of Silence: The Trauma of Incest.* (Volcano, CA, Volcano Press, 1978, 1985, 1996)
38. David Finkelhor, *Sexually Victimized Children,* (New York, NY, The Free Press 1979, 1981)
39. Diana E.H. Russell, "The Incidence and Prevalence of Intrafamilial and Extrafamilial Sexual Abuse of Female Children." *Child Abuse and Neglect,* 7 (1983): 133-146.
40. CHILDHELP history: http://www.childhelp.org/pages/ (Accessed July 1, 2014)
41. Supra Note 32 at 101, 105-106
42. Katharine Ramsland, "The McMartin Day Care Case," Crimelibrary. Available at: www.crimelibrary.com/criminal_mind/psychology/mcmartin_daycare/1hltm
43. Sena Gurvin et al., "More Than Suggestion: The Effects of Interviewing Techniques from the McMartin Preschool Case. Journal of Applied Psychology, 83, no. 3 (1988) 347-359.
44. Supra Note 32 at 207
45. Supra Note 32 at 5, 174-175
46. Diana Russell, "The Great Incest War: Moving Beyond Polarization." Introduction to the second edition of *The Secret Trauma: Incest in the Lives of women and Girls,* (New York: Basic Books/Perseus Press, 1999) xvii-xlii. Reprinted in *Coalition Commentary: A Publication of the Illinois Coalition Against Sexual Assault*, (Spring, 2000): 1, 3-15
47. Id
48. Supra Note 32 at 123
49. Supra Note 32 at 134
50. Supra Introduction, Note 9 at xv
51. Supra Note 32 at 162
52. The Leadership Council on Child Abuse and Interpersonal Violence: www.leadershipcouncil.org
53. Mo Therese Hannah, "Truth Commission: Findings and Recommendations," In Mo Therese Hannah and Barry Goldstein

235

(Eds.) *Domestic Violence, Abuse, and Custody: Legal Strategies and Policy Issues*, (Kingston, NJ, Civic Research Institute, 2010) 8-1

54. Domestic Violence Legal Empowerment and Appeals Project: www.dvleap.org
55. Child Justice: www.child-justice.org
56. Protective Parents Coalition: www.ppcforchange.com
57. Mothers Against Court Custody Abuse: www.maccabuse.org
58. Safe Kids International: www.safekidsinternational.org
59. Supra Introduction Note 2
60. Supra Note 32
61. Supra Introduction Note 3
62. Supra Introduction Note 1
63. Supra Note 32 at 174
64. Supra Note 32 at 191
65. Supra Introduction Note 9
66. Mo Therese Hannah and Barry Goldstein (Eds.) *Domestic Violence, Abuse, and Custody: Legal Strategies and Policy Issues*, (Kingston, NJ, Civic Research Institute, 2010).
67. Barry Goldstein and Elizabeth Liu, *Representing The Domestic Violence Survivor: Critical Legal Issues; Effective Safety Strategies*, (Kingston, NJ, Civic Research Institute, 2013).
68. Barry Goldstein, *The Quincy Solution: Stop Domestic Violence and Save $500 Billion*, (Brandon, OR, Robert D. Reed Publishers, 2014).
69. See for example: Wendy Titleman, *A Mother's Journal, Book One: Let My Children Go!* (New Orleans, LA, Kinderlex Books, 2003); Maralee McLean, *Prosecuted But Not Silenced: Courtroom Reform for Sexually Abused Children*, (Mustang, Oklahoma, Tate Publishing, 2012); Doreen Ludwig, *Motherless America: Confronting Welfare's Fatherhood Custody Program*, (Amazon, 2015).
70. Supra Introduction, Note 9 at 10
71. Id at 36
72. Supra Introduction Note 1 at 163
73. Supra Chapter 1 Note 1 at 34-35
74. Supra Introduction Note 9 at 12
75. Evan Stark, *Coercive Control: The Entrapment of Women in Personal Life*, (Oxford, Oxford University Press, 2007)
76. Id at 205
77. Supra Note 32 at 29

78. Lundy Bancroft and Jay Silverman, *The Batterer as Parent: Addressing the Impact of Domestic Violence in Family Dynamics.* (Sage Publications, Sage Series on Violence Against Women, Thousand Oaks, CA, 2002) Chapter 4

79. Rahila Gupta, "'Victim' vs. 'Survivor': Feminism and Language," *50.50 Inclusive Democracy*, June 16, 2014. Available at: www.opendemocracy.net/5050/rahila-gupta/victim-vs-survivor-feminism-and-language, (Accessed 11/11/2016).

Chapter 3

1. U.S. Census Bureau, "Births, Deaths, Marriages and Divorces," *Statistical Abstracts of the United States 2012*, 65. Available at: http://www.census.gov/prod/2011pubs/12statab/vitstat.pdf (Accessed July 8, 2014)

2. Robert H. Mnookin, "Child-Custody Adjudication: Judicial Functions in the Face of Indeterminacy." *Law and Contemporary Problems*, 39, no. 3 (1975): 234-236.

3. Ramsey Laing Klaff, "The Tender Years Doctrine: A Defense," *California Law Review*, 70, no. 2 (1982): 336

4. Id at 344

5. Eleanor E. Maccoby and Robert H. Mnookin, *Dividing the Child: Social and Legal Dilemmas of Custody.* (Cambridge, MA, Harvard University Press, 1992, 1994), 284

6. Linda Henry Elrod, "Federalization of Child Support Guidelines", *Journal of the American Academy of Matrimonial Lawyers*, 6, *(1990): 106*

7. Alison Clarke-Stewart and Cornelia Brentano, *Divorce: Causes and Consequences.* (New Haven, CT, Yale University Press, 2007), 10

8. Supra Note 6 at 111

9. For early history of the Fathers Rights Movement see: http://www.marylandfathers.org/ FUERhistory.html (Accessed July 22, 2014)

10. David Levy, "Children's Advocate Paul Robinson Passes Away At 88." *National Parents Organization*, Our Blog (undated). Available at: https://nationalparentsorganization.org/blog/ 18949-childrens-advocate (Accessed July 8, 2014)

11. Leora N. Rosen, Molly Dragiewicz and Jennifer C. Gibbs, "Fathers' Rights Groups: Demographic Correlates and Impact on

Custody Policy," *Violence Against Women*, 15, no.5, (May 2009):513-531

12. Supra Note 6 at 124
13. Supra Introduction Note 7 at 10, Sheila Heim et al., 2002
14. American Bar Association, Center on Children and the Law, August, 1989: Available at: http://www.americanbar.org/groups/child_law/tools_to_use/attorneys/joint_custody.html (Accessed July, 8, 2014)
15. Dianne Post, "Arguments Against Joint Custody," *Berkeley Journal of Gender, Law and Justice*, 4, no. 2, (September 1989): 316-325
16. Gabrielle Davis, et al., *Dangers of Presumptive Joint Physical Custody*, (Battered Women's Justice Project, Minneapolis, MN, May 2010). Available at: http://www.thelizlibrary.org/liz/Dangers-of-Presumptive-Joint-Custody.pdf (Accessed July 8, 2014)
17. Supra Note 5 at 284-285
18. U.S. Census Bureau, *Custodial Mothers and Fathers and Their Child Support: 2011. Series P60-246, Current Population Survey, Table 9.* (Washington, D.C., U.S. Department of Commerce, April 2012) Available at: https://www.census.gov/people/child support/data/files/chldu11.pdf. (Accessed July 8, 2014).
19. Supra Note 5 at 113
20. Id at 100-101
21. Id at 199-201
22. Id at 137
23. Id at 152
24. Janet R. Johnston, "High Conflict Divorce," *The Future of Children*, 4. No. 1 (1994), 168
25. Dennis P. Saccuzzo, Nancy E. Johnson, and Wendy J. Koen, Mandatory *Custody Mediation: Empirical Evidence of Increased Risk for Domestic Violence Victims and Their Children.* National Criminal Justice Reference Service, Report No. 195422, April 2003, NIJ Grant No. 1999-WT-VX-0015
26. Id at 17
27. Supra Note 5 at 294
28. Id at 148
29. Id at 91
30. Supra Note 23
31. Supra Note 24 at 28
32. Supra Introduction Note 1 at 62

33. Id at 141-43
34. Gender Bias Study of the Court System in Massachusetts, New England Law Review, 24 (Spring 1990): 745
35. Id at 840
36. Id at 844
37. Supra Introduction Note 2 at xiv
38. Joyanna Silberg, How Many Children Are Court-Ordered Into Unsupervised Contact With Abusive Parents After Divorce? The Leadership Council on Child Abuse and Interpersonal Violence, September 22, 2008, Available at: http://www.leadership council.org/1/med/PR3.html (Accessed Nov 4, 2016).
39. The Women's Law Center of Maryland. (2004). Custody and financial distribution in Maryland: An empirical study of custody and divorce cases filed in Maryland during fiscal year 1999. Towson, MD. http://www.wlcmd.org/pdf/Custody Financial DistributionInMD.pdf
40. Mary A. Kernic et al., "Children in the Crossfire: Child Custody Determinations Among Couples With a History of Intimate Partner Violence," *Violence Against Women*, 11 no. 8 (2005): 991-1021
41. Mary A. Kernic, (2015). Impact of legal representation on child custody decisions among families with a history of intimate partner violence study. Final Report, National Institute of Justice grant No. 2010-IJ-CX-0022
42. Supra Introduction Note 4
43. Supra Chapter 3 Note 6; See also Supra Note 39
44. Supra Note 36 at 79
45. Kathleen Coulborn Faller, and Ellen DeVoe, "Allegations of Sexual Abuse in Divorce," *Journal of Child Sexual Abuse*, 4, no. 4 (1995): 1-25.
46. Amy Neustein and Anne Goetting, "Judicial Responses to the Protective Parents' Complaint of Child Sexual Abuse." *Journal of Child Sexual Abuse*, 8, no. 4 (1999): 103-122
47. Supra Introduction Note 6
48. Supra Introduction Note 7, Sheila Heim, 2002
49. Supra Introduction Note 7, Dianne Post, 2003 p 48
50. Joan Meier, Custody Outcomes in Cases with Abuse and Alienation Allegations. Domestic Violence Legal Empowerment Project.

Chapter 4

1. H.CON.RES.172—Expressing the sense of Congress that, for purposes of determining child custody, credible evidence of physical abuse of ones spouse should create a statutory presumption that it is detrimental to the child to be placed in the custody of the abusive spouse. Enacted October 26, 1990.

2. Resource Center on Domestic Violence: Child Protection and Custody, a project of the Family Violence and Domestic Relations Program (FVDR) of the National Council of Juvenile and Family Court Judges (NCJFCJ). "Domestic Violence as a Factor to be Considered in Custody/Visitation Determinations." Available at: http://www.ncjfcj.org/ sites/default/files/chart-custody-dv-as-a-factor.pdf, (Accessed 11/7/2016.)

3. National Council of Juvenile and Family Court Judges, *Model Code on Domestic and Family Violence*, (Reno, Nevada, National Council of Juvenile and Family Court Judges, January 1994). Available at: http://www.ncjfcj.org/resourcelibrary/ publications/model-code-domestic-and-family-violence (Accessed July 3, 2014)

4. Id at 33

5. Rebecca E. Shiemke, "Domestic Violence: Legal Remedies in Other States." *Michigan Bar Journal, Domestic Violence Awareness,* September 2011, 37. Available at: https://www.michbar.org/journal/pdf/pdf4article1908.pdf (Accessed August 4, 2014).

6. Allison C. Morrill et al., "Child Custody and Visitation Decisions When the Father Has Perpetrated Violence Against the Mother," *Violence Against Women,* 11, no. 8(2005): 1076-1107;

7. California Legislative Information, SB-1716 Child custody proceedings: allegations of sexual abuse. (1999-2000) Available at: http://leginfo.legislature.ca.gov/faces/billNavClient.xhtml? bill_id=199920000SB1716&search_keywords= (Accessed July 10, 2014)

8. California Legislative Information, SB-33 Child sexual abuse (2005-2006). Available at: http://leginfo.legislature.ca.gov/ faces/billNavClient.xhtml?bill_id=200520060SB33&search_key words= (Accessed July 10, 2014).

9. California Legislative Information, AB-2893 Sex offenders: child custody and visitation. (2005-2006) Available at: http://leginfo.

legislature.ca.gov/faces/billNavClient.xhtml?bill_id=200520060 AB2893&search_keywords= (Accessed July 10, 2014)

10. California Legislative Information, AB-612 Child custody evaluations. (2007-2008) Available at: http://leginfo.legislature. ca.gov/faces/billNavClient.xhtml?bill_id=200720080AB612& search_keywords= (Accessed July 10, 2014).

11. California State Auditor, Report 2009-109 Summary, January-2011. Available at: http://www.bsa.ca.gov/reports/summary /2009-109 (Accessed July 15, 2014)

12. California Legislative Information, AB-939 Family law proceedings (2009-2010.) AB-1050 Child custody: preferences of child. (2009-2010) Available at: http://leginfo.legislature. ca.gov/ faces/billNavClient.xhtml?bill_id=200920100AB1050& search_keywords= (Accessed July 10, 2014).

13. California Legislative Information, AB-1050 Child custody: preferences of child. (2009-2010). Available at: http://leginfo. legislature.ca.gov/faces/billNavClient.xhtml?bill_id=200920100 AB1050&search_keywords=(Accessed July 10, 2014).

14. California Legislative Information, SB-924 Damages: childhood sexual abuse: statute of limitations. (2013-2014) Available at: http://leginfo.legislature.ca.gov/faces/billNavClient.xhtml? bill_id =201320140SB924&search_keywords= (Accessed July 10, 2014).

15. Joan S. Meier, Pilot data for "Child Custody Outcomes in Cases Involving Parental Alienation or Abuse Claims," http://nij.gov/ funding/awards/pages/award-detail.aspx?award=2014-MU-CX-0859 (last visited August 13, 2016)(on file with author)

16. William Glaberson, "Determined to be Heard," The New York Times, October 2, 1988, Available at: http://www.nytimes.com /1988/10/02/magazine/determined-to-be-heard.html? pagewanted=all, (Accessed July 11, 2016

17. Crocker Stephenson, "Boy at Center of Famous 'Poor Joshua!' Supreme Court Dissent Dies," The Journal Sentinel, November 11, 2015. Available at: http://archive.jsonline.com/news /obituaries/joshua12b99614381z1-346259422.html, (Accessed July 11, 2016.)

18. DeShaney v. Winnebago Department of Social Services, 812 F. 2d 298, at p. 304

19. DeShaney v. Winnebago County Department of Social Services (No. 87-154) Supreme Court Decision, Available at:

https://www.law.cornell.edu/supremecourt/text/489/189, (Accessed July 11, 2016)

20. Supra, Note 17.
21. Idividually and as Next Best Friend of Her Deceased Minor Children, Gonzales et al. Certiorari to the United States Court of Appeals for the Tenth Circuit, No. 04-278. Argued March 25, 2005—Decided June 27, 2005.
22. Inter-American Commission on Human Rights, Report No. 80/11, Case 12.626, Merits, Jessica Lenahan (Gonzales) et al. United States, July 21, 2011
23. David J. Lansner, "The Nicholson Decisions: New York's Response to 'Failure to Protect' Allegations," *American Bar Association Commission on Domestic Violence eNewsletter*, 12, (Fall 2008). Available at: http://www.americanbar.org/content /newsletter/publications/cdv_enewsletter_home/vol12_expert 1. html, (Accessed November 7, 2016)
24. Jack B. Weinstein, *Memorandum of Finding of Fact of Law and Order*, United States District Court, Eastern District of New York, Nicholson v. Scopetta, (March1, 2001) 158. Available at: http://news.findlaw.com/hdocs/docs/nyc/nchlsnwllms030102 drft.pdf. (Accessed July 6, 2014)
25. Id at 168
26. Michelle Etlin, "Slavery, Misogyny, and Child Oppression: The Common Denominator," *Journal of the Task Group on Child Custody Issues of the National Organization of Men Against Sexism*, 8, no.1 (Spring 1996): 1-9
27. Rashida Manjoo, Report of the Special Rapporteur on Violence Against Women, Its Causes and Consequences: Addendum, Mission to the United States of America," *United Nations General Assembly, Human Rights Council, Seventeenth Session, Agenda Item 3: Promotion and Protection of All Human Rights, Civil, Political, Economic, Social and Cultural, Including the Right to Development.* June 6, 2011

Chapter 5

1.   Joseph Sorge and James Scurlock, *Divorce Corp.*, (Jackson, WY, DC Books LLC, 2013) xv
2.   Id at 15
3.   Id at 123

4. Phillip Greenspun's weblog, posted November 12, 2014 http://blogs.harvard.edu/philg/2014/11/12/the-billion-dollars-of-premarital-property-oklahoma-divorce/
5. Anne Stevenson , "Dying For Custody (Part 1): DOJ Announces Investigation Into Connecticut Court." *Communities Digital News*, January 25, 2014. Available at: http://www.commdig inews.com/life/dying-for-custody-part-1-doj-announces-investigation-into-connecticut-court-programs-4659/; Michael Volpe, "Making Divorce Pay." *Capital Research Center*, July 2015. Available at: www.capitalresearch.org (Accessed 11/29/2016).
6. Supra Introduction Note 14, Keith Harmon Snow at 22.
7. Statement Regarding Divorce Corp. from Judge Sol Gothard available at: http://www.centerforjudicialexcellence.org/wp-content/uploads/2014/02/Sol-Gothard-Divorce-Corp-Statement.pdf (accessed October 10, 2016)
8. Supra Chapter 2 Note 69, Maralee McLean
9. Supra Chapter 2 Note 69, Wendy Titelman, at 110
10. Supra Chapter 2 Note 69, Doreen Ludwig
11. Supra Introduction, Note 14, Keith Harmon Snow at 212
12. Supra Note 5, Michael Volpe.
13. Anne Stevenson, "CT Court Employees Face Tough Questions Over Conflicts of Interest." *The Washington Times Communities*. May 20, 2013. Available at: http://www.thelizlibrary.org/mothers/130520-wash-times.pdf
14. Supra Introduction, Note 14, Keith Harmon Snow at 139
15. Supra Note 13
16. Id.
17. Meyer Elkin Interviewed at his home by David Kordoba available at: https://libraries.usc.edu/sites/default/files/elkin_meyer.pdf (accessed October 10, 2016)
18. Family Court Review Hofstra: An Interdiscilinary Journal. Available at: http://onlinelibrary.wiley.com/journal/10.1111/(ISSN)1744-1617
19. M.J. Ackerman and M.C. Ackerman, "Child Custody Evaluation Practices: A 1996 Survey of Psychologists." Family Law Quarterly, 30, no. 3 (1996): 565-585.
20. (M.J. Ackerman and T.B. Pritzl, "Child Custody Evaluation Practices: A 20-Year Follow-Up." Family Court Review, 49, (2011): 618-628.

21. J.N. Bow and P. Boxer, "Assessing Allegations of Domestic Violence In Child Custody Evaluations." *Journal of Interpersonal Violence,* 18, no. 12 (2003): 1394-1410

22. L.S. Horvath, T. Logan, and R. Walker, "Child Custody Cases: A Content Analysis of Evaluations in Practice." *Professional Psychology: Research and Practice,* 33 (2002): 557-565.

23. Nancy E. Johnson, Dennis P. Saccuzzo, and Wendy J. Koen, "Child Custody Mediation in Cases of Domestic Violence: empirical Evidence of a Failure to Protect," *Violence Against Women,* 11, no. 8 (2005): 1022-1053.

24. Murray Straus, "The Conflict Tactic Scales and its Critics: An Evaluation and New Data on Validity and Reliability," In M.A. Straus and R.J. Gelles (Eds.), (pp. 48-73). New Brunswick, N.J.: Transaction Publishers.

25. Shannon Catalano, *Special Report: Intimate Partner Violence: Attributes of Victimization 1993-2011,* Bureau of Justice Statistics, Office of Justice Programs, U.S. Department of Justice, November, 2013.

26. Michael Johnson, "Patriarchal Terrorism and Common Couple Violence: Two Forms of Violence Against Woman," *Journal of Marriage and the Family,* 57 (1995): 283-294

27. Michael P. Johnson, "Conflict and Control: Gender Symmetry and Asymmetry in Domestic Violence, *Violence Against Women,* 12, no.11 (2006): 1003-1018.

28. Leora N. Rosen, "Origin and Goals of the 'Gender Symmetry' Workshop," *Violence Against Women,* 12, no. 11 (2006): 997-1002.

29. Joan S. Meier, "Johnson's Differentiation Theory: Is It Really Empirically Supported?" *Journal of Child Custody,* 12 (2015): 4-24.

30. Michael P. Johnson, *A Typology of Domestic Violence: Intimate Terrorism, Violent Resistance, and Situational Couple Violence,* (2008): Northeastern University Press, p 330.

31. Irene H. Frieze, "Investigating the Causes and Consequences of Marital Rape," *Signs,* 8 (1983): 532-553; Irene H. Frieze and M.C. Hughe, "Power and Influence Strategies in Violent and Nonviolent Marriages," *Psychology of Women Quarterly,* 16 (1992): 449-465.

32. J.V. Frye, J. Manganello, Jacquelyn C. Campbell et al., "The Distribution of and Factors Associated with Intimate Terrorism and Situational Couple Violence Among a Population-Based

Sample of Urban Women in the United States," *Journal of Interpersonal Violence*, 21, no. 10 (2006): 1286-1313.

33. Nancy Ver Steegh and Clare Dalton, "Report From The Wingspread Conference on Domestic Violence and Family Courts." *Family Court Review*, 46, no. 3 (2008):458; Nancy Ver Steegh, "Differentiating Types of Domestic Violence: Implications for Child Custody,: *Louisiana Law Review*, 65 (2005): 1379-1431. Victims of Intimate Terrorism need comprehensive safety planning, especially around the time of separation when the perpetrator's need to control may escalate. p 1390

34. Id Report From The Wingspread Conference on Domestic Violence and Family Courts

35. Jason S. Hans, Jennifer L. Hardesty, Megan L. Haselschwerdt and Laura M. Frey, "The Effects of Domestic Violence Allegations s on Custody Evaluator's Recommendations." *Journal of Family Psychology*, 28, no. 6 (2014): 957-966.

36. Daniel G. Saunders, Kathleen C. Faller, and Richard M. Tolman, "Child Custody Evaluators' Beliefs About Domestic Abuse Allegations: Their Relationship to Evaluator Demographics, Background, Domestic Violence Knowledge and Custody-Visitation Recommendations," Final Report to the National Institute of Justice, Grant #2007-WG-BX-0013, June, 2012, p. 69

37. Id at 67.

38. Michael S. Davis, Chis S. O'Sullivan, Kim Susser et al., "Custody Evaluations When There Are Allegations of Domestic Violence: Practices, Beliefs, and Recommendation of Professional Evaluators," Final Report Submitted to the National Institute of Justice, Grant #2007-WG-BX-0001, November 2010.

39. Gardner, R.A. (1987). The Parental Alienation Syndrome and the differentiation between fabricated and genuine child sex abuse. Cresskill, NJ: Creative Therapeutics.

40. Bruch, C.S. (2001). Parental Alienation Syndrome and Parental Alienation: Getting it wrong in child custody cases. Family Law Quarterly, 35, 527–552, p 550

41. Id

42. Supra Introduction Note 4

43. Faller, K.C. (1998). The Parental Alienation Syndrome: What is it and what data support it?. Child Maltreatment, 3(2), 100–115.

44. Joan S. Meier, "A Historical Perspective on Parental Alienation Syndrome and Parental Alienation," Journal of Child Custody, 6 (2009) p 240

45. Id at 239; NDAA: http://www.ndaa.org/ncpcaupdate_v16_no7.html

46. Stephanie Dalam, "Dr. Richard Gardner: A review of his theories and opinions on atypical sexuality, pedophilia, and treatment issues," *Treating Abuse Today*, 8, no. 1 (1998): 15–22.

47. Kelly, J.B., & Johnston, J.R. (2001). The alienated child: A reformulation of Parental Alienation Syndrome. Family Court Review, 39(3), 249–266.

48. Id at 255

49. Id at 257

50. Id at 258

51. Supra Note 40 at 246

52. Johnston, J.R. (2005). Children of divorce who reject a parent and refuse visitation: Recent research and social policy implications for the alienated child. Family Law Quarterly, 38, 757–775.

53. Association of Family and Conciliation Courts, *Guidelines for Examining Intimate Partner Violence: A Supplement to the AFCC Model Standards of Practice for Child Custody Evaluation*. April, 2016.

54. Supra, Note 44 at 234

55. Sandra A. Graham Berman and Jeffrey L. Edelson (Eds.) *Domestic Violence in the Lives of Children: The Future of Research, Intervention, and Social Policy*. (Washington, DC, American Psychological Association, 2002), p 3.

56. Evan Stark, " Comments on AFCC Proposed Guidelines on Custody and IPV," Undated Memorandum Sent to Peter Salem and Loretta Frederick.

57. Supra Note 36 at 92

58. Jennifer L. Hardesty, Jason S. Hans, Megan L. Haselschwerdt, Lyndal Khaw, and Kimberly A. Crossman, "The Influence of Divorcing Mothers' Demeanor on Custody Evaluators' Assessment of Their Domestic Violence Allegations." *Journal of Child Custody*, 12, no. 1 (2015): 47-70.

59. Supra Note 56

60. Pamela C. Alexander, "Stages of Change and Group Treatment of Batterers," *Final Report to The National Institute of Justice*, Grant # 2004-WG-BX-0001, August 2009

61. Nancy S. Erickson, "Use of the MMPI-2 in Child Custody evaluations Involving Battered Women: What Does Psychological Research Tell Us?" Family Law Quarterly, 39 (2005): 87-89

62. Peter Salem, Debra Kulak, and Robin M. Deutch, "Triaging Family Court Services: The Connecticut Judicial Branch's Family Civil Intake Screen." *Pace Law Review*, 27, no. 4 (2007): 741-783

63. Id at 758.

64. Id at 764.

65. Pennsylvania Bar Association, *Commission for Justice Initiatives, Changing The Culture of Custody in Pennsylvania: Report and Recommendations.* May, 2007. Available at: https://www.pabar.org/public/committees/CJI/Changing%20t he%20Culture%20of%20Custody%20Committce%20Report% 20and%20Recommendation.pdf

66. Id at 25

67. Id at 29

68. Peter G. Jaffe, Claire V. Crooks, and Nicholas Bala, "A Framework for Addressing Allegations of Domestic Violence in Child Custody Disputes," *Journal of Child Custody*, 6 (2009): 169-188, p 180.

69. Id at 32

70. Nancy Ver Steegh, Gabrielle Davis, and Loretta Frederick, "Look Before You Leap: Court System Triage of Family Law Cases Involving Intimate Partner Violence." *Marquette Law Review*, 95, (2012): 955-991

71. Id at 989

72. Supra Chapter 3 Note 40

73. Supra Note 56 at 380

74. Supra Chapter 2 Note 29

75. Supra Introduction Note 7, Sheila Heim et al 2002

76. Supra Introduction Note 7, Dianne Post, 2003

77. Rita Berg, "Parental Alienation Analysis, Domestic Violence, and Gender Bias in Minnesota Courts," *Law and Inequality*, 29, 5-31, 2011.

78. Keith Harmon Snow, CT Court Case Histories and Summaries, The Conscious Being Alliance, available at: http://www.consciousbeingalliance.com/2013/01/summary-of-connecticut-court-judicial-abuse-cases-january-2013#more (Accessed November 29, 2016).

79. Joyanna Silberg, How Many Children Are Court-Ordered Into Unsupervised Contact With Abusive Parents After Divorce? The Leadership Council on Child Abuse and Interpersonal Violence, September 22, 2008, Available at: http://www.leadership council.org/ 1/med/PR3.html (Accessed November 4, 2016)

80. Joan S. Meier, Pilot data for "Child Custody Outcomes in Cases Involving Parental Alienation or Abuse Claims," http://nij.gov/funding/awards/pages/award-detail.aspx?award= 2014-MU-CX0859 (last visited August 13, 2016)(on file with author) The author was awarded a three-year grant from the National Institute of Justice to expand this research; the results will be available by the end of 2017.

Chapter 6

1. Lisa M. Seghetti and Jerome P. Bjelopera, "The Violence Against Women Act: Overview, Legislation, and Federal Funding," *Congressional Research Service Report for Congress*, 7-5700, R42499 (Washington, D.C., Library of Congress, May 10, 2012.)

2. Public Hearing Before Assembly Task Force on Domestic Violence, (Trenton NJ, March 6, 1998) 132-133: http://www. njleg.state.nj.us/legislativepub/Pubhear/030698lb.PDF (Accessed July 2, 2014).

3. H.Con.Res. 182 (105th): *Expressing the Sense of Congress With Regard to Child Custody, Child Abuse, and Victims of Domestic and Family Violence*, Available at: https://www.govtrack.us/ congress/bills/105/hconres182 (Accessed November 29, 2016).

4. H.R. 3514: Violence Against Women Act of 1998(105th), March 19 1998. Available at: http://congress-bills.findthebest.com/l/ 88189/105-h-3514 (Accessed July 3, 2014)

5. Supra Note 1

6. Id

7. The Violence Against Women Reauthorization Act of 2013. Available at: http://www.gpo.gov/fdsys/pkg/BILLS-113s47enr /pdf/BILLS-113s47enr.pdf (Accessed July 3, 2014).

8. Memorandum from Bonnie Campbell, Director, Violence Against Women Office to Noel Brennan, Deputy Assistant Attorney General, Office of Justice Programs, RE: *Children Being Placed in Custody of Alleged Perpetrators of Physical and Sexual Child Abuse*, May 28, 1998.

9. Supra Chapter 2 Note 27
10. Id at 17-22
11. ICF International, *The Greenbook Initiative Final Evaluation Report, National Institute of Justice Grant No. 2000-MU-MU-0014.* (ICF International, Fairfax, VA, February 2009) Available at: http://aspe.hhs.gov/hsp/08/sr/greenbook/report.pdf (Accessed July 3, 2014).
12. Id at 47
13. Battered Women's Justice Project, "OVW Child Custody Differentiation Project: Progress Summary." (Battered Women's Justice Project, Minneapolis MN 2012) Available at: http://www.bwjp.org/files/bwjp/files/Custody_Project_History _and_Future_Directions.pdf (Accessed July 3, 2014).
14. Subcommittee on the District of Columbia, Committee on Government Reform and Oversight, House of Representatives, Hearing, HR 1855, To Amend Title 11 District of Columbia Code, To restrict the Authority of the Superior Court Over Certain Pending Cases Involving Child Custody and Visitation rights, August 4, 1995, 7-8. Available at: http://www.gpo.gov/fdsys/ pkg/CHRG-104hhrg36561/pdf/CHRG-104hhrg36561.pdf (Accessed July 9, 2014)
15. United States Court of Appeals for the District of Columbia Circuit (Appeal No. 97cv00929) Argued September 11, 2003, decided December 16, 2003 No. 02-5224, Doris R. Foretich et al., Appellants v. United States of America Office of the Attorney General and Jean Elizabeth Morgan Appellees, 11.
16. Id
17. Jonathan Turley, "Elizabeth Morgan Act and Legislating Family Values," November 20, 2007. Available at: http://jonathan turley.org/2007/11/20/elizabeth-morgan-act-and-legislating-family-values/ (Accessed July 9, 2014)
18. Supra Note 14 at 9
19. Talia Carner, *Puppet Child*, Otsego, MI, PageFree Publishing, Inc., July, 2002.
20. The Protective Parent Reform Act is available at: http://www.taliacarner.com/puppet-child/the-protective-parent-reform-act/
21. Nacha Cattan, "Rabbi Blau Weighs in on Custody Case," *Forward Magazine*, December 5, 2003.
22. Jennifer Friedlin, "Mothers Push Reforms in Family Courts' Handling of Custody Cases," *Forward Magazine*, December 17,

2004, Available at: http://forward.com/news/4005/mothers-push-reforms-in-family-courts-e2-80-99-handling/ (Accessed 11/15/2016).

23. Shauna R. Prewitt, "Giving Birth to a "Rapist's Child": A Discussion and Analysis of the Limited Legal Protections Afforded to Women Who Become Mothers Through Rape," *The Georgetown Law Journal*, 98, (2010): 827-862.

24. National Conference of State Legislatures, "Parental Rights and Sexual Assault," Available at: http://www.ncsl.org/research/human-services/parental-rights-and-sexual-assault.aspx (Accessed November 7, 2016)

25. H.R.1257 - Rape Survivor Child Custody Act, Available at: https://www.congress.gov/bill/114th-congress/house-bill/1257/text, (Accessed November 7, 2016)

26. Rape Abuse and Incest National Network, "Termination of Rapists Parental Rights Laws," Available at: https://apps.rainn.org/state-laws/landing-page/ (Accessed February 27, 2017)

27. Jason V. Owens, "Did Massachusetts Pass a Law Granting Parental rights to Rapists?" Stevenson, Lynch & Owens P.C., February 19, 2016. Available at: http://stevensonlynch.com/did-massachusetts-pass-a-law-granting-parental-rights-to-rapists/, (Accessed November 11, 2016)

28. Maryland State Bar Association, Position Statement to the House Judiciary Committee, March 3, 2016, House Bill 646-Family Law – Child Conceived Without Consent – Termination of Parental rights (Rape Survivor Family Protection Act). Position: Oppose. Available at: http://www.mcasa.org/_mcasaWeb/wp-content/uploads/2016/03/MSBA-Opposition-to-HB-646.pdf (Accessed November 11, 2016)

29. Overview of the Americans with Disabilities Act. Available at: www.ada.gov/ada_intro.htm

30. Overview of ADA 2008 Amendments, Available at: https://www.eeoc.gov/laws/regulations/ adaaa_fact_sheet.cfm

31. Karin Huffer, *Overcoming the Devastation of Legal Abuse Syndrome, Karin Huffer,* June 1995; Karin Huffer; Karin Huffer, *Legal Abuse Syndrome: 8 Steps for Avoiding the Traumatic Stress Caused by the Justice System*, Bloomington, IA, AuthorHouse, June, 2013.

32. Equal Access Advocates, Available at: www.equalaccessadvocates.com: Accessed 11/18/2016.

33. Karin Huffer, "New Opportunities to Learn How to Assist People

as a Certified ADA Advocate in Family Court," *Divorce in Connecticut,* September 4, 2016, Available at: http://divorcein connecticut.blogspot.com/search/label/DR.%20KARIN%20HUF FER (Accessed November 18, 2016).

34. H.Con.Res.150 - Expressing the sense of Congress that child safety is the first priority of custody and visitation adjudications, and that state courts should improve adjudications of custody where family violence is alleged. Available at: https://www. congress.gov/bill/114th-congress/house-concurrent-resolution /150. (Accessed November 18, 2016).

Chapter 7

1. Laura Morgan, Chair, Child Support Subcommittee, Family Law Section of the American Bar Association. Child Support Enforcement in the United States and the Role of the Private Bar. http://www.csecouncil.org/industry/reports/role-of-bar/#II

2. Id

3. Title IV-D paternity establishment (see https://www.law. cornell.edu/uscode/text/42/658a). NOTES: Good cause for noncooperation exceptions—physical or emotional harm including DV http://www.acf.hhs.gov/programs/css/resource/ good-cause-for-refusing-to-cooperate

4. National Conference of State Legislatures. Child Support 101: State Administration http://www.ncsl.org/research/human-services/ child-support-adminstration.aspx

5. Supra Note 1

6. Public Law 104-193-Aug. 22, 1996. Available at: http://www. gpo.gov/fdsys/pkg/PLAW104publ193/pdf/PLAW-104publ193. pdf (Accessed June 24, 2014).

7. Office of Child Support Enforcement, Evaluation of the Child Access Demonstration Projects. DCL-97-11. Available at: http://www.acf.hhs.gov/programs/css/resource/ evaluation-of-child-access-demonstration-projects (Accessed June 24, 2014).

8. Office of Child Support Enforcement, Administration for Children and Families, U.S. Department of Health and Human Services. "Access and Visitation Grant Program: FY 2013 Update."

9. Department of Health and Human Services Office of the Inspector General. *Effectiveness of Access and Visitation Grant Programs*, October 2001, OEI-05-02-00300. Available at: https://oig.hhs.gov/oei/reports/oei-05-02-00300.pdf (Accessed June 24, 2014).

10. Office of Child Support Enforcement, Final Rule: Grants to States for Access and Visitation Programs. AT-99-07, April 28, 1999. Available at: http://www.acf.hhs.gov/programs/css/ resource/final-rule150-grants-to-states-for-access-and-visitationprograms (Accessed June 24, 2014).

11. Dick Woods' open letter to Fathers' Rights organizations. Available at: http://web.archive.org/web/20000819085224/www.ncfc.net/aef.txt (Accessed June 24, 2014)

12. Letter from Dick Woods to Iowa State Representative Minette Doderer, December 21, 1992.

13. Obituaries: David G. Ross, commissioner with judge dies at 77, *Washington Post*, July 2, 2013. Available at: http://www.washingtonpost.com/local/obituaries/david-gross commissioner-and-judge-dies-at77/2013/07/02/08ba9fb6-e266-11e2-80eb-3145e2994a55_story.html (Accessed June 24, 2014).

14. Ron Haskins, "Work Over Welfare: The Inside Story of the 1996 Welfare Reform Law," (Washington, D.D., Brookings Institute, 2006).

15. Children's Rights Council, Family Advisory Board. Available at: http://www.crckids.org/about-us/who-we-are/familyadvisory-board/ (Accessed June 24, 2014)

16. Jessica Pearson & David Price, "Access and Visitation Programs: Promising Practices." Department of Health and Human Services, Administration for Children and Families, Office of Child Support Enforcement, 2004, p. ii

17. Id at ii

18. Sarah Avellar et al., Catalog of Research: Programs for Low-Income Fathers. OPRE Report 2011-20. Mathematica Policy Research, June 2011., p. 295

19. Supra Note 16, at 59.

20. Id 26

21. The NCAOC Access and Visitation Program. Available at: http://www.nccourts.org/Citizens/CPrograms/AVisitation/Documents/NCmodel.pdf (Accessed June 24, 2014).

22. Hamil R. Harris and Carol Morello, "Suspect Sought Ex-Wife in Md." *Washington Post, October* 30th 2002. Available at: http://www.washingtonpost.com/wpdyn/content/article/200 5/07/28/AR2005072800809_pf.html (Accessed June 24, 2014)

23. See Note 16 Supra at 56

24. Supra Note 8

25. Supra Note 16, at 64

26. Carmen Solomon-Fears, "Fatherhood Initiatives: Connecting Fathers to their Children", *Congressional Research Report for Congress*, Congressional Research Service, 7-5700, RL31025, January 28, 2014, 1 http://fas.org/sgp/crs/misc/RL31025.pdf (Accessed June 24, 2014)

27. Id at 8

28. Carmen Solomon-Fears, "Child Support Enforcement: New Reforms and Potential Issues," *CRC Report for Congress*, order code 97-408 EPW, Updated February 6 2002, 6. Available at: http://digital.library.unt.edu/ark:/67531/metacrs2806/m1/1/ high_res_d/97408epw_2002Feb06.pdf (Accessed June 24, 2014).

29. Supra Note 26 at 3

30. Theodora Ooms, Jacqueline Boggess, Anne Menard, Mary Myrick, Paula Roberts, Jack Tweedie, and Pamela Wilson "Building Bridges Between Healthy Marriage, Responsible Fatherhood, and Domestic Violence Programs: A Preliminary Guide." *Center for Law and Policy*, December 2006. http://www.clasp.org/resources-and-publications/archive/02 08.pdf (Accessed June 24, 2014)

31. Id at 8

32. Congressional Update, "New Law Would Establish Police-Station Type Transfers for Children," *Speak Out for Children*, Fall 2000/ Winter 2001, 14

33. Letter to Yevgenia Shockome from Dianne Witter, Director, YWCA Supervised Visitation Program, YWCA of Dutchess County, New York, August 12, 2003.

34. Supra Note 26 at 1

35. Sara McLanahan and Gary Sandefur, *Growing Up With a Single Parent: What Hurts, What Helps*, (Cambridge, MA, Harvard University Press, 1997) 3.

36. See for example, Sandra Graham-Berman, et al. "The Impact of Intimate Partner Violence and Additional Traumatic Events on Trauma Symptoms and PTSD in Preschool-Aged Children."

Journal of Traumatic Stress, 25, no. 4 (2012): 393-400; Christopher P. Fagundes, Robert Glaser, and Janice Kiecolt-Glaser, "Stressful Early Life Experiences and Immune Dysregulation Across the Lifespan," *Brain, Behavior and Immunity*, Jan: 27, no. 1 (2012): 8-12.

37. For example, the CRC Report (Supra Note 26 p. 8) notes that in the waiver evaluation, criminal history was the norm rather than the exception.

38. See R. L. Coley and B.L. Medeiros, "Reciprocal Longitudinal Relations Between Nonresident Father Involvement and Adolescent Delinquency." *Child Development,* 78, no. 1 (2007): 132–1; V. King, and J.M. Sobolewski, "Nonresident Fathers' Contributions to Adolescent Well-Being." *Journal of Marriage and Family* 68, no. 3 (2006): 537–557; S.R. Jaffee, et al., "Life With (or Without) Father: The Benefits of Living With Two Biological Parents Depend on the Father's Antisocial Behavior." *Child Development*, 74, no. 1 (2003): 109–126.

39. David S. DeGamo, "Coercive and Prosocial Fathering, Antisocial Personality, and Growth in Children's Post-Divorce Non-compliance," *Child Development*, March: 8, no. 2 (2010): 503-516.

40. Antisocial personality disorder (ASPD) is common in prison settings. Surveys of prisoners worldwide indicate a prevalence of antisocial personality disorder of 47% for men and 21% for women, See S. Fazel, and J. Danesh, "Serious Mental Disorder in 23,000 Prisoners: A Systematic Review of 62 Surveys." *Lancet*, 359 (2002): 545–550. The prevalence of ASPD in the general population is estimated to be only 0.6%. See M.F. Lenzenweger, et al, "DSM-IV Personality Disorders in the National Comorbidity Survey Replication." *Biological Psychiatry,* Sep 15; 62, no. 6 (2007): 553-564.

41. Anne Stevenson, "Connecticut Court Failure: The Deadly Rebranding of Joshua Komisarjevsky." *Communities Digital News*, February 25, 2014. Available at: http://www.commdig inews.com/life/connecticut-court-failure-the-deadly-rebranding-of-joshua-komisarjevsky-10607/ (Accessed June 23, 2014)

42. Office of the Assistant Secretary for Planning and Evaluation, "The National Evaluation of the Responsible Fatherhood, Marriage and Family Strengthening Grants for Incarcerated and Reentering Fathers and Their Partners" *Research in Brief,* May

2013. Available at: http://aspe.hhs.gov/hsp/13/MFSIPI mplementation/rpt_mmfsip.html (Accessed June 24, 2014).

43. Office of the Assistant Secretary for Planning and Evaluation, "Addressing Domestic Violence in Family Strengthening Programs for Couples Affected by Incarceration." *Research in Brief*, March 2013. Available at: http://aspe.hhs.gov/hsp/13/ MFSIPDomesticViolence/rb_domestic.cfm (Accessed June 24, 2014).

44. Supra Note 42

45. Jacinta Bronte-Tinkew, Jennifer Carrano, Sara Ericson & Kassim Mbwana, "Promising Practices in Self-Sufficiency & Employment Programs for Fathers: Evidence-Based and Evidence-Informed Research findings. *National Responsible Fatherhood Clearinghouse*, June 22nd, 2009

46. David Mandel & Associates, "Safe Engagement of Fathers When Domestic Violence is Present: Building A Model Response to Domestic Violence Within Responsible Fatherhood Programming." *David Mandel & Associates*, Canton, CT, 2009.

47. Supra Note 18

48. Pamela Holcomb et al., "In Their Own Voices: The Hopes and Struggles of Responsible Fatherhood Program Participants in the Parents and Children Together Evaluation." OPRE Report 2015-67. Mathematica Policy Research, June, 2015

49. Doreen Ludwig, "Motherless America: Confronting Welfare's Fatherhood Custody Program." Create Space Independent Publishing, 2015, p 204-205

50. John S. Martinez Fatherhood Initiative of Connecticut http://www.ct.gov/fatherhood /site/ default.asp

51. Supra Note 45, p. 53

52. Supra Note 45, p. 56

53. Supra Note 46

54. United States Government Accountability Office, "Healthy Marriage and Responsible Fatherhood Initiative: Further Progress is needed in Developing a Risk-based Monitoring Approach to Help HHS Improve Program Oversight." *Report to the Chairman, Committee on Finance, U.S. Senate*, GAO-08-1002, September 2008. Available at:http://www.gao.gov/assets/ 290/281743. pdf (Accessed June 24, 2014).

55. Liz Schott, LaDonna Pavetti & Ife Floyd. "How States Use Federal and State Funds Under the TANF Block Grant." *Center*

on Budget and Policy Priorities, Washington, D.C. October 15, 2015.

56. Memorandum "Temporary Assistance to Needy Families (TANF) Expenditure Report." from Michael Gilbert, Assistant Director, Division of Financial Services, Sate of Connecticut Department of Social Services, to Senator Marilyn Moore, Co-Chairperson, Representative Catherine Abercombie, Co-Chairperson, Human Services Committee, and Representative Toni Walker, Co-Chairperson, Senator Beth Bye, Co-Chairperson, Appropriations Committee, January 12, 2015.

57. Spreadsheet prepared by Jane McNichol of the Legal Assistance Resource Center of CT based on Temporary Family Assistance for Needy Families (TANF) Expenditure Reports submitted periodically by the Connecticut Department of Social Services to the co-chairs of the Legislature's Human Services and Appropriations Committees" but for serious research purposes you probably want to get the appropriate documents from DSS.

58. John S. Martinez Multi Agency MOU, Available at: http://www.maccabuse.org/documents/pdfs/MOU_Multi_Agen cy_AgreementCT%20FATHERHOOD%20PROGRAMS.pdf

59. Supra Note 49 at 288-289

Chapter 8

1. National Clearinghouse for the Defense of Battered Women, *The Impact of Parental Kidnapping Laws and Practices on Domestic Violence Survivors. Report to Congress*, Philadelphia, PA, August, 2005. OVW Grant no.2002-x-2338-WT-PA

2. Patricia M. Hoff, "The Uniform Child Custody Jurisdiction and Enforcement Act," *Juvenile Justice Bulletin*, (Office of Juvenile Justice and Delinquency Prevention, U.S. Department of Justice, Washington, D.C., December 2001), 2.

3. Supra Note 2 at 3

4. Supra Note 2 at 4

5. Joan Zorza, "Child Custody Roundtable II: Proposed Solutions," *Domestic Violence Report*, 16, no. 6 (August/September 2011): 85

6. Supra Note 1 at 10

7. Id at 11-13

8. Id at 26

9. Id at 27-31

10. Id at 33-34
11. Id at 32
12. Id at 34
13. The Hague Convention on the Civil Aspects of International Child Abduction. Available at: http://www.hcch.net/index_en.php?act=conventions.text&cid=24 (Accessed July 9, 2014)
14. Kilpatrick Townsend, *Litigating International Child Abduction Cases Under the Hague Convention* (National Center for Missing and Exploited Children, Alexandria, VA, 2012) pages 53-54. Available at: http://www.missingkids.com/en_US/HagueLitigat ionGuide/hague-litigation-guide.pdf (Accessed July 9, 2014).
15. Sudha Shetty and Jeffrey Edelson, "Adult Domestic Violence in Cases of International Parental Child Abduction," *Violence Against Women,* 11, no. 1 (2005), 121.
16. Jeffrey L. Edelson et al., Multiple Perspectives on Battered Mothers and Their Children Fleeing to the United States for Safety: A Study of Hague Convention Cases. Final Report, NIJ #2006-WG-BX-0006, Washington, D.C., November 2010. Available at:https://www.ncjrs.gov/pdffiles1/nij/grants/232624.pdf (Accessed July 9, 2014)
17. Id at 346-351
18. Office of Juvenile Justice and Delinquency Prevention, *The Crime of Family Abduction: A Child's Perspective.* (U.S. Department of Justice, Office of Justice Programs, Washington, D.C. 2010), 17. Available at: https://www.ncjrs.gov/pdffiles1/ojjdp/229933.pdf (Accessed July 9, 2014).

Chapter 9

1. Supra Chapter 2 Note 32 at 199
2. Supra Introduction Note 1
3. Supra Chapter 8 Note 5 at 85-86, 94-96
4. Supra Chapter 2 Note 27
5. Supra Introduction Note 7, Sheila Heim et al., 2002
6. Bernice Young, "Girl, Interrupted," SF Weekly News, (Wednesday December 18, 2002). Available at: http://www.sfweekly.com/2002-12-18/news/girlinterrupted/full/ (Accessed July 9, 2014)
7. For more information see http://www.barrygoldstein.net /important-articles/safe-child-act (Accessed July 29, 2014).

8. Id
9. Supra, Chapter 2, Note 68.
10. Supra, Chapter 2, Note 62.
11. Evan Stark, "Rethinking Custody Evaluation in Cases Involving Domestic Violence" *Journal of Child Custody*, 6, no. 3, (2009), 315.
12. Supra, Chapter 7, Note 46.
13. Supra, Chapter 7, Note 49 at 282-286.
14. See: http://www.childabusesolutions.com (Accessed November 9,2016).

Chapter 10

1. Betty Freidan, *The Feminine Mystique*, (New York, W.W. Norton & Company; Reprint, September 17, 2001).
2. Supra Introduction Note 14, Keith Harmon Snow, 2016
3. Supra Chapter 8 Note 5
4. See: "Family Court Enhancement Projects" Available at: https://www.justice.gov/opa/pr/ justice-department-selects-four-courts-identify-promising-practices-custody-and-visitation. (Accessed November 9, 2016)
5. Trocme, N., & Bala, N. (2005). "False Allegations of Abuse and Neglect When Parents Separate," *Child Abuse and Neglect*, 29(12), 1333–1345.
6. Supra Chapter 8 Note 5 at 94
7. Congress recognized and attempted to address this problem by passing the International Marriage Broker Regulations Act (IMBRA) as part of the VAWA 2005 reauthorization. This Act requires, among other things, disclosure of criminal convictions for various crimes including domestic violence and child abuse by petitioners for foreign brides.
8. Supra Chapter 2 Note 78 at 99-119.
9. Supra Chapter 8 Note 5 at 95.
10. Supra Chapter 8 Note 5
11. Violence Against Women Act of 2005. Available at: http://www.gpo.gov/fdsys/pkg/BILLS-109hr3402enr/pdf/BILLS-109hr3402enr.pdf (Accessed July 9, 2014).
12. Supra Chapter 8 Note 5
13. Supra Chapter 3 Note 40

Index

200, 202, 208, 219, 225, 227
U.S. Constitution, 39, 77, 78, 81,
82, 84, 87, 89, 151, 215
U.S. Department of Health and
Human Services (DHHS), 22,
123, 124, 126, 130, 132, 152,
158, 172
U.S. Department of Housing and
Urban Development (HUD),
22
U.S. Department of Justice (DOJ),
123, 128, 130, 132, 147, 199

Ver Steegh, Nancy, 116
Victims of Child Abuse Laws
(VOCAL), 30
Violence Against Women Act
(VAWA), 23, 89, 98, 122-129,
168, 184, 185, 188, 193, 200,
226
Violence against women
movement, 15, 19, 20, 32
Visitation: and child support, 50;
and custody, 72, 73, 74, 75, 98,
122, 124, 126, 127, 128, 129,
130, 137, 141, 142, 144, 147,
176, 184; father, 63, 70, 71,
138, 139, 167; and fatherhood
programs, 152-165; mothers'
loss of rights to, vii, 4, 25, 34,
63; rapists' right to, 143; and
safety concerns, 62, 69, 71, 72,
126, 127, 147, 168, 202, 208;
supervised, 72, 105, 113, 116,
144, 153, 156, 168, 169, 208;
unsupervised, 63, 64, 102,
119, 126, 137, 138
Waller, Garland, ix
Weinstein, Jack, 82, 83, 84, 87
Wellesley Center on Women, viii,
64

Winner, Karen, vii, 37
Wolf, Frank, 137
Woods, Dick, 158, 159

Zorza, Joan, 191, 202, 217, 219,
221, 223-227

About the Author

Leora N. Rosen obtained her PhD in Social Anthropology from Witwatersrand University in Johannesburg, South Africa, and a Masters in Public Health from Columbia University in New York. She worked as a social science analyst at the Walter Reed Army Institute of Research where she conducted original research on military families and women in the military. Later she worked as a senior social science analyst at the National Institute of Justice where she managed research programs related to violence against women and family violence. She retired from government service in 2007.

Dr. Rosen became aware of the problems facing protective mothers in the 1980s, and devoted much of her time to advocacy and research on their behalf. In 1996 she published *"The Hostage Child: Sex Abuse Allegations in Custody Disputes,"* co-authored with Michelle Etlin.

Dr. Rosen was also co-editor of a textbook on the Military Family, and has published numerous articles in peer-reviewed journals on military families and military personnel including articles on sexual harassment, the impact of child abuse histories on psychological wellbeing and adjustment to military life, and on the prevalence and correlates of intimate partner violence among military personnel.

She was co-editor of two special issues of the journal *Violence Against Women* dealing with violence against women in the military, and co-editor of one special issue on domestic violence and custody. She has also conducted and published research on fathers' rights groups.

www.ingramcontent.com/pod-product-compliance
Lightning Source LLC
Chambersburg PA
CBHW051855170526
45168CB00001B/117